T0319742

Institutions, Industrial Upgrading, and Economic Performance in Japan

To my daughter, Clare 'Tankobu', and her husband, Pete,
who were married in September, 2004 – with all the best wishes
for their happy and bright future.

Institutions, Industrial Upgrading, and Economic Performance in Japan

The 'Flying-Geese' Paradigm of Catch-up Growth

Terutomo Ozawa

Professor of Economics, Colorado State University and Research Associate, Center on Japanese Economy and Business, Columbia Business School, USA

Edward Elgar

Cheltenham, UK • Northampton, MA, USA

Published by
Edward Elgar Publishing Limited
Glensanda House
Montpellier Parade
Cheltenham
Glos GL50 1UA
UK

Edward Elgar Publishing, Inc.
136 West Street
Suite 202
Northampton
Massachusetts 01060
USA

A catalogue record for this book
is available from the British Library

ISBN 1 84376 959 X

Printed and bound in Great Britain by MPG Books Ltd, Bodmin, Cornwall

Contents

Figures

Tables

Abbreviations

AFL-CIO	American Federation of Labor–Congress of Industrial Organizations
ARPA	Advanced Research Project Agency
ASEAN	Association of Southeast Asian Nations
BT	Biotechnology
CAD	Computer-Aided Design
CIO	Chief Information Officer
CRM	Customer Relationship Management
DKB	Dai-Ichi Kangyo Bank
DVD	Digital Video Disk
EDI	Electronic Data Interchange
ERP	Enterprise Resource Planning
FDI	Foreign Direct Investment
FG	Flying Geese
GDP	Gross Domestic Product
GHQ	General Headquarters
GNP	Gross National Product
GPS	Global Positioning System
Icann	Internet Corporation for Advanced Names and Numbers
ICU	International Christian University
ID	Inner-Dependent
IDP	Investment Development Path
IS–EP	Import Substitution–Export Promotion
IT	Information Technology
JETRO	Japan External Trade Organization
KM	Knowledge Management
LCD	Liquid Crystal Display
LDP	Liberal Democratic Party
LSI	Large Scale Integration
M&A	Merger and Acquisition
METI	Ministry of Economy, Trade, and Industry
MITI	Ministry of International Trade and Industry
MNC	Multinational Corporation
NIE	Newly Industrializing Economy
NOI	Net Outward Investment

NT	Nano-technology
OECD	Organization for Economic Cooperation and Development
OF	Outer-Focused
PC	Product Cycle or Personal Computer
PCA	Parts, Components, and Accessories
QC	Quality Control
R&D	Research and Development
RCA	Revealed Comparative Advantage
SCM	Supply Chain Management
TDP	Technology Development Path
TFP	Total Factor Productivity
UNCTAD	United Nations Conference on Trade and Development
VCR	Video Cassette Recorder
VLSI	Very Large Scale Integration
WWI	World War I
WWII	World War II
www	World Wide Web

Foreword

The so-called 'flying-geese' theory of economic development introduced by Kaname Akamatsu, a professor of economics at the Hitotsubashi University, Tokyo, in the early 1930s, has recently gained in popularity and reputation against the backdrop of the phenomenal economic growth of East Asia (first Japan, then the NIEs, and the ASEAN-4, and most recently, China) during the latter half of the twentieth century. References to this theory are now frequently found in the academic literature on economic development, international trade, and foreign direct investment. The media also have come often to use the term 'flying geese', especially in describing the catching-up growth patterns of developing countries on the heels of more advanced countries.

Professor Terutomo Ozawa of Colorado State University has written most extensively on this subject outside Japan. He and I have had opportunities to exchange ideas, collaborate in research, and co-author several publications on the topic. In this book, Ozawa brings together and expands on many fascinating ideas that he has developed in his previous works over many years. These include 'economies of hierarchical concatenation', 'increasing factor incongruity', 'comparative advantage (or market) recycling', 'the Ricardo–Hicksian trap of industrial production', 'Smithian growth élan', 'triumvirate pro-trade structural transformation', 'knowledge creation vs. knowledge diversion', 'the price–knowledge/industry-flow mechanism à la David Hume', 'the syndrome of institutional incongruity', 'socially justifiable moral hazard vs. degenerative moral hazard', and many others – all these richly nuanced concepts being used as the critical building blocks for his flying-geese (stages) model of industrial upgrading in a catching-up country.

His ideational/theoretical foundations are built not only on contemporary neoclassical economic concepts (such as 'scope and scale economies', 'factor abundance and intensity', 'externalities', and 'agglomeration economies') but also more broadly on the dynamic classical economics of David Hume, Adam Smith, David Ricardo, John Stuart Mill, and the development theories of Joseph Schumpeter, Colin Clark, Alexander Gerschenkron, Arthur Lewis, and Hollis Chenery, as well as on the institutional perspectives of Thorstein Veblen and Douglass North. His approach to conceptualization is iconoclastic and innovative – in the best tradition of Akamatsu who always strove to be original and iconoclastic, challenging conventional ideas.

Moreover, what makes this book truly distinctive is his emphasis on evolutionary analysis and a political economy framework, within both of which the various roles of institutions (inclusive of politics) are treated and explored as determinants of economic performance and molders of international business, along with market-coordinated activities that the institutions support and complement – but sometimes hinder – in a cumulative-causational manner. His analysis is carried out using Japan's postwar – and up to the present – experience as the primary focus to reveal and illustrate the salient features of catch-up growth, flying-geese style, that delineate a dynamic process of scaling the ladder of economic development by learning from and emulating the advanced countries. His stages approach is not a mere typology. He explores in detail the *causality* of how the Japanese economy has progressed from one stage to the next on the road of structural upgrading, each step coordinated and promoted by both autonomous market forces and institutional factors.

Akamatsu's theory has three different patterns of flying-geese formation: (a) from imports to domestic production, and finally to exports, (b) from low-end product manufacturing to high-end product manufacturing, and (c) an alignment of countries at different stages of economic development. Ozawa reinterprets and puts Akamatsu's third pattern in a much broader 'international political economy' framework of what he calls 'hegemon-led growth clustering'. He then zeros in, and elaborates, on the second pattern in terms of his dynamic stages model of industrial upgrading à la Schumpeter, treating the other two patterns as functional/enabling forces for industrial upgrading.

This book presents quite a few interesting concepts that may be useful in further theorizing the flying-geese process of structural transformation and formulating some empirical tests. It should be noted, however, that Ozawa presents an amended framework (his *own* reformulated version) of Akamatsu's model, since Akamatsu's original ideas could be elaborated on in a number of ways from different perspectives. In short, Ozawa succeeds in extending, building up, and joining the Akamatsu–Kojima lineage of this unique Japan-born theory of economic development from a fresh, unconventional, and discerning perspective.

Koganei, Tokyo
Summer, 2004

Kiyoshi Kojima
Emeritus Professor of Economics
Hitotsubashi University

Preface/Acknowledgments

Japan's postwar economic growth in that space-confined, mountainous, and resource-scarce archipelago, about the size of the State of Montana in the US, but with almost a half of America's population, is nothing but a story of great structural transformation, a transformation that has made Japan join the ranks of the advanced economies as the world's second largest economy over as short a span of time as less than three decades after World War II.

It has been nearly four decades since I began to study some early phases (1950–75) of Japan's transformation and the roles of foreign direct investment (FDI) and knowledge transfer as facilitators of industrial upgrading. With an eye to achieving the national goals of caching up with the advanced West, Japan created a unique set of institutions in the early postwar period, and actively employed industrial – and other macro-organizational (Dunning, 1992) – policies to assist its private sector to gain international competitiveness in a number of high-productivity manufacturing sectors. The upshot was high growth throughout the 1960s.

As the decade of the 1960s drew to its close, furthermore, Japanese multinational corporations' (MNCs) activities began to become noticeable worldwide. In the early 1970s, their overseas investment grew very rapidly in both numbers and value, against a backdrop of rising labor shortages at home, the ever-expanding need to secure overseas supply sources of industrial resources, and the appreciation of the yen that made home-based production and exports increasingly more costly but overseas production more profitable. These early phases of Japan's economic growth and Japanese MNCs' international operations were examined in my books, *Japan's Technological Challenge to the West, 1950–1974: Motivation and Accomplishment* (MIT Press, 1974) and *Multinationalism, Japanese Style: The Political Economy of Outward Dependency* (Princeton University Press, 1979; paperback edition in 1982).

Ever since, I have kept track of the evolution of the Japanese economy and its accompanying cross-border business activities. My continued analyses have been published in conference volumes, journal articles, book chapters, and books – just to cite a few monographs, for example, *Japan's General Trading Companies: Merchants of Economic Development* (co-authored with Kiyoshi Kojima; OECD, 1984); *Recycling Japan's Surpluses for Developing Countries* (OECD, 1988); *Business Restructuring in East Asia: Cross-Border*

M&As in the Crisis Period (co-authored with James Zhan; Copenhagen Business School Press, 2001). The present volume draws, and expands, on many ideas presented in publications, and presents my most recent thinking and ideas on the vicissitudes and current state of synergistic interactions between Japan's structural transformation and international business operations.

Indeed, many significant changes have occurred – are occurring – in the motivations, characteristics, and patterns of international business activities emanating from and penetrating into the Japanese economy, as it has gone through a series of structural upgrading from low to higher, and still much higher, value-added stages since the end of World War II. At the start of the 1970s Japan was already on its way to joining the ranks of advanced countries, but its industry was still dominated by traditional heavy and chemical industries that caused some serious environmental and ecological problems at home – all the more because of its cramped homeland space. Japan then strove to build up less-resource-intensive, environmentally less straining, higher value-added, and knowledge-based industries, notably automobiles and electronics.

One major accomplishment of such efforts has been the successful innovation of world-class assembly techniques that has converted mass production into so-called 'lean production' (originated as the Toyota production system). It is the new method of organizing production in such a way to eliminate wastes in work processes, work-related motions, materials, and material handling. This homespun organizational and technological innovation has given a decisive support for Japan's structural transformation, export competitiveness, and overseas investment activities.

With the newly gained strength in manufacturing, exporting, and international business operations, Japan's industrial activities inevitably outgrew the domestic market and became inexorably outer-bound and outer-dependent, thereby advancing into the global economy. Home was no longer an optimal base for manufacturing and service production. Particularly notable was Japan's ever-deepening economic integration with other East Asian economies, constituting a geographical cluster that is now the world's fastest growth region. Japan's industrial production has become increasingly embedded in East Asia as a unitized/integral space of operations, though its marketing and procurement networks are spun around the world. Paradoxically, the success of economic nationalism (originally intended to avoid reliance on foreign interests and secure self-autonomy) has thus deepened Japan's dependence on the rest of the world, forcing Japan to play the game of both regionalism and globalization.

Japan's rapid catch-up modernization in the postwar period was, indeed, the first sign of the East Asian miracle. Japan's success did exert, and still continues to exert, a significant impact on neighboring economies as a role model to emulate. On the other hand, a host of economic and institutional predicaments recently experienced by Japan may equally serve as reminders of the undesirable consequences of Japanese-style catch-up strategy that other countries need to heed and avoid.

The major focus of this study is the process of industrial upgrading that Japan went through during the second half of the last century and on the roles of institutions and the political economy in facilitating or retarding such structural transformation. The so-called 'flying-geese' theory of economic development is used as the overall framework of analysis, along with many other conceptual models, to examine from an evolutionary perspective how Japan has climbed the ladder of economic growth one rung at a time. The stages framework is used, but the inter-stage *causal* links are the primary focus of analysis.

Completion of this study owes a great deal to many who have long encouraged me to finish this new monograph. Professor Emeritus Kiyoshi Kojima of Hitotsubashi University, Tokyo, the main torch-carrier of the original flying-geese theory in Japan as a protégé of Professor Kaname Akamatsu, who introduced the theory in the 1930s, has been a constant source of inspiration and intellectual guidance. I am greatly appreciative of his long-lasting friendship and constructive exchanges of ideas with me.

A word of deep-felt gratitude also goes to Professor Emeritus John H. Dunning of both Reading University, UK, and Rutgers University, US, for more than 20 years' warm friendship and tutelage. He honored me with an appointment as a Visiting Esmee Fairbairn Senior Research Fellow at the University of Reading, UK, in 1983. I have also been invited to many of the numerous academic conferences he has organized, several of which were held in such memorable places as Lake Como (Italy), Brussels (Belgium), Bangkok (Thailand), Rotterdam (the Netherlands), and Madrid (Spain). As a result I have had invaluable opportunities to explore the key topics related to international production, Japanese MNCs, and East Asian industrial dynamism. Many of the ideas presented in this study originated from my participation in his conferences.

I am similarly indebted to Professor Jean-Louis Mucchielli of the University of Paris I: Panthéon-Sorbonne, France. He kindly invited me to the Sorbonne as a short-term visiting professor on three occasions (May 1994, February 1996, and May 1996) – and as a speaker at the 1994 Sorbonne Colloquium on Stratégies des Firmes Multinationales et Impacts des Délocalisations (June 9–10, 1994) and at the 1996 Sorbonne Colloquium on Globalisation et Régionalisation dans les Investissements et le Commerce (May 30–31, 1996). I am deeply grateful for his generous hospitality and the intellectual stimuli he gave me. Some of the ideas I explored and presented at the Sorbonne are incorporated in this book.

I must also add Professor Colin Dodds, President of Saint Mary's University, Halifax, Canada, and Professor Emeritus Gavin Boyd of the same institution, to my list of individuals to whom I owe an intellectual debt. They organized a series of conferences on different aspects of international business starting in 1998 and invited me to three of those conferences as a speaker. This book includes many of the analyses I presented at Saint Mary's University.

I likewise enjoyed the good fortune to conduct research and organize my thoughts on the topic of this book as a Visiting Foreign Professor (*Gaikokujin Kyakuin Kyoju*) at the Institute of Social Science, the University of Tokyo, during the fall semester of 1996. I am thankful to the Institute for the kind hospitality and generous financial support that made my stay not only productive but quite enjoyable as well. Special thanks go to Professor Tetsuo Abo, then at the Institute, my personal host, who graciously made a number of privileged professional arrangements for me, the most important of which was to lecture in his seminar class. I benefited immensely from interacting with, and learning, from other faculty members of the Institute, notably Professor Haruki Wada, then director of the Institute, Professor Akira Kudo, Professor Masahiro Kawai, Professor Juro Hashimoto, and Professor Hirokuni Obata.

The three-month research fellowship awarded to me at the East-West Center, Hawaii, in the spring of 2001 was equally supportive of, and highly conducive to, my study. Dr Dieter Ernst of the Center was an excellent host during the tenure, according me an intellectually productive environment that greatly enhanced my research output – despite the enticing distractions of the beautiful Hawaiian beaches.

More recently, I have become enormously indebted to Professor Hugh Patrick of Columbia Business School, who has generously given me strong support in various ways such as writing letters of recommendation and painstakingly commenting on my paper on the flying-geese paradigm (which was later published in the *Journal of Asian Economics*). Above all, the appointment he kindly gave me as Research Associate at the Center on Japanese Economy and Business, Columbia Business School, is one of the greatest honors and privileges I have received in my academic career.

Last but not least, my most recent appointment as a Visiting Professor of International Economics and Business Administration at the International Christian University (ICU), Tokyo, during the spring quarter of 2004 was an additional god-sent opportunity to observe first-hand how the Japanese economy was rebounding from a more than a decade-long stagnation. I am thankful to Dr Norihiko Suzuki, President of the ICU, and Professor Kano Yamamoto for inviting and giving me a memorable spring and an early summer in Japan. At the start of the spring term I fully enjoyed the gorgeous canopies of cherry blossom for which the ICU campus is well known.

In short, this book contains a synthesis of many of my thoughts and ideas presented in a number of published articles, book chapters, books, and at numerous conferences. To be more specific, Chapter 1 draws in part on, and combines, 'Pax Americana-Led Macro-Clustering and Flying-Geese-Style Catch-Up in East Asia: Mechanisms of Regionalized Endogenous Growth', *Journal of Asian Economics*, **13** (6), 2003, 699–713, and 'Towards a Theory of Hegemon-Led Macro-Clustering', in Peter Gray (ed.), *Extending the Eclectic Paradigm in International Business*, Cheltenham, UK: Elgar, 2003, 143–58. Chapters 2 and 3 are partly based on 'Strategic Organization and Structural Dynamism: Spatial Underpinning of Japan's Phase-Based Industrial Competitiveness', *CEMS Business Review*, **2** (Suppl.), 1997: S19–S35. Chapter 4 expands on '"Managed" Growth, Relocation and Restructuring: The Evolution of Japan's Motor Industry into a Dominant Multinational Player', in Peter Buckley and Jean-Louis Mucchielli (eds), *Multinational Firms and International Relocation*, Cheltenham, UK: Elgar 1997, 161–188. The appendix to Chapter 5 is a short revised version of 'Japan: The Macro-IDP, Meso-IDPs, and the Technology Development Path (TDP)', in John Dunning and Rajneesh Narula (eds), *Foreign Direct Investment and Governments*, London: Routledge, 1996, 142–173. Chapter 8 draws on 'Japan's Network Capitalism in Evolution', in John Dunning and Gavin Boyd (eds), *Alliance Capitalism and Corporate Management*, Cheltenham UK: Elgar, 2003, 230–248. And finally, Chapter 9 is an expanded version of 'Japan in an Institutional Quagmire: International Business to the Rescue?', *Journal of International Management,* **9** (3), 219–236, reprinted in part with permission from Elsevier, copyrighted 2003. I am grateful to Professor Emeritus Peter Gray of Rutgers for his helpful comments on this last chapter.

Terutomo Ozawa

Fort Collins, CO, USA,
at the foot of the beautiful Rockies,
Summer 2004

PART I

Post-WWII growth clustering and Japan as a second goose

1. Hegemon-led growth clustering and the flying-geese paradigm of catch-up growth

1.1. TWO HEGEMONIES AND TANDEM GROWTH

It is important to keep in mind that Japan's phenomenal economic growth, both pre- and post-World War II, has been a derivative of the spread of global capitalism, early on under the Pax Britannica and more recently under the Pax Americana. In other words, Japan's rapid industrialization would have been inconceivable if it had not been for the roles of Great Britain and the United States as the successive hegemons that created a favorable global environment for trade, investment, and technology transmission. The postwar US hegemony in particular has brought about a host of ideal opportunities for Japan to capitalize on in crafting and pursuing its own brand of catch-up growth.

The Pax Britannica and the Pax Americana both constitute a global economic system of what may be called 'hegemon-led growth clustering' (a hegemon-driven process of tandem growth) (Ozawa, 2003c), when looked at from an economics point of view (though it has many other dimensions). Growth clustering is a phenomenon in which a hegemon economy propagates growth stimuli to its closely aligned cohort of countries that are at *various* stages of development and structural transformation. The stimuli include dissemination of technology, knowledge, information, skills, and demand (via access to the hegemon's home market), and provision of development finance – and above all, transplantation of growth-inducing institutional arrangements of open market capitalism; this all contributes to higher levels of industrial productivity, efficiency, and per capita income. The lower-echelon countries can 'free ride' and thrive on those stimuli, so long as they are willing to follow in the ideological steps of the hegemon. In other words, there are what may be called 'economies of hierarchical concatenation' (Ozawa, 1995b) that the follower countries can reap from the forces of hegemon-led growth clustering.

At the same time, the hegemon itself and other high-echelon countries in turn garner benefits from rapid integration with lower-echelon countries, as well as from the latter's vigorous economic development and growth which create demand for goods and services from the upper-echelon countries. (Such

3

benefits, for example, have most recently been seen in the information technology boom in the US which was in no small part stimulated by the low prices of computers and telecommunications equipment outsourced in East Asia and made available to more companies and individuals.) Their synergistic interactions result in agglomeration economies, enabling the *entire* hierarchy of countries to mutually gain, grow, and prosper.

The cross-border trade and investment created under the regime of growth clustering are fundamentally market-driven (profit-motivated and guided) under capitalism, though individual countries, especially those in the lower echelons, are usually involved in *dirigiste* strategies. Growth clustering is geographically expansive, geocentric, and intertemporally concatenated. *Markets, hierarchies*, and *institutions* play their respective requisite roles in governing the hegemon-led system. Put simply, a hierarchy of countries led by a *lead* country matters – and matters a lot, not only for the individual cohort countries' economic development and growth but also for the entire hegemonic sphere's prosperity.

1.2.   ECONOMIES OF HIERARCHICAL CONCATENATION AND LEARNING EXTERNALITIES

1.2.1.   Classical Economists' Foresight: Ideas from Adam Smith, John Stuart Mill, and Karl Marx

The concept of 'economies of hierarchical concatenation' brought about by the forces of hegemon-led growth clustering draws in part on the insights of Adam Smith (1776/1908):

> Private people who want to make a fortune, never think of retiring to the remote and poor provinces of the country, but resort either to the capital, or to some of the great commercial towns. *They know that where little wealth circulates, there is little to be got; but that where a great deal is in motion, some share of it may fall to them.* The same maxim which would in this manner direct the common sense of [individuals] … should make a whole nation regard the riches of its neighbours as a probable cause and occasion for itself to acquire riches. *A nation that would enrich itself by foreign trade is certainly most likely to do so when its neighbours are all rich and industrious.* (vol. 1: 378, emphasis added)

What is described here is more than the 'neighborhood' effect. Smith is thinking in *hierarchical* terms where some countries ('the capital' and 'great commercial towns') are rich, while others ('remote and poor provinces') are undeveloped or underdeveloped. Those developing countries, if they are to develop ('to make a fortune'), need to establish close commercial contact with the hegemon ('the capital') and the advanced subregional countries ('great commercial towns'). In other words, the former can capitalize on gaps in incomes (purchasing power) and industrial knowledge (technology) vis-à-vis the more advanced.

In Smith's day, trade was the main form of international business operations whereby to exploit such economies of concatenation. Foreign direct investment (FDI) (international production as we know it today) obviously did not exist – except in the nascent colonial type of overseas investments, investments made to support early settlements in the New World by chartered trading companies such as the Plymouth Company and the Hudson Bay Company from the Old World (McNulty, 1972). Besides, Smith himself considered the logistic costs of making investments abroad too high to be justified: '[the fortune] of the trader who is obliged frequently to commit it, not only to the winds and the waves, but to the more uncertain elements of human folly and injustice, by giving great credit in distant countries to men, with whose character and situation he can seldom be thoroughly acquainted' (Smith, 1776/1908: 291).

Hence, Smith advocated free trade as a means of making the best use of the prevailing hierarchy of nations at that time. For him, indeed, free trade was the most effective development tool for any underdeveloped country to use, if it was determined to catch up and become 'equal' with the advanced countries: 'Nothing seems more likely to establish this equality of force than that mutual communication of knowledge and of all sorts of improvements which an extensive commerce from all countries to all countries naturally, or rather necessarily, carries along with it' (Smith, 1776/1908, vol. 2: 140). In other words, trade provides opportunities to emulate and learn from each other. It is more than mere exchanges of goods, but it is more importantly a knowledge-transfer mechanism.

On this score, John Stuart Mill (1848/1909) made a further elaboration:

> ... the economic benefits of commerce are surpassed in importance by those of its effects which are intellectual and moral. It is hardly possible to overrate the value, for the improvement of human beings, of things which bring them into contact with persons dissimilar to themselves, and with modes of thought and action unlike those with which they are familiar ... it is indispensable to be perpetually comparing [one's] own notions and customs with the experience and example of persons in different circumstances ... *there is no nation which does not need to borrow from others.* (pp. 581–2, emphasis added)

The total gains from trade, therefore, consist of more than the mere *static* gains arising from exchanges of goods and from trade-induced specialization; more important dynamic gains come in the form of *mutual learning*. Yet, in a hierarchical world of nations operating at different stages of development, the lower-echelon ones no doubt enjoy the availability of much more abundant opportunities to learn from their higher-echelon (more advanced) counterparts than vice versa. These learning opportunities are the *core* of economies of hierarchical concatenation – and latecomer advantages.

Relevant also is a similar observation made by Karl Marx: 'The country that is more developed industrially only shows, to the less developed, *the image of its own future*' (emphasis added, as cited in Palma, 1978: 7). For Marx, the cross-border spread of capitalism from the most advanced to the less advanced is inexorable and unavoidable, ultimately creating competitors for the former as the capitalist mode of production is transplanted onto the less advanced. The hegemon economy innovates and disseminates to the rest a new pattern of production and consumption, which is 'the image of its own future' for the latter. *The wealth-producing power of capitalism was considered so strong that it could not be contained and monopolized within the advanced world alone and would necessarily spread to the less developed.*

1.2.2.   The 'Price-Knowledge/Industry-Flow' Theory *à la* David Hume

The inevitability of the spread of economic growth under capitalism had actually been stressed much earlier by David Hume (1754/1985), a couple of decades earlier than the publication of Adam Smith's *An Inquiry into the Nature and Causes of the Wealth of Nations* (1776/1908). Hume zeroed in on the transmission of growth (hence wealth) from the rich to the poor countries in connection with his argument that British hegemony and one-sided prosperity would prove only transitory because of the inexorable catch-up of other countries. He started out by observing 'a happy concurrence of causes in human affairs, which checks the growth of trade and riches, and hinders them from being confined entirely to one people' (Hume, 1754/1985: 283). Hume's point was that no single nation would be able to keep prosperity all to itself without eventually sharing it with the less developed. He continued:

> Where one nation has gotten the start of another in trade, it is very difficult for the latter to regain the ground it has lost: because of the superior industry and skill of the former, and the greater stocks [i.e., the first-comer advantages]. But these advantages are compensated, in some measure, by the *low price of labour* in every nation which has not an extensive commerce, and does *not much abound in gold and silver. Manufactures, therefore, gradually shift their places, leaving those countries and provinces which they have already enriched, and flying to others, whither they are allured by the cheapness of provisions and labour, till they have enriched there also and are again banished by the same causes* ... [I]n general, we may observe, that the dearness of everything, from plenty of money, is a disadvantage, which attends an established commerce, and sets bounds to it in every country, by enabling the poorer states to under sell the richer in all foreign markets. (Hume, 1754/1985: 283–4, emphasis added)

What is so insightful in Hume's observation is that he clearly grasped the key roles played by labor cost (as well as the costs of other inputs) and the reserves of 'gold and silver' whose relative abundance invariably would affect prices and the market exchange rates, triggering cross-border flows of those precious metals under a bimetallic monetary standard (as posited in his 'price-specie-flow' theory). Because of changes in these two variables which would become relatively unfavorable for the rich countries (hence relatively favorable for the poor), the manufactures would be 'flying to others, whither they are allured by the cheapness of provisions and labour, till they have enriched there also and are again banished by the same causes ...'. This process may be called the 'price-knowledge/industry-flow' theory as the 'real' sector counterpart of Hume's 'price-specie-flow' theory for the 'money' sector.

A *trans-migratory* shift of manufacturing across borders was thus recognized by Hume as a development-transplanting and wealth-spreading activity across countries. He was thus talking about the phenomenon of what may be called 'comparative advantage (or industrial/market) recycling' down the hierarchy of nations (Ozawa, 1993; UNCTAD 1995). In a nutshell, he boldly elucidated the two principal mechanisms – low labor costs and currency undervaluation (real depreciation) – through which a poor nation (a follower economy) might be able to catch up in manufacturing activities.

In this regard, although Stephen Hymer (1960/1976), who theorized a process of international business operations at the firm level, is considered the *father* of the *micro*economic theory of FDI, we can unarguably call David Hume the *father* (better still the great, great, great grandfather?) of the *macro*economic theory of FDI (which necessarily transplants industry across borders). Labor cost and exchange rates are now recognized as among the key macroeconomic determinants of overseas investment, especially in labor-intensive manufacturing. (These two factors are, indeed, currently so powerful that the US economic upturn of 2003–4 initially had difficulty immediately creating jobs and was dubbed 'jobless – or even job-loss – recovery' in the American media, at least partly because of the 'flying' of jobs to China and India. In this respect, we are justified in saying that Hume was already concerned with the issue of 'off-shoring' (outsourcing abroad). Hume's theory of industrial transmigration will be revisited in Chapter 7 after we study the postwar Japanese experience of catch-up growth in the following chapters.

1.2.3. Hume's Theory of Endogenous Retrogradation

In addition to the labor costs and exchange rates that move against the interests of the advanced nations, Hume (1754/1985) also argued that *'When the arts and sciences come to perfection in any state, from that moment they naturally, or rather necessarily decline, and seldom or never revive in that nation, where they formerly flourished'* (p. 135, emphasis in original). The ineluctable decline of an advanced economy is likewise caused by an internal decay in the arts and sciences as well. Elmslie (1995) calls such a climactic 'Hume's Theory of Endogenous Retrogradation'. (Hume was concerned mainly about Britain's eventual retrogradation, but as will be seen in Chapter 6, Japan is presently confronted with the phenomenon of endogenous retrogradation in sciences and engineering among the youth – and what may be called 'institutional retrogradation' in Chapter 9.)

1.2.4.   Catch-up Growth by Emulating and Learning

These observations made by Smith, Hume, Mill, and Marx are intuitively powerful and perspicacious. They provide support for the notion of economies of hierarchical concatenation, the essence of which is *the existence of opportunities for catch-up growth by emulating and learning* mainly on the part of the lower-echelon countries. There are so many poor countries, however, with extremely low wages and depreciated home currencies, yet they are unable to industrialize, failing to take turns in *emulative growth*, as envisaged by Hume. The learning initiative needs to be started from the part of developing countries themselves, and 'learning how to learn' is the most critical first step. We need, therefore, more detailed explanations of under what circumstances and in what ways the less developed can catch up with – and in some cases, even surge ahead of, in some industrial activities – the 'lead' country or any other higher-echelon countries. In other words, we need to specify the *operational causal mechanisms* through which the benefits of hierarchical concatenation are engendered and exploited by the constituent countries of a particular regime of growth clustering.

The Japanese experience (explored in this book) provides one model of 'catch-up growth by emulating and learning', which proved to be a success story – thanks in many ways, however, to the unique circumstances that surrounded Japan in the early postwar period. Each developing country must ultimately formulate its own catch-up strategy (model) that is both compatible and effective with the prevailing *external* and *internal* circumstances. (We already know that other Asian countries have successfully been pursuing development policies of their own that are quite different from the Japanese model.) In what follows, a new overarching framework of evolutionary analysis will be introduced for the purpose of elucidating the driving forces of hegemon-led growth clustering in terms of a reformulated version of the so-called 'flying-geese' theory of economic development.

1.3. AN AMENDED 'FLYING-GEESE (FG)' MODEL OF INDUSTRIAL UPGRADING

As introduced and explained elsewhere (Ozawa, 1992, 1993, 2001a, 2003a), a model of industrial upgrading can shed light on the evolutionary process of hegemon-led tandem growth. This model is a reformulated version of the so-called 'flying-geese (FG)' theory, which originated in Akamatsu (*inter alia*, 1935, 1962), expanded conceptually in Kojima (*inter alia*, 1958, 2000, 2003, and 2004), and Kojima and Ozawa (1984a, 1985). There are many other scholars who have used Akamatsu's framework, either explicitly or implicitly, for analyses of trade and investment patterns, as well as economic development patterns among different countries. Noteworthy (to cite a few of those published in English) are Shinohara (1972, 1982), Rapp (1967), Meier (1980), Yamazawa (1990), Chen (1993), UNCTAD (1995), Radelet and Sachs (1997), Korhonen (1998), and Ito (2001). (For a recent literature survey, see Kojima [2000]). Most of them, however, have not really elaborated on Akamatsu's original ideas, especially on the idea of a *sequence* – and its causal *mechanisms* – of structural upgrading, particularly from an institutional and evolutionary perspective, which is the main focus of this book.

1.3.1. Akamatsu's Three Patterns of Sequential Development

In his writings published back in the 1930s and also after WWII, the late Kaname Akamatsu of Hitotsubashi University introduced *three* patterns of flying-geese formation. The first FG analogy came from his empirical findings of the sequential pattern of 'importing→domestic production→exporting (M→P→E)' in several prewar Japanese industries, which he identified as the *fundamental* FG pattern of industrial development. This represents a strategy of import-substitution-cum-export-promotion. He found this pattern of sequence statistically in the industry development of cotton yarn, cotton cloth, spinning and weaving machinery, and machines and tools, as shown in Figure 1.1. It should be noted that prewar Japan pursued the 'M→P→E' strategy to cash in on the forces of Pax Britannica-led growth clustering. In other words, this fundamental FG pattern is nothing but the 'natural/rational' behavior of the follower-goose countries emulating and learning from the lead-goose (hegemon) economy.

A second FG pattern is *a sequence of product development* not only in the order of 'capital goods following consumer goods' but also 'in the progression from crude and simple goods to complex and refined goods' (Akamatsu, 1961). Both types of qualitative product transformation/improvement are themselves made possible by way of a catching-up country's M→P→E strategy. Hence, the FG pattern of concomitant industrial and product

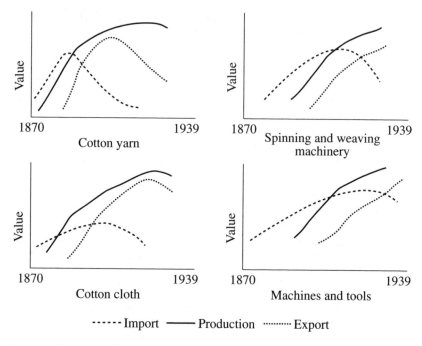

Source: Akamatsu (1962)

Figure 1.1   Akamatsu's wild-geese-flying patterns

development can be considered a *derivative* of the fundamental FG formation, a pattern that is also correlated with the phenomenon of industrial upgrading (to be detailed in the next section).

A third FG pattern is what Akamatsu (1961) called 'the alignment of nations along the different stages of development'. In his own words,

> ... the underdeveloped nations are aligned successively behind the advanced industrial nations *in the order of their different stages of growth in a wild-geese-flying pattern*. For example, when Japan passes the third stage of growth, India and China, which are less developed than Japan, will proceed to the second stage, where they will become homogeneous with Japan in consumer goods industries, and Japan's consumer goods exports to them will decrease. However, Japan will proceed from domestic production and use of capital goods to their production for export, creating a relationship of *advanced differentiation* with these backward nations. On the other hand, Japan will show an *advanced uniformization* with respect to the advanced industrial nations. (Akamatsu, 1961: 208, emphasis added)

The first and second FG patterns are specific to the catching-up processes experienced by *individual* developing countries, while the third pattern is a phenomenon observable within a hegemon-led *hierarchy* (group) of countries. The notions of 'differentiation' and 'uniformization' are synonymous with those of 'divergence' and 'convergence' in the jargons of present-day development theories. The adjective 'advanced' (though not explained by Akamatsu) connotes a process of ratcheting, rung by rung, up the ladder of industrial upgrading. It is not a one-shot climb but a *step-by-step* sequence of *continuous advance* in learning over time along the trail of industrialization pioneered and already blazed by the more developed countries. As Akamatsu (1962) put it, 'It is impossible to study the economic growth of the developing countries in modern times without considering the *mutual interactions* between these economies and those of the advanced countries' (p.1, emphasis added). Thus, his thought can be captured in terms of the notion of economies of hierarchical concatenation.

What is implied in the above quote is also that Japan as a second-ranking goose needs to be mindful not only of closing the gap with 'the advanced industrial nations' but more importantly of how fast the follower-geese countries in the third-rank echelon are in turn advancing, thereby closing the gap vis-à-vis Japan. There is always a 'danger' for Japan of being overtaken by other follower geese and experiencing the problems – and new opportunities – of 'uniformization' in industrial relationships.

1.3.2.   A Stages Model of Industrial Upgrading *à la* Schumpeter

This book concentrates on Akamatsu's first and second patterns in terms of the Japanese experience of industrial upgrading. The third pattern requires a separate analysis of Japan's relationships with other Asian economies – that is, an examination of Asia-wide FG formation as a unit of analysis.[1]

Although Akamatsu's ideas are riveting and thought-provoking, he only outlined his paradigm with very broad strokes of a brush so to speak, leaving its many important dimensions unelaborated. The reformulated model of industrial upgrading (Ozawa, 1992, 1993, 2001a, 2003a) presented in this book is a 'leading growth-sector' stages theory *à la* Joseph Schumpeter (1934), in which *a sequence of growth is punctuated by stages* (five stages as will be seen below) in the wake of 'the perennial gale of creative destruction'. In each stage a certain industrial sector can be identified as the main engine of structural transformation enabling the economy to scale the ladder of industrial development.

This conceptualization is in sharp contrast to the neoclassical view of growth as a smooth incremental accumulation of capital and jibes with what W.W. Rostow (1960) emphasizes:

> At any period of time, the rate of growth in the sectors will vary greatly; and it is

possible to isolate empirically certain leading sectors, at early stages of their evolution, whose rapid rate of expansion plays an essential direct and indirect role in maintaining the overall momentum of the economy. For some purposes *it is useful to characterize an economy in terms of its leading sectors; and a part of the technical basis for the stages of growth lies in the changing sequence of leading sectors*. In essence it is the fact that sectors tend to have a rapid growth phase, early in their life, that makes it possible and useful to regard economic history as *a sequence of stages rather than merely as a continuum, within which nature never makes a jump*. (p. 14, emphasis added)

How 'the perennial gale of creative destruction' persistently provides the fundamental impulse to structural transformation and modernization is explained better still in Schumpeter's (1942) own words:

The essential point to grasp is that in dealing with capitalism we are dealing with an *evolutionary* process ... *Capitalism, then, is by nature a form or method of economic change and not only never is but never can be stationary*. And this evolutionary character of the capitalist process is not merely due to the fact that economic life goes on in a social and natural environment which changes and by its change alters the data of economic action; this fact is important and these changes (wars, revolutions and so on) often condition industrial change, but they are *not* its prime movers. Nor is this evolutionary character *due to a quasi-automatic increase in population and capital* or to the vagaries of monetary systems of which exactly the same thing holds true. The fundamental impulse that sets and keeps the capitalist engine in motion comes from *the new consumers' goods, the new methods of production or transportation, the new markets, the new forms of industrial organization* that capitalist enterprise create. (pp. 82–3, emphasis added)

In other words, the evolutionary progress is *not* input-driven incrementally (not 'due to a quasi-automatic increase in population and capital') but is set in motion by innovations, which then lead to rapid capital formation in new industries, *necessarily destroying the value of the existing old capital*. Hence, the capitalist process can be neither incrementally additive nor cumulative in capital accumulation as posited by neoclassical economists.

Japan's high growth period was driven by a process of sequential upgrading through which its whole industrial structure is upgraded by a leading growth sector. It is more than a mere increase in total factor productivity (TFP) as usually perceived by neoclassical economists as an upward shift of a *given* aggregate production function. A *new* aggregate production function of the entire industrial structure replaces the existing old one – that is to say, the new continually (periodically) destroy the value of the existing production function in a wave-like fashion, as schematically illustrated in terms of a series of structural upgrading in Figure 1.2. This feature will be made clear in the following chapters that describe how the Japanese economy has gone through the different stages of industrial transformation.

This dynamic stages-delineated evolutionary/mutational approach is similar

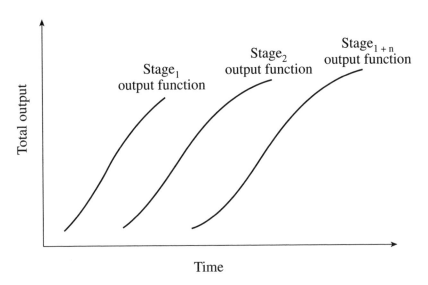

Figure 1.2 Mutating aggregate production functions, FG-style

in growth pattern to the idea of what Aoki and Yoshikawa (Aoki and Yoshikawa, 1999; Yoshikawa, 2000) call 'demand-creating innovations', although the latter emphasizes the demand side more strongly than our model of structural catch-up which is more supply-sided in comparison, as will be seen below. Luckily, Japan's catch-up growth, especially in its earlier phases, had no problem with demand. Arguably an 'excessive' number of producers were engaged in manufacturing a particular type of 'new' product (new to Japan but already in existence in the West) in the post-WWII period of catch-up growth, yet their oversupply was, on the whole, taken care of – thanks to their export markets in the West, as well as the rapidly growing home markets. More importantly, furthermore, they were able to adopt, adapt, and improve on, imported technologies by basically concentrating on the technology absorption-cum-production (supply) side (Ozawa, 1974). Put differently, postwar Japanese innovations have largely been 'supply-creating innovations' to paraphrase Aoki and Yoshikawa's nomenclature. Now that Japan is close to the existing top rung of the development ladder (which is ever more consumer-oriented than the earlier rungs), however, 'demand-creating innovations' are, indeed, the *sine qua non* for growth in Japan.

The model of industrial upgrading under the forces of hegemon-led growth clustering is based on the Japanese experience with structural transformation. The sequence of industrial upgrading Japan has gone through, however, is *not* Japan's own creation. Instead, it is laid out clearly in the scheme of global capitalism driven by the Anglo-American hegemonies.

1.4.   A SEQUENCE OF INDUSTRIAL UPGRADING UNDER THE TWO HEGEMONIES

The world economy has so far seen five tiers of leading growth industry emerge in wave-like progression ever since the Industrial Revolution in England: the five tiers which are illustrated in Figure 1–3. The first dominant industry that appeared was what may be called '*Heckscher-Ohlin*' *endowments-driven* (*natural resources-* or '*raw*' *labor-intensive*) *light industries* best represented by cotton textiles – named after the Heckscher–Ohlin trade theory which explains the basis for trade (the doctrine of comparative advantage) in terms of differences in factor proportions between countries. It was soon entailed by the '*non-differentiated Smithian*' *scale-driven* (*physical capital-intensive, natural resource-processing*) *heavy and chemical industries*, such as steel and basic chemicals (basically homogeneous/non-differentiated goods). This second stage is named after Adam Smith who stressed the dynamic gains from increasing returns to scale.

Indeed, the Golden Age of Capitalism, Mark I (1870–1914) stemmed from the rapid growth of these first two phases of industrial development under the Pax Britannica. That age's need – and its search – for natural resources (e.g., iron ore and copper ore) and overseas markets for textiles and capital goods led to colonialism. And scale-driven heavy and chemical industrialization was pursued relentlessly under imperialism as part and parcel of an arms race among the imperial powers (including Japan, which engaged in authoritarian nation building under the banners of '*Fukoku Kyohei* [Rich Nation and Strong Army]' and '*Shokusan Kogyo* [Nurture Industry and Promote Production]') (Samuels, 1994).   The stability of currencies was maintained under the international gold standard of the period, with London as the world's financial center.

The rise of the Pax Americana originated from US ingenuity in the innovation of interchangeable parts and assembly-line operations, which eventually culminated in the American manufacturing paradigm of mass production – and the American-initiated pattern of mass consumption (especially after WWII) that would set the tone for the rest of the world. The '*differentiated Smithian*' *assembly-based industries* (*notably automobiles*) emerged as the leading growth sector in the United States, following the introduction of Ford's assembly-lines and Frederick Taylor's scientific management ('time and motion study'). Fordism-cum-Taylorism thus became the dominant manufacturing paradigm, which was aimed at exploiting increasing returns to scale through standardization of products (as initially exemplified by the Model T), work processes, and parts and components.

With the entry of other producers, however, automobiles became increasingly differentiated in engineering, designs, functions, optional

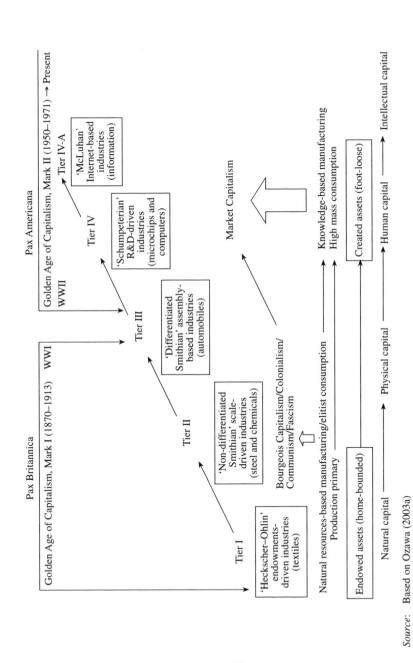

Source: Based on Ozawa (2003a)

Figure 1.3 Structural upgrading under Pax Britannica-led and Pax Americana-led growth-clustering

features, and add-on accessories to satisfy consumers' diversified preferences, although this type of differentiation was normally of the 'skin-deep' (on the surface) nature. Nevertheless, the stage of assembly-based industries, which also included electric machinery and appliances, became by nature far more *consumer-oriented* and far more responsive to diversified consumer tastes than its previous counterpart of heavy and chemical industrialization. The business concept of 'marketing' (as opposed to 'production') and the practice of 'market research' came into use in the United States where the 'differentiated Smithian' stage first saw its highest state of evolution ahead of any other countries – particularly with the rapid rise of the middle-income class of households underpinning the viable mass-consumption markets.

Such a new industrial structure necessitated strong market democracy where people are able to vote by their dollars in determining the desirable types of consumer goods. Individual freedom of choice became the *sine qua none* of the age of high mass consumption. Consumerism was the market ideology of US-led global capitalism – and the hallmark of the Golden Age of Capitalism, Mark II (1950–71). The US magnanimously (by then prevailing standards) opened its markets to foreign manufactures (particularly for Japanese exports, as will be seen in Chapter 3).

Rising consumerism then spurred R&D activities in corporate America in search of new products. As a consequence, especially in the post-WWII period, the *'Schumpeterian' R&D-driven industries* came to represent the subsequent stage of economic growth, innovating *knowledge-based* goods, one after another – such as TV sets, computers, semiconductors, washers and dryers, dishwashers, microwave ovens, tape-recorders, and antibiotics. In the 1950s and 1960s, many large companies in science-based industries began to set up corporate R&D centers. Notable were IBM's Watson Labs and AT&T's Bell Labs. The 'age of corporate laboratories' (Best, 2000) was thus ushered into the US economy, leading to America's industrial leadership in many high-tech sectors. 'Created' assets began increasingly to substitute for and replace 'endowed' natural assets.

Indeed, this structural transformation of the US economy was captured in the product-cycle (PC) theory of trade and investment (Vernon, 1966; Hirsch, 1967). It describes (i) why new high-income goods and labor-saving processes are first introduced in, and exported from, the US ahead of any other countries, but (ii) why such US exports are soon to be replaced by overseas production once the technology involved has been perfected and standardized, making it easy for the follower firms in other countries to imitate. In the end, furthermore, the US is actually to wind up importing these goods, the very goods it has initially innovated at home and exported. Hence, the PC theory can be interpreted as a theory of innovation and cross-border knowledge dissemination.

In addition to this PC theory (Type 1), Vernon (1979) introduced the PC theory, Type II, in which R&D activities themselves are, in turn, widely dispersed throughout the world via networks of multinationals' FDI – instead of being centered only in the US. The PC theory, Type II, thus can be construed as a theory of R&D capability dispersion overseas. A full range of R&D activities (from basic research to commercialization, involving product and process engineering, designing, and development) may still be controlled and managed by US multinationals, but many such knowledge-creating activities, especially downstream, are now carried out in foreign host countries. This dispersion of R&D facilitates immediate local production in the host countries – without the prolonged product-cycle sequence of innovations at home→exports→technology transfers and local production→imports as envisaged in the PC theory, Type 1.

In this connection, another version of the PC theory (Type III) is proposed to describe how in the early upstream stages of R&D, American firms have often been induced to sell basic/seed technologies abroad through licensing or other non-equity transactions – instead of fully developing and commercializing them at home first, often even giving up commercialization efforts altogether. The PC theory, Type III, is quite relevant to Japan's postwar strategy to secure under license state-of-the-art technologies in 'crude' (un- or underdeveloped) form from Western firms and commercialize them into successful products (more on this in Chapter 5). As rapidly catching-up economies (such as the NIEs and China) develop R&D capabilities of their own, the Japanese experience is most likely to be replicated.

The latest stage of economic growth driven by information technology (IT) has emanated from the configuration of Schumpeterian industries. The new stage is built on the Internet and other forms of IT, which have revolutionalized the telecommunications industry. This IT revolution has given birth to the *'McLuhan' Internet-enabled phase of economic growth* in which we now live – named after Marshall McLuhan, the guru of mass communications (Ozawa, 2001b). Indeed, the phenomena of 'The Media is the Message' (McLuhan and Fiore, 1967) and 'The Global Village' (now Web-enabled) (McLuhan and Powers, 1989) are the hallmarks of our present age of information. This new growth sector was pioneered in the US, particularly during the latter half of the 1990s. (The salient features of the McLuhan stage will be examined further in Chapter 6.)

In addition to the above five stages, moreover, an additional phase of growth is actually in the making as another spin-off from the Schumpeterian industries and as a subsystem of the New Economy. It is based on the biotechnology (BT) revolution, though still in its infancy as a lead sector. A tentative nomenclature can be assigned to this promising industry: the 'Watson–Crick' stage of growth – named after James Watson and Francis

Crick, Nobel prize winners who discovered the famous double helix in the DNA molecular structure in the early 1950s. In addition, yet another technology revolution is in the offing: a nano-technology (NT) revolution. The world will thus soon witness a fuller unfolding of the New Economy, a new economic structure that is molded not only by IT but by BT – and soon by NT as well. It is said that a comeback of presently depressed Silicon Valley depends upon its capability to ride 'the next big wave of innovation after the internet: the convergence of bio-, info- and nano-technologies'.[2]

We can recapitulate the sequential path and nature of modern industries introduced under global capitalism as follows. What the Pax Britannica introduced were initially the labor-intensive light industries (the 'Heckscher–Ohlin' stage) as typified by textiles and then the resource-intensive, scale-driven heavy and chemical industries (the 'non-differentiated Smithian' stage) as epitomized by steel, basic chemicals, and heavy machinery. In contrast, the Pax Americana created the highly components-intensive, assembly-based, genuinely consumer-oriented, and R&D-intensive industries (the 'differentiated Smithian' and the 'Schumpeterian' stages) as best represented by automobiles and electronics – and most recently, the Internet-enabled information-intensive industries (the 'McLuhan' stage), which may soon be joined by the BT and NT revolutions. In particular, the IT-driven industries are built on 'intellectual and entrepreneurial capital' and strongly geared to the needs of final consumers. The New Economy is the latest creation of US-led consumer capitalism.

Furthermore, the three tiers of industries developed under the Pax Americana all require market democracy as the *sine qua non*, where individual freedom and the free enterprise system prevail, along with safeguarded human rights. As Baumol (2002) argues, free market capitalism is the most efficient innovation machine to produce a stream of innovations, satisfying consumer needs and demands – because of its 'survival-of-the-fittest' force of fierce competition:

> ... what differentiates the prototype capitalist economy most sharply from all other economic systems is free-market pressures that force firms into a continuing process of innovation, *because it becomes a matter of life and death for many of them*. The static efficiency properties that are stressed by standard welfare economics are emphatically *not* the most important qualities of capitalist economies. Rather, what is clear to historians and laypersons alike is that *capitalism is unique* in the extraordinary growth record it has been able to achieve; in its recurring industrial revolutions that have produced an outpouring of material wealth unlike anything previously seen in human history. (p. viii, emphasis original)

Open free-market capitalism is therefore the necessary institution for Pax-Americana-nurtured industries, especially for the New Economy, where individuals are increasingly empowered more fully to exercise freedom of choice and communicate with each other at the grass roots more freely than ever before in real-time exchange of information at the click of a mouse, thanks to the IT revolution.

In contrast, the Old Economy industries (especially the 'smoke-stack' industries) are the legacies of the Pax Britannica. They were once developed and thrived as the leading growth sectors in the advanced countries in the pre-WWII period – under a variety of economic systems; unfettered bourgeois capitalism and colonialism (early on in Great Britain and other capitalist powers), communism (in the Soviet Union and China), fascism (in Germany, Italy, and Japan), and welfare/socialist capitalism (in Scandinavia).

In short, the evolutionary sequence of growth under capitalism has compelled the entire world economy, notably in the recent past, irrevocably to move toward market democracy as an *institutional requirement* for growth. In this sense, Amartya Sen's (1999) vision of 'individual freedom' as the ultimate goal of development ('development as freedom') is no longer an exogenous element that needs to be attained as the objective; it is all but endogenously and autonomously achievable under the internal logic of evolutionary capitalism.

1.5.   THE GOLDEN STRAITJACKET

The apt concept of the 'Golden Straitjacket' (Friedman, 1999) has been introduced to describe the newly emerged institutional requirements for countries to survive and thrive in this age of globalization and mega-competition that has replaced the era of the Cold War. The Cold War era divided the world into the Free World bloc, the Soviet Communist bloc, and the Third World which played the game of pitting the US and Soviet superpowers against each other. (Japan as a designated bulwark against communism was one of the most fortunate beneficiaries of the era, as will be detailed in Chapter 9.)

The collapse of the USSR created an entirely new world, in which the US suddenly found its total hegemony and began to mold the rest of the world in its own image. Thatcher-Reaganism was first targeted at deregulation and marketization at home but soon to spread overseas, forcing other countries to wear the Golden Straitjacket if they were to partake of the benefits of global capitalism (stepped-up economic integration). The rules of the Golden Straitjacket (or what has come to be known as the 'Washington Consensus') are the requirements of responsible macroeconomic policies (tight monetary and fiscal policies), a 'hands-off' small government, flexible labor markets, deregulation, privatization, liberalization, opening of the domestic markets for trade and investment.

Rodrik (2000) incorporates the idea of the Golden Straitjacket into what he calls 'the political trilemma of the world economy', a trilemma stemming from three policy choices: international economic integration, nation-state, and mass politics, as illustrated in Figure 1.4. The trilemma allows us to choose a combination of two policy choices, not all three:

> If we want true international economic integration, we have to go either with the nation-state, in which case the domain of national policies will have to be significantly restricted, or else with mass politics, in which case we will have to give up the nation-state. If we want highly participatory political regimes, we have to choose between the nation-state and international economic integration. (Rodrick, 2000: 180)

Japan was once able to pursue a combination of nation-state and local politics (which was quite ethnocentric/nationalistic) at the cost of international economic integration (i.e., protecting domestic industries and controlling capital flows across border) under the Bretton Woods compromise, which, in fact, permitted restrictions on trade and capital flows to a considerable extent, although the overall trend was in the direction of freer exchanges of goods.

As will be detailed in Chapter 9, such an ethnocentric *dirigiste* catch-up policy turned out to be effective during the Bretton Woods-cum-the Cold War period. But the post-Cold-War age of the IT revolution (which ushered the New Economy into the world) has been compelling Japan to shift away from the axis of nation-state and local politics and toward that of nation-state and global integration. In other words, Japan has recently begun to wear the

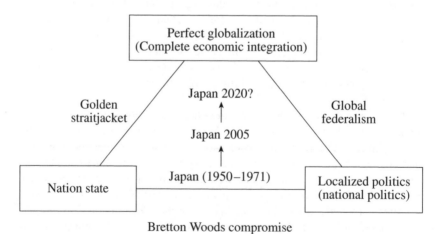

Source: Based on Rodrik (2000)

Figure 1.4   The political trilemma of the world economy

Golden Straitjacket – albeit initially reluctantly and even now somewhat gingerly (as illustrated by arrows in Figure 1.4).

1.6. COMMON FEATURES AND DISSIMILARITIES BETWEEN THE TWO HEGEMONS

There are at least six important common features (though there are obviously many dissimilarities as well) between the two strands of hegemon-led growth clustering.

1.6.l. Leader's Stance

Both types of growth clustering are based on a *hierarchy* of diverse economies in terms of degree of technological advance and levels of per capita income. Each hegemonic economy (as may be interchangeably called the 'first lead goose' in terms of the flying-geese model of tandem growth discussed earlier) initially even adopted a unilateral free-trade stance. This created the vast and readily available markets to which the emulating economies were able to export goods. The hegemon thus provided a crucial external market (demand) so that the follower countries could supplement their underdeveloped internal markets and even earn foreign exchange (dominant currency).

The only difference between Great Britain and the United States as a lead economy was that the former at least initially restricted technology outflows to retain trade competitiveness at home, while the latter was much more willing to impart its technological and organizational knowledge overseas (as evidenced by America's various programs of technology transfer and economic aid in the post-WWII period) – most importantly, because of the huge technological gap that existed at the end of the war and America's Cold War geopolitics to create industrially strong allies.

1.6.2. Layers of Emulators

Both British and American hierarchies had layers of challengers. In the British hegemony, as Rostow (1960) shows in his stages theory of growth, Britain had a take-off lead over the 1783–1802 period, followed by 'take-off Class II (1830–50)' (e.g., US, France, and Germany), then 'take-off Class III (1870–1901)' (e.g., Sweden, Japan, Russia, Italy, Canada, and Australia), and 'take-off Class IV (1933 onward)' (e.g., Argentina, Turkey, Brazil, Mexico, Iran). Although Rostow is concerned only with identifying when the take-off (and subsequently 'the drive to technological maturity and high mass consumption') has occurred in different countries, his classification of countries demonstrates the time lags involved among what he calls the 'four graduating classes'. It is also of interest to note that Japan was already in the third graduating class, along with such other countries as Sweden and Italy, under the forces of Britain-led growth clustering in the pre-World War I (WWI) period.

The British hegemony ended by WWI, and the between-the-wars period witnessed a global stagnation. The US, a member of the second graduating class, whose economy dramatically expanded during WWII, emerged decisively as a new hegemon after the war. Thus, the America-led clustering was clearly a continuation of the Britain-led clustering. In turn, the America-led Pacific Rim clustering has been a sequence of tandem growth: US→Japan→NIEs→ASEAN-4→China. That is to say, the flying-geese pattern of tandem growth has been a regional manifestation of America-led clustering. (It should be noted, however, that this sequence of tandem growth has become *no longer* so linear and monotonic as depicted in the FG pattern in some industries, notably electronics and the Internet-enabled industries. That is to say, the FG formation becomes 'un-orderly', though its essence – knowledge transfer – remains unchanged.)

1.6.3.   Emulators' Catch-up Policy – 'Infant Industry' Protection

The Britain-led clustering indicates that the emulating nations all used dynamic 'infant-industry' protection (import substitution) policies. Interestingly, Friedrich List (1841) greatly influenced both Germany and the US (of the second graduating class or the second geese) in adopting protection as a means of building up national manufacturing industries in their efforts to catch up with Britain. Surprisingly enough, it is not widely known that List himself was actively involved in the early protectionist movement and the formulation of the early tariff policies of the US. He was in exile from Germany in the US from 1825–1830 to escape a ten-month sentence received for his liberal ideas, which were too far advanced for the government of the time (Bell, 1953).

Japan as a second goose under the American hierarchy similarly pursued a dynamic infant-industry protection strategy, as did South Korea and Taiwan (the third-ranking geese). On the other hand, China is currently engaged in a new form of protection, what may be called 'infant market protection', involving the participation of many foreign multinationals in local industrial development in its still protected markets (Ozawa, 1999b).

It is worth noting that even Britain's rise to power in the wake of the Industrial Revolution may itself be interpreted as an outcome of import substitution involving Indian cotton cloth. Textile machinery was invented for the very purpose of manufacturing 'the cotton yarn that European hands were too clumsy to produce by methods long used in India' (Rostow, 1990: 22).

1.6.4. Emulators' Technological Contributions

A successful catch-up process is not a mere borrowing of advanced knowledge (technology and skills) from the hegemonic economy. It involves original knowledge creation, normally as improvements on – or alternatives to – existing knowledge. Among the most notable innovations made by the followers during the British-based period were, as mentioned earlier, the interchangeability/standardization of parts and assembly-line mass production (Fordism/Taylorism) in the US. Later on, under the America-led clustering, mass production in turn came to be replaced by flexible or lean production (to be discussed in Chapter 5) in Japan. Japan's consumer electronics industry also made a significant contribution to innovating and commercializing a slew of sleek and wondrous gadgets, devices, and components (ranging from pocket-sized transistor radios in the late 1950s to business-card-sized calculators, the quartz watch, portable stereos, VCRs in the 1970s to LCDs and camcorders in the 1980s to CD players, digital cameras, and high-definition flat TVs in the 1990s, and now DVDs and other digitalized devices). The simultaneous existence of the technologically capable second geese is critical in augmenting and further spreading the forces of macro-clustering initially set in motion by the lead goose. The role of the second geese as a technological augmenter cannot be overemphasized.

1.6.5. Trade and Factor Movement

In both hierarchies, multilateral patterns of trade ensued. Britain (the first goose) and its close emulators, continental Europe and the US, focused on manufacturing, while the primary producing countries (mostly colonies) specialized in producing and providing raw materials to the industrial North. And a new international division of labor developed between Britain and other newly industrialized European countries and the US, in which Britain tended to specialize in the old industries (steel, ships, rail, and related goods) and services (especially international finance and insurance), while Europe and the US specialized in the new industries (chemicals and electrical goods) (Landes, 1969).

Furthermore, the British growth clustering was strongly characterized by international labor migration and capital (mostly debt capital) from the Old World to the New World. Kevin O'Rourke and Jeffrey Williamson's *Globalization and History: The Evolution of a Nineteenth-Century Atlantic Economy* (1999) is the first attempt to present a comprehensive analysis of

Britain-led clustering in terms of a received neoclassical framework, the Heckscher–Ohlin–Samuelson factor-endowment theory. O'Rourke and Williamson's aim is to examine cliometrically if income (real wage) convergence occurred among major economies during the 1850–1914 period. They argue that the driving mechanisms of what they call 'globalization' (which is equivalent to the notion of growth clustering) are (i) cross-border factor movements (labor migration and capital flows) and (ii) international trade – both of which were substantially liberated due to cost reductions in transportation and communications (railroads, steam ships, and the telegraph) and the hegemon's (Britain's) free trade stance. They stress that 'Our results suggest that the ability to exploit international factor markets was *the* crucial variable determining relative performance' (O'Rourke and Williamson, 1999: 282, emphasis added). Capital flows were mostly debt capital (bonds) at that time. Put in terms of our lexicon, the more successful a catching-up country (the New World) was in attracting immigrants and capital inflows, the more effective it was in riding on the hegemon-led wave of growth clustering. This thus explains the success of the US to later emerge as the heir of global capitalism.

In contrast, the US-led growth clustering, especially as it is regionalized in East Asia, has been quite different, since labor migration was out of the question, and capital flows were initially constrained under the Bretton Woods (original IMF) regime. Trade and knowledge flows were *the* crucial variables determining relative growth. This was, indeed, the very situation Japan exploited to its advantage, as will be seen in subsequent chapters. Later on, furthermore, capital movement, once liberalized, has turned to rapid cross-border flows of FDI, portfolio equity investment, and bank loans.

As was the case with the British hegemony, its American counterpart has been supporting industrial production in the rest of the world by securing and governing the supplies of raw materials and fuels (now, oil and natural gas) from the Third World. In addition, a new division of labor has developed between the US and East Asia, in which the former has become ever more service-oriented (e.g., R&D, banking, finance, and insurance), while the latter has increasingly specialized in manufacturing. These patterns of multilateralism are the reflections of trade based on differences in the stages of growth and structural upgrading.

1.6.6.　Currency Stability

Both the Britain- and America-led regimes produced a Golden Age of Capitalism, as seen earlier – chronologically speaking, 1820–1913 for the former and 1950–73 for the latter, respectively. During the Britain-led golden age the GDPs and exports of constituent countries rose phenomenally by then-prevailing standards; 2.2 per cent (1820–70) to 2.5 per cent (1870–1913) in growth rates, and 4.0 per cent (1820–70) and 3.9 per cent (1870–1913) in export expansion. During the America-led golden age, there was 4.9 per cent in growth and 8.6 per cent in export expansion (Maddison, 1982, as cited in Glyn et al., 1990). Thus, 'global economic involvement' (Gray, 1999), another way of describing a process of globalization, intensified. The golden-age growth of the Pax Britannica was facilitated by the gold standard, and that of the Pax Americana first by the Bretton Woods system of fixed exchange rates, but later also by its ability to adapt to and manage flexible rates when this proved vital. Most recently, America's balance-of-payments conditions are such that many developing countries (notably China) have been able to keep their currencies undervalued vis-à-vis the US dollar so as to remain competitive in trade (causing the Humean 'flying of manufactures' phenomenon) and stock up on foreign exchange reserves.

1.6.7. Disruptions in Growth Clustering

The Britain-led clustering was ended by WWI, while its US-led counterpart has so far been interrupted by oil crises (in 1974 and 1978) and most recently by a series of financial crises, notably in Asia and Latin America. But the hegemonic power of the US continues – especially with the recent information technology revolution (more on this in Chapter 6).

1.7. RUSSIA AND JAPAN AS 'TAKE-OFF CLASSMATES': COMMUNISM VS. CONSUMERISM[3]

As pointed out earlier, the US-led growth clustering has been built on strong consumerism and market democracy. In this connection it is worth paying attention to the collapse of the USSR where consumer goods were once in short supply and it was difficult to shop – say, in comparison to postwar Japan where all manner of consumer goods came to abound, raising the people's standard of living dramatically.

Interestingly enough, Russia and Japan initially had many common characteristics as late starters at industrialization. Both began to industrialize at about the same time – and under the imperial tutelage of their respective rulers, the tsar in the former and the Meiji emperor in the latter. As discussed earlier, in categorizing countries into four different classes with respect to their 'take-off' periods, Rostow (1960) grouped Russia and Japan together in the take-off Class III (1870–1901). Russia and Japan thus began as classmates, so to speak, in the take-off stage of economic development. To be more exact, Rostow identified the Russian take-off as approximately from 1890 to 1914, and Japan's from 1878 to 1899. In the next stage of 'the drive to maturity' (in which 'a society has effectively applied the range of [then] modern technology to the bulk of its resources'), 1950 was a 'rough symbolic date for technological maturity' for Russia, and 1940 for Japan.

Consequently, Japan was slightly ahead of Russia through the 'drive-to-maturity' stage. But Japan's lead accelerated, especially after 1950 when it regained political autonomy upon the signing of the San Francisco Peace Treaty, and its economic miracle was soon to be made on the back of market democracy – with an ever-widening gap vis-à-vis Russia. For the next stage (after the 'drive-to-maturity' phase) is the age of high mass consumption in which Russia was victimized by its own political system, totalitarian communism, since such a system proved incompatible with the democratic consumerism needed to make mass-consumption capitalism flourish. The collapse of communism was the telling testimony to the intrinsic incompatibility between the age of consumerism and the centrally planned and military-dominated totalitarian society.

Rostow's (1960) prognosis concerning the self-contradictory course of Soviet communism back in the late 1950s shows great foresight:

We come now to the age of high mass-consumption, where, in time, the leading sectors shift towards durable consumers' goods and services: a phase from which Americans are beginning to emerge [in the 1950s]; whose not unequivocal joys Western Europe and Japan are beginning energetically to probe; and *with which Soviet society is engaged in an uneasy flirtation.* (p. 10, emphasis added)

For the United States, the turning point was perhaps Henry Ford's moving assembly line of 1913–14; but it was in the 1920s, and again in the post-war decade, 1946–56, that this stage of growth was pressed to, virtually, its logical conclusion. In the 1950s Western Europe and Japan appear to have fully entered this phase, accounting substantially for a momentum in their economies quite unexpected in the immediate postwar years. The Soviet Union is technically ready for this stage, and *by every sign, its citizens hunger for it: but communist leaders face difficult political and social problems of adjustment if this stage is launched.* (p. 11, emphasis added)

The basic incompatibility between totalitarian communism and the age of consumerism gave the communist leaders only one option: in order to retain power, they had to keep the Soviet economy in the pre-consumerism phase of industrial production, namely, heavy and chemical industrialization. In the meantime, the West, including Japan, quickly proceeded to the phase of high mass consumption, as its political system, democracy, turned out to be structurally congruous with the new age of consumer capitalism. No wonder, then, that the Soviet bloc came tumbling down in the late 1980s. The same forces of Pax Americana-led growth clustering likewise tapped the shores of communist China, which began pragmatically to adopt a market economy by

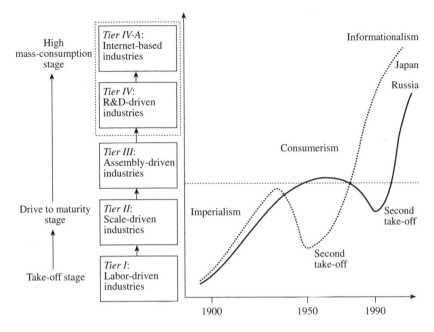

Source: Based on Ozawa (1996b)

Figure 1.5   Sequential catch-up development: Japan vs. Russia

opening its door to the Free World in 1987.   These developments are
schematically illustrated in Figure 1.5.

Why did the US win the Cold War? In a nutshell, it was not so much the
build-up of US military power under Ronald Reagan as the affluence of the
masses made possible by consumerism – that is, the power of Pax Americana-
led growth clustering, that proved decisive. In other words, consumerism and
individualism triumphed over communism and collectivism. That is to say,
Adam Smith triumphed over Karl Marx, as so often remarked in the media
after the fall of the Berlin Wall. And now the former communist bloc is in the
orbit of US-led global capitalism.

1.8. SUMMING UP

We cannot deny the fact that we are living in a world economy driven by
global capitalism under the aegis of the Pax Americana. The US-led regime
is a growth-spreading system, even at some cost to the hegemon's own

economic interests. As Hume emphasized, this is supposed to be due to 'a happy concurrence of causes in human affairs, which checks the growth of trade and riches' only in one particular people, namely the hegemon people. In other words, growth and prosperity cannot be monopolized by the hegemon alone – nor, for that matter, by any higher-echelon countries, since the hegemon-led global system is so structured that growth inevitably spreads – or 'flies' in Hume's own word – to lower-echelon countries. And this process is now accelerating thanks to the IT revolution (which leads to the death of time and space) and the on-going process of institutional reforms (deregulation, privatization and liberalization) and corporate business restructuring (involving the outsourcing, shedding and transfer of value-added activities both at home, abroad, and across borders).

In the subsequent five chapters, we will examine in detail how postwar Japan has benefited from the economies of hierarchical concatenation engendered by the forces of Pax-Americana-led growth clustering as Japan has climbed, rung by rung, the ladder of industrial upgrading. The climb has not necessarily been an easy task, since Japan encountered a different set of obstacles and accompanying problems at each rung. It will be shown that its catch-up growth, flying-geese style, has been the fundamental outcome of *incessant learning* (learning-by-borrowing, learning-by-emulating, and learning-by-alliancing), which has been made possible in terms of crafting economic policies and pre-arranging the requisite institutions designed to make the best use of the prevailing politico-economic conditions both at home and overseas at each stage of catch-up.

NOTES

1. Another book by Ozawa (forthcoming) on the third pattern is in progress, *Regionalized Endogenous Growth in Asia: The Flying-Geese Paradigm of Tandem Catch-Up*.
2. *The Economist*, July 19, 2000.
3. This section draws on Ozawa (1996b).

PART II

Out of, and beyond, the limit of borrowed knowledge and home-spun goods

2. Labor-driven stage – and logic – of reconstruction

2.1. LOGIC OF THE HECKSCHER–OHLIN TRADE THEORY

This chapter explores the process and logic of industrial upgrading and structural dynamism associated with the labor-driven (Heckscher–Ohlin) phase of catch-up growth in postwar Japan. Any developing country must rely on its relatively abundant factor in the early stages of industrialization. For a country with scarce natural resources but an abundant supply of labor, its initial development strategy is to mobilize labor so as to exploit the logic of the Heckscher–Ohlin factor endowment theory of trade. Actually, Japan's resource scarcity (except labor) has turned out to be a disguised blessing, since labor-driven economic development leads to a much *quicker* rise in wages – hence in the overall level of living standards for workers – than its resource-based counterpart (Ozawa, 1997c). In contrast, resource-abundant countries are often victimized by their dependence on primary exports, which are subject to a secular decline in the terms of trade in the world market. Resource exploitation is also subject to diminishing returns, especially on the part of labor, with the consequence of a skewed income distribution in favor of landowners but against workers, who would be trapped in poverty. This is not an ideal condition for kick-starting industrialization, since it often leads to social instability. Often cursed are the haves in natural resources, and blessed are the have-nots.

2.2. LABOR SURPLUS AS A CATAPULT FOR INDUSTRIAL UPGRADING

In the early postwar period, approximately from the start of the 1950s to the mid-1960s, Japan pursued labor-driven industrialization as a way of creating local employment and of exporting low-wage-based manufactures in order to earn badly needed foreign exchange. This type of development strategy is now considered the most basic and sensible one for any labor-abundant developing country to achieve rapid economic development. After all, Japan was then still a developing economy – with its industrial capacities in a shambles at the war's end. It also had an abundant supply of labor, both unemployed and underemployed, and its wage rate was low, as low as only one-eighth of the US level. Besides, labor-driven growth was indeed the 'natural and rational' course to take, since Japan had already built extensively competitive light industries in the prewar period, such as textiles, light machinery, household appliances, toys, and a host of others. The industrial experience and institutional arrangements thus had clearly existed, and it was relatively easy to quickly restore and expand such manufacturing activities for both home and export markets.

Japan similarly had its basic heavy and chemical industries, such as steel, shipbuilding, air craft, and chemicals, which had been fairly well established in connection with the pursuit of Japan's military objectives – but whose physical facilities after the war lay overused and damaged by air raids. Yet, human capital in the heavy and chemical industries remained. Before those war-damaged heavy and chemical industries could recover and be converted to peacetime production, however, Japan had to depend on more easily restored light industries for export and foreign exchange earnings.

The most serious problems Japan faced immediately after the war were very high rates of unemployment and underemployment and the rampant poverty caused by war devastation and defeat. As is vividly described by Uchino (1983),

> Japan had sustained crushing damage to its own economy during the war and, with defeat, it had found itself completely deprived of its former empire. The loss of Manchuria, China, and Southeast Asia reduced the territory of the Japanese empire to 56 percent of its peak during the war. As nearly 6 million demobilized soldiers and repatriated civilians flooded into Japan from these lost territories, the cessation of military production threw another 4 million people out of work to make a total 13.1 million unemployed at the end of the war. Even after making allowances for those who could be absorbed into the agricultural sector, the economy would have to create employment for approximately 10 million people. (pp. 17–18)

Since wartime bombing had reduced 119 major cities to rubble, 'approximately 2.2 million homes were lost ... and 9 million people were driven into the streets with only the clothes on their backs' (Uchino, 1983: 15). Many families found shelter in the rural areas, often eking out a living as marginal farm laborers for their relatives and acquaintances or in rural cottage industries. Those who remained in the cities had to find employment as day laborers in alley shops and a host of service jobs that catered for the occupation forces. These abnormal labor market conditions created an abundant supply of low-cost yet hard-working, skilled workers for labor-intensive industries.

The situation was akin to Arthur Lewis's growth model of unlimited labor supply (1954) and Charles Kindleberger's account of Europe's postwar growth (1967), which was framed in terms of Lewis's model. Kindleberger's analysis is highly conscious of the role of geography and labor migration. He found strong evidence that 'the major factor shaping the remarkable economic growth which most of Europe has experienced since 1950 has been the availability of a large supply of labor' (Kindleberger, 1967: 3).[1] Specifically for the German miracle, 'the *sine qua non* was the elastic labor supply which held down wages and maintained profits and investment' (p. 30). Similarly, in early postwar Japan, a large reserve army of workers, either unemployed or underemployed, provided a basis for rapid growth, because it ensured low wages, thereby relieving any immediate pressure of a profit squeeze on businesses. This phenomenon may also be interpreted as akin to Paul Krugman's notion of 'input-driven' growth, in which available labor and capital were merely mobilized to raise output with the use of existing technologies (i.e., without any increase in total factor productivity) (Krugman, 1994).

Luckily, Japanese industry had a long tradition of producing and exporting labor-intensive manufactures, the activities pursued most actively by small and medium-sized firms throughout Japan ever since its modernization in the mid-nineteenth century. Their exports were assisted by a large number of wholesale traders and trading companies. In fact, Japan's widespread small-scale cottage industry is the legacy of Japan's latecomer capitalism. Japan did not have the *laissez-faire* capitalism that preceded imperialism in England; instead, Japan's industrial revolution occurred simultaneously with global imperialism as a backdrop, with the consequence of the emergence of the 'peculiar nature of the development of capitalism in Japan' (Okazaki, 1954).[2] Drawing on this observation, Takahashi (1968) points out the peculiarities of the modern Japanese economy: *inter alia*, an abundance of small and dwarf-sized enterprises, the poverty of the peasants, a narrowness of the domestic market, and a thirst for foreign markets.

All these features combined to prevail in highly export-oriented, small-scale, mostly family-owned household workshops. Interestingly, these small light-industry enterprises even now form a large number of regionally clustered production bases, which are known in Japan as *jiba-sangyo* (community-based industrial clusters). Before we proceed to examine the *jiba-sangyo*, it is appropriate to first describe the very favorable trade environment provided to Japan under the benevolent tutelage of the United States in the early postwar period.

2.3. THE US AS A BENEVOLENT VICTOR

As discussed in Chapter 1, the success of East Asian growth should be interpreted as a sequence of strong chain reactions created within the US-led hierarchy of countries. Their economic development did not occur simultaneously, but took place in tandem, flying-geese style. Japan was the very first of the Asian countries to exploit the growth stimuli of the Pax Americana, initially by pursuing labor-driven industrialization and exporting labor-intensive goods to the West. The United States was, in fact, the promoter of such a catch-up strategy.

It should be noted, however, that the occupying Allied Forces, at first, intended to punish Japan by stripping machinery and equipment from its factories and shipping them out as war reparations to other Asian countries that had suffered Japan's military aggression. But the communist takeover of mainland China and the start of the Cold War forced the occupation authorities to reverse their policy in favor of Japan's economic reconstruction. For example, the removal of as many as 2466 pieces of equipment was proposed in 1946, but this program was suspended in spring 1949, with the result that only 160 pieces had been removed by that time (Tsuru, 1993).

For the sake of defending the Free World against communism, the United States was clearly in a position to sacrifice its own economic interests to some extent because of its then unprecedented dominance as an economic power. As a byproduct of wartime economic mobilization, the US came to dominate the world in practically every industry at the end of the war. It ended up possessing a full set of all manufacturing industries, a complete set ranging from the most technologically sophisticated all the way down to even the most labor-intensive standardized industries.

Thus, at the start of the postwar period, the US was able to produce practically everything in self-sufficiency, enjoying superiority and competitiveness in every single industry, as well as in agriculture, forestry, and other natural resources. Ironically, however, this very US dominance contained a built-in mechanism to foster challengers and to disperse the sources of economic prosperity to its cohort member countries.

As the hegemon (lead goose) economy, the US could not afford to remain a secluded colossus. It had to take the initiative to revitalize Europe and Japan by promoting freer trade and investment in order to stem the rising tide of communism, the biggest threat to capitalism and democracy. The Marshall Plan and other magnanimous aid programs exemplified the concrete positive measures taken by the US to promote economic reconstruction, particularly against the background of the deepening Cold War. As a consequence, America's industrial hegemony and leadership served as a nursery, as it were, for the quick recovery and miraculous economic growth of Europe and Japan.

The favorable environment created by the US is well described by Krasner (1987):

... through the 1960s the United States presided over a global economic system that was theoretically based upon liberal principles and diffuse reciprocity, but which operated in fact to promote the economic prosperity and political stability of its major allies even if this meant accepting practices that discriminated against America itself. This *strange* world was one the United States could accept because of its unique global position. The extraordinary political, military, and economic dominance it was bequeathed by the consequences of World War II made it possible for the United States to adopt a very long time-horizon and pursue generous policies. Japan and Western Europe could act as *free riders on the liberal economic regime* without incurring the wrath of the United States, which was more concerned with political and economic stability than with strict adherence to liberal rules. (pp. 2–3)

In this respect, for geopolitical reasons the US selected Japan, only yesterday's enemy, as *the* pivotal ally in East Asia. With respect to America's postwar policy toward Japan, Hersh (1993) observes:

Just as German recovery was expected to stimulate economic growth in Europe, it was thought that by promoting the revitalization of Japan, the EROA [Economic Recovery in Occupied Areas] would indirectly contribute to a favorable economic climate in the Far East. In March 1948, Wall Street investment banker, William Draper, explained to a Congressional Foreign Affairs Committee that Japan – cut off from its regional and traditional supplies and markets – would be unable to export enough to the United States to pay for the import of essential American raw materials. Accordingly, a precondition for breaking out of this vicious circle was to ensure Japan access to non-dollar sources of supply. *The goal of a self-supporting Japanese economy thus became a cornerstone of US Asian policy.* Assistance to the reconstruction of Japan received even higher priority than aid to the Chinese nationalists facing defeat at the hands of Mao Zedong. In William Draper's view, *it was the revival of Japan – and not the fate of China – which was the prerequisite for the establishment of the area.* Japan was to provide the 'focal point in the whole recovery of the East from the effects of the war'. (pp. 17–19, emphasis added)[3]

Furthermore, despite America's absolute supremacy in nearly all industries, what mattered as a basis for trade in the early postwar period was essentially the working of comparative advantage. Being abundantly endowed with capital, natural resources, and superior technology, the US obviously had a very strong comparative advantage in high value-added industries ('Schumpeterian' and 'differentiated Smithian'), only a weak comparative advantage in medium value-added industries ('nondifferentiated Smithian'), and definitely a comparative disadvantage in low value-added (labor-intensive) industries ('Heckscher–Ohlin'). On the other hand, early postwar Japan had a strong comparative advantage in labor-intensive industries such as textiles and toys.

The sources of competitiveness in Japan's textile exports in those days were succinctly explained by Kenen (1960) in terms of two trade theories of comparative advantage:

The structure of wage costs from industry to industry is not the same in every country. Japan ... has lower wage costs per unit of textile output than the United States, and successfully competes in our market ... our textile wages are below average American wages; and [that] Japanese textile wages are below typical Japanese wages. But *Japan's textile industry is as productive as ours*. Hence the average absolute wage difference between Japan and the United States is not offset by a difference in efficiency, and Japan can compete in our market ...

Our competitive advantage in the manufacture of machinery has little to do with wage rates in our machine-producing industry; workers there are not underpaid compared to workers in similar industries abroad. Our advantage stems, instead, from the fact that the American machine-producing industry is more efficient compared to other American industries than are machine-producing industries abroad compared to other industries abroad. (pp. 31–2)

In other words, Japan's textile industry has a comparative advantage because of lower wages even though efficiency (technology level) is almost identical (as postulated in the Heckscher–Ohlin factor endowment theory of trade), while the US machinery has a comparative advantage since it has a superior technology (as envisaged in David Ricardo's theory of comparative advantage built on different technological levels).

In those days, interestingly enough, American labor unions themselves were promoting free trade by fully embracing the doctrine of comparative advantage. In the late 1950s, George Meany, president of the AFL-CIO, declared that it was in the interest of the United States to freely import small Volkswagens from Germany and toys from Japan, so that the Germans and Japanese could in turn purchase American goods. The AFL-CIO even officially declared rather hyperbolically in strong support of free trade:

Without 'free trade' ... at least half of the American people would be doomed to a life of poverty. The nation would be consumed by crime, civil disorder, race riots, violence, forcing an end to all civil and industrial liberties. America's roads would be clogged with masses of wandering, homeless people, threatening the existence of the family as an institution and giving rise to a generation of juvenile delinquents. Sickness and disease would plague the population. Demagogues would harangue the people and mislead and confuse them. The crisis would convulse the nation, threatening private property and democratic political institutions alike. (Donahue, 1992: 23)[4]

As a consequence, the doctrine of comparative advantage and free trade was eagerly espoused and put into practice with decisive support and endorsement from labor unions. Japan was clearly a great beneficiary of such US trade policy. In fact, the US even encouraged Japan to manufacture and export cotton textiles by using the cotton the US government supplied on generous credit, because the prewar source of cotton supply from China had been cut off and no longer available (Arisawa, 1967). Consequently, in the 1950s the

Japanese textile firms started out as low-cost subcontractors for American's then Big Five apparel makers: Regal Accessories, Republic Cellini (Hy Katz), Marlene, Spartan Mayro, and CBS (Jack Clark), all southern US manufacturers who produced low-end apparel in Japan (Bonacich and Waller, 1994). And in those days, most of the textiles imported into the US were from Japan:

> The Far East was to the southern United States what the South was to the Northeast: an opportunity to cut costs. The early apparel importers worked almost exclusively with the large Japanese trading companies, especially Mitsui. *U.S. importers would take sample products they had either brought or made themselves and have them made in Japan at a lower price.* As one source put it, 'We taught them how to make the garments, about thread tension, how to pack a carton, etc.'. (Bonacich and Waller, 1994: 81, emphasis added)

Surely, the Japanese already knew how to produce basic textiles and garments, but had to learn how to design and stitch those high-quality, brand-differentiated apparel goods which would be marketable in postwar America's affluent consumer market.

To recapitulate, the United States was doubtlessly a magnanimous victor (even though geopolitics compelled the US to be so in its own self-interest). In an interview the late Saburo Okita, former foreign minister of Japan (who popularized the notion of the flying-geese formation of East Asian economies at the fourth Pacific Economic Cooperation Conference in Seoul, South Korea, in 1985), remarked that 'America was generous and open ... although Japan was still an occupied country, the Americans were extremely kind to us' (Hara, 1991: 48). Such a favorable external institutional environment was no doubt the most critical factor in Japan's quick industrial recovery and expansion in the early postwar period.

2.4.   *JIBA-SANGYO* THE INDUSTRIAL CLUSTER

Given the abundant supply of labor immediately after WWII, in what way did Japan launch its labor-driven industrial recovery and growth? How was it organized institutionally? There are no less than 300 *jiba-sangyo* locations (micro-regional industrial clusters) throughout Japan from its northern island, Hokkaido, to its southern major island, Kyushu. Although the share of *jiba-sangyo*'s output in Japan's total manufacturing has declined with the growth of more capital-intensive, large-scale industries in Japan, they once did serve as the key export-manufacturing locations for labor-intensive goods in which early postwar Japan once again found a strong comparative advantage.

In 1970, for example, even two and a half decades after the war, these *jiba-*

sangyo still remained strongly export-focused, namely 40.6 per cent as a whole with some variations across industries, ranging from 67.5 per cent for light machinery to 36.7 per cent for textiles. In the 1950s and 1960s, they were doubtlessly even more export-oriented because the domestic market was still relatively small. These production regions were inhabited by small and mid-sized firms; in 1974, firms with five persons or fewer accounted for 70.8 per cent, and those with 50 persons or fewer for as high as 96.0 per cent of firms in textiles (Yamazaki, 1980: 13).

Production regions can be classified into two types: rural and urban types. Which type is more important depends on the industries, but the rural type was numerically dominant in both production regions, 262 vs. 45 in 1972, and enterprises, 72 699 vs. 11 714 in 1972. Yet the urban type was somewhat more significant in terms of production share for such industries as textiles and machinery and metal products, 59 per cent and 44 per cent, respectively (Yamazaki, 1980: 30). A high degree of social division of labor existed in the *jiba-sangyo* industry. Primary and secondary subcontractors accounted for somewhat more than half of the enterprises that constituted production regions. Wholesalers often served as production organizers by providing raw materials, technical guidance, and operating capital. This was basically a *putting-out* system. In the rural *jiba-sangyo* regions, at the bottom of such a production hierarchy, were the part-time farmers who were willing to work for relatively low wages – without leaving their farms.

The origin of Japan's rural *jiba-sangyo* is actually found in the poverty of an agricultural community.

> … it was the poverty of the farmers in each area which promoted the development of these [regions]. The farmers were very poor, and had large facilities and small areas of arable land to work. It was difficult for them to maintain an acceptable standard of living by farming alone, and they had to find other means of obtaining income. In this sense, the farmers can be called the founders of industry. (Yamazaki, 1980: 45)

Similarly, the urban *jiba-sangyo* was also born as a result of equally widespread poverty. Small town workshops employed those 'who were willing to be employed for the lowest possible wages and under the worst possible working conditions' (Takahashi, 1968: 85).

Given such a historical legacy of light industrial development, it is no wonder that immediate postwar poverty and unemployment sought – and found – solutions in the expansion of labor-intensive manufacturing throughout Japan. Japan's early postwar comparative advantage in light industries was thus locationally embedded in the *jiba-sangyo*.

It should be noted in passing, however, that those 'made-in-Japan' goods produced by small cottage industries in the early postwar period were often poor in quality and had an ignominious reputation as 'cheap shoddy goods'. Consequently, for the sake of promoting exports the Ministry of International Trade and Industry (MITI) had to provide guidance and set quality standards. An important role was thus played by the state in the otherwise highly market-driven process of economic development.

2.5. *JIBA-SANGYO*: MARSHALLIAN VS. SMITHIAN INDUSTRIAL CLUSTERS

Since *jiba-sangyo* is a regional industrial cluster (or a micro region), Alfred Marshall's notion of 'industrial district' (1920) may immediately be conjured up. The three enabling features of Marshall's manufacturing cluster – namely labor pooling, specialized suppliers, and information flows – are useful ideas. In this regard, however, although Marshall is usually credited with initiating discussion on and introducing the idea of spatial agglomeration, it is worth making a short digression here to stress that Adam Smith (1776) had much earlier – indeed, as many as 144 years earlier than Marshall – conceptualized the growth of industrial clustering (Ozawa, 2000; Ozawa and Ferror, 1997) and that the Smithian model is *more relevant to* Japan's export-oriented *jiba-sangyo*.[5]

Observing the nascent stages of British industrialization, Smith first emphasized the intersectoral growth complementarity between 'country' (agriculture) and 'town' (manufacturing) as the first-phase meso-level division of labor. Here the Smithian town represents an agglomeration of small manufacturers ('artificers' in Smith's own words) who settle initially in response to the needs of farmers – and, thereafter increasingly, to the needs of each other, as explained in the following passage:

> Without the assistance of some artificers, indeed, the cultivation of land cannot be carried on, but with great inconveniency and continual interruption. Smiths, carpenters, wheel-wrights, and plough-wrights, masons, and bricklayers, tanners, shoe-makers, and tailors, are people, whose service the former has frequent occasion for. Such artificers too stand, occasionally, in need of the assistance of one another, and as their residence is not, like that of the farmer, *necessarily tied down to a precise spot, they naturally settle in the neighbourhood of one another, and thus form a small town or village.* The butcher, the brewer, and the baker, soon join them, together with many other artificers and retailers, necessary or useful for supplying their occasional wants, and who *contribute still further to augment the town.* (Smith, 1776/1908: 481, emphasis added)

As manufacturing develops around 'an inland country naturally fertile and easily cultivated' (which, however, is unable to export surplus 'corn' because of high inland transportation costs but which instead can provide surplus food and materials for local manufacturing), it starts to produce surplus artifacts which then become exportable:

> ... as the fertility of the land had given birth to the manufacture, so that progress of the manufacture re-acts upon the land, and increases still further its fertility. The manufacturing first supply the neighborhood, and afterwards, as their work improves and refines, more distant markets ... *The corn, which could with difficulty have been carried abroad in its own shape (on account of the expense of land carriage, and inconveniency of river navigation), is in this manner virtually exported in that of the complete manufacture, and may easily be sent to the remotest corners of the world.* (Smith, 1776/1908, 430–1, emphasis added)

This process of micro-regionalization thus involves what may be called 'surplus-resource transmogrification' – that is, surplus corn (wheat) is transmogrified into manufactures as exportables in towns (i.e., micro-industrial clusters). In fact, this *roundabout* way of exporting corresponds to what is known as the Smithian 'vent-for-surplus' theory of trade (Myint, 1958), which stresses the activation of surplus resources and surplus capacities through trade. The surplus-resource transmogrification, however, represents 'a vent for surplus' through *indirect* (roundabout) trade.

And once these manufacturing clusters begin to export, productivity growth is further sparked and enhanced by trade expansion itself (due to increasing returns to scale, learning, and agglomerations), as expounded in Smith's famous dictum: 'the division of labor is limited by the extent of the market'. It is, indeed, to this dynamic micro-regionalization process that Smith attributed the rise of Leeds, Halifax, Sheffield, Birmingham, and Wolverhampton as England's dominant industrial clusters. Smith thus clearly saw and conceptualized how trade was both influenced by and in turn reinforced the process of geographical industrial agglomeration in Britain. He therefore identified the critical nexus between trade and geography more than 200 years earlier than Porter (1990) and Krugman (1991), who are often credited with bringing geography into trade and growth theory.

Indeed, the differences between Marshall's and Smith's conceptualizations of industrial clustering are quite sharp. In contrast to Marshall's *single*-sector manufacturing-centered, close-economy model of regional agglomeration, what Smith had in mind was actually a *three*-sector, *open*-economy model, in which the 'town' initially provides artifices to the 'country' in exchange for surplus farm produce, but soon ends up exporting its own surplus artifices overseas. And trade exerts favorable feedback on the 'town' (manufacturing cluster). Smith's concept is far more dynamic, more structural in terms of sectoral interactions, and more explicitly focused on the role of trade. It is based on virtuous cycles and cumulative causation. Marshall's industrial agglomeration is compatible with the static model of perfect competition, whereas Smith's concept is not, since it involves both external and internal economies (increasing returns), as well as export-induced technological progress. Japan's *jiba-sangyo* fits Smith's model much better than Marshall's.

2.6.   THE PARADOX OF LABOR SHORTAGES IN A LABOR-ABUNDANT ECONOMY

Labor-surplus and low-wage conditions in Japan did not last long. The more successful the expansion of Japan's labor-driven industrialization and labor-intensive exports, the greater the demand for young workers and the more rapid the rise in wages. This development is exactly what the Heckscher–Ohlin theory of trade would predict: a relatively abundant factor, labor, will gain from trade when a country's comparative advantage prevails in labor-intensive industries. Moreover, an increased overseas demand for exports exerts a pronounced upward pressure on wages, a phenomenon known as a 'factor price magnification' effect for the Heckscher–Ohlin type of trade (Stolper and Samuelson, 1941). In this sense, *trade-based comparative advantage is self-destructive*.

The shortages of young workers began to appear in the early 1960s and became serious in its latter half. The ratio of job offers to job seekers for the 19-and-under age group stood at 157 per cent in 1965 and continued to rise. The ratio reached 506 per cent in 1970; that is, each job seeker of this age category received five offers on the average (Ozawa, 1979b). Many factors on both the supply and the demand sides of the industrial labor market contributed to this development. First, Japan's overall demographic structure soon grew older with a decline in the absolute number of 15- to 19-year-olds in the labor force, a category previously bolstered by the 'baby boom' of the immediate postwar period. It declined from 12.4 per cent of the total labor force in 1955 to 5.7 per cent in 1970.[6]

Rising incomes and Japan's tradition of education meritocracy, as reflected in the education-based promotion system in both business enterprises and government bureaus, encouraged an ever-increasing number of young people to seek higher education. The educational opportunities for higher learning were created as part of the postwar modernization/democratization programs introduced by the occupation authorities. As many as 55 new universities were created, one in each prefecture throughout Japan; consequently, the percentage of junior high school graduates who entered employment declined from 38.6 percent in 1960 to 18.7 percent in 1969.[7] Although this type of labor shortage did create a short-term problem for the expanding, labor-intensive industries, it initiated a process of human capital formation, namely, the creation of a better educated labor force that Japan would soon need for its higher-tier phases of growth.

At the same time, as the supply of young workers in the labor market decreased, Japan's economic growth brought about a surge in the demand for young workers who were highly adaptable, both physically and mentally, to modern industrial operations. In addition to the *jiba-sangyo*, larger-scale, factory-based manufacturing activities rapidly grew *pari passu* with the growth of new consumer goods such as motorcycles (e.g., Honda's 'cubs' or light motorcycles); portable radios and tape recorders (e.g., Sony's transistor radios and tape recorders); musical instruments (e.g., Yamaha's organs and pianos); electrical household appliances (e.g., Matsushita's washing machines, refrigerators, and air-conditioners); and TV sets, first monochrome in the 1950s and then color in the late 1960s (e.g., Sharp's TVs and Sony's transistor TVs).

New large-scale factories were rapidly built to mass-produce these consumer durables. Many of them became Japan's new earners of foreign exchange. The expansion of the new industries and the rising per-capita incomes also resulted in demand for industrial and social infrastructure such as highways, bridges, railroads, airports, telephone lines, and other transportation and communications facilities. This new development became an important support base for the next phase of heavy and chemical industrialization, as will be described below. Although the products were more capital-intensive than Japan's traditional exports, their mass production processes were at least initially quite dependent on low-cost factory labor, especially on the 19-year-and-under group of workers.

Labor shortages began to occur in the late 1960s. In 1971, for example, as many as seven job offers became available to each young job seeker. With an ever-increasing abundance of employment opportunities for young people, they grew particularly fastidious about working conditions and the social status associated with their occupations. Japanese enterprises began to experience the difficulty of recruiting young people for physically strenuous work such as metal casting or for unclean jobs such as skinning and tanning. They showed more interest in what they considered clean and glamorous service industries, such as department stores, airlines, travel agencies, and Japan's emerging leisure industry.

Despite their gleaming modern facilities, even large manufacturing enterprises had trouble attracting and hiring young people for shop-floor work, work considered tedious and monotonous by youth, and had to pay unconventionally high wages by the prevailing standards. By and large, however, fast-growing manufacturers with hot products, such as Sony and Matsushita, had no trouble in recruiting, since they were able to offer social prestige and job security as well as larger bi-annual bonuses than others. In contrast, small and medium-sized firms, especially those in the urban *jiba-sangyo*, were hardest hit. Their working facilities and conditions were still primitive and the least attractive for youth.

The upshot was the paradox of labor shortages in a labor-abundant economy. In short, this irony can be explained, however, in terms of economic and socio-institutional factors: (i) the wage-magnification effect of the Heckscher–Ohlin type of trade, (ii) the growth-induced increase in demand for higher education (that causes a decline in the supply of young shop-floor workers) due to Japan's high cultural propensity for learning and the enhanced postwar opportunities for higher education, and (iii) the growth-induced change in the occupational preferences of young workers away from physical toil and toward 'cleaner' office jobs.

2.7. LABOR-DRIVEN LOGIC OF OUTWARD FDI

As a way of escaping from the tightened labor market at home, Japanese manufacturers, especially small- and medium-sized ones, began to seek labor abroad.[8] Luckily, at that time, Japan's neighboring economies, that is, Taiwan, South Korea, Hong Kong, Singapore, and Thailand, had a plentiful supply of young labor, because more than 50 per cent of their population in the 1960s was under 19 years of age as compared to Japan's 33 per cent.[9] At that time, the rate of participation in higher learning was much lower in those countries than in Japan. And all the Asian economies were switching from inward-oriented development strategies to more outward-focused, export-oriented strategies. Taiwan and Korea, in particular, became eager to attract foreign investment, since US economic aid was about to cease in the mid-1960s.

As a consequence, the first wave of Japan's manufacturing investment was characterized by some unique features of abnormality or immaturity by then-prevailing Western standards of overseas production (Ozawa 1979a: 73–5).

(a) The outward expansion of Japanese firms occurred after 1968 and continued during the 1969–73 period. This first wave of FDI was a sudden phenomenon instead of an evolutionary one typical of its Western counterparts. Western firms grew large enough in size and financial power to become multinational corporations.[10] Komiya (1990) identifies the year 1972 as the decisive beginning of Japanese FDI:

> The year 1972 was called the '*gannen*' of Japan's overseas (direct) investment. The *gannen* is the first year of

the reign of an emperor in China or Japan. Japan's overseas FDI increased sharply in 1972 and 1973. In these two years many Japanese firms for the first time considered, planned, and undertook FDI as an important and integral part of their business activities. While Japan's outward FDI flows for the twenty-one years 1951 to 1971 add up only to 3.6 billion U.S. dollars, the total for just two years, 1972 and 1973, amounts to 5.8 billion. (p. 18)

(b) Japan's manufacturing investments were clustered in Asia, namely in neighboring countries, and were bundled together in labor-intensive or technologically standardized goods such as textiles, sundries, metal products, and the relatively unsophisticated lines of household electric appliances and chemicals. In fact, textiles, electric appliances, and sundries accounted for 63.5 per cent of the total cumulative value of Japan's investment in Asia at the end of 1975; 65.5 per cent of the total cumulative value of Japan's investment in textiles, 50.2 per cent of that in electrical appliances, and 60.7 per cent of that in sundries were located in Asia. This was considered peculiar by the then-prevailing Western theory of FDI.

(c) Japan's small- and medium-sized manufacturers, that is, those with either a capital of Y100 million or less, or a total number of employees of 300 or less, were the most active investors.

About 42 per cent of the number of overseas manufacturing investments were made by this category of enterprise and their ventures were concentrated in Japan's neighboring economies. They accounted for 70.0 per cent of Japan's manufacturing investment in South Korea and 58.6 per cent of investment in Taiwan in 1975.

(d) Japanese multinationals were highly dependent on external sources of funds to finance their foreign direct investment in those years. Thirty-four per cent of their overseas investment funds came from government-affiliated financial institutions, notably the Export-Import Bank of Japan and the Overseas Economic Cooperation Fund; 32.8 per cent came from private financial institutions, mostly the city banks whose liquidity was, in turn, created by the Bank of Japan; and the remainder from the investing firms' own internal funds.

(e) Group investment was often organized by general trading companies (*sogo shosha*) as providers of capital, information, organizational skills, and access to markets (Kojima and Ozawa, 1984b).

These immature features reflected the special macro-structural changes, that is, the sharp decline in the labor–capital ratio, which Japanese industry found itself experiencing as it initially pursued the avenue of labor-driven reconstruction of the war-torn economy. The first phase of Japan's overseas investment can be summarized in the following way:

> ... given the influence of the peculiar macro-economic forces on the Japanese economy, the *more competitive* the industry (that is, the less technologically sophisticated the product and the smaller the firm-specific advantage), the *greater* the need so far for the Japanese manufacturing sector to resort to overseas production in developing countries – a phenomenon not envisioned in the prevailing monopolistic theory of direct foreign investment. (Ozawa, 1979a: 89)

This type of macro-motivated FDI emerges under the forces of *increasing factor incongruity* (to be elaborated on in Chapter 7). Simply put, the very success of labor-driven and export-focused industrialization causes labor shortages and wage increases, and destroys the country's comparative advantages in labor-intensive products. As a consequence, there inevitably emerges the phenomenon of factor incongruity between the promoted labor-intensive production and exports and the country's newly altered factor prices. This principle led to Japan's low-wage-seeking type of overseas investment toward the end of its labor-driven stage of postwar reconstruction.

The low-wage-seeking type of FDI in standardized, traditional manufactures such as textiles and sundries continued to be made throughout the 1970s, accentuated by the first two rounds of appreciation of the yen in 1971 and 1973, which further destroyed Japan's labor-intensive exports, whose competitiveness had depended on price rather than non-price factors.[11] This type of FDI can be called the 'elementary or immature' type, since it seeks a more favorable production milieu in which to operate rather than aiming at exploiting the firm's monopolistic advantage or market power; it is *macro-structurally induced*. The industries in which the early Japanese MNCs operated were highly competitive in market structure. They were not characterized by the monopolistic or oligopolistic features which are posited in the Hymerian monopolistic theory of FDI.

In those days, for example, Vernon (1970) observed: 'Multinational enterprises are not identified with the manufacture of such *standardized* products as steel bars and rods, gray cloth, or plywood; but they are identified with products whose specifications are in flux' (p. 383, emphasis added). And Kindleberger (1969) similarly argued: 'For direct investment to thrive there must be some imperfection in markets for goods or factors, including among the latter technology, or some interference in competition by government or by firms, which separates markets ... It does not occur in *standardized* goods produced by competitive industries such as textiles, clothing, flour milling, and distribution ...' (pp. 13–14, emphasis added). Nevertheless, Japanese investments in standardized light industry goods did occur.

The driving mechanism for the labor-driven logic of growth and the elementary type of FDI can be schematically summarized in terms of Hegelian triadic dialectics (Ozawa, 2003e), as shown in Figure 2.1. The 'wage magnification' effect of trade and the 'price-knowledge/industry-flow (*à la* Hume)' mechanism set in motion *both* the market and institutional forces for outward FDI in labor-intensive industries and for advancing into capital-intensive industries, first modernizing the prewar-built heavy and chemical industries. The increased enrollment in higher education (human capital formation) and the high rate of savings (financial capital accumulation) reinforced Japan's efforts to upgrade its industrial structure.

The elementary type of outward FDI represents the typical first stage of such activity from the export-oriented countries in the Third World. The NIEs have already gone through this stage, and the ASEAN-4, notably, Thailand and Malaysia, were just entering it, as they experienced the sharp rising wages at home in the pre-crisis period. It is worth keeping in mind that in the immediate post-war period and throughout the 1950s, Japan itself was still a 'newly industrializing economy (NIE)' (Kudo, 1995).

2.8.   SUMMING UP

Japan's experience with the labor-driven reconstruction of its early postwar economy clearly illustrates the importance of the international political

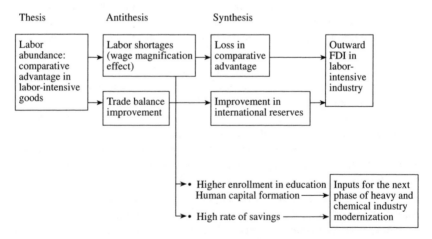

Figure 2.1   Labor-driven economic development, wage magnification, and outward FDI (the 'price-knowledge/industry-flow' mechanism à la Hume at work)

economy and institutional factors as facilitators of trade-led growth. Obviously, the pattern of a country's comparative advantage does not automatically come into existence, but needs to be purposely organized, reinforced, and managed at both external (transnational) and internal (domestic) levels.

Contrary to the expectations of the Heckscher–Ohlin factor proportions theory of trade, there are many labor-abundant countries that are simply incapable of developing any export competitiveness in labor-intensive products. Myint (2001) succinctly puts it, 'economic growth with export expansion in developing countries cannot be fully explained purely in terms of formal international trade theory unless we take into account the changes in the domestic institutional setting' (p. 520). What makes it possible for a labor-abundant economy to capitalize on exports as an engine of growth is the trade-conducive international environment and the domestic institutional arrangements, both accidental/path-dependent and policy-guided, with which the economy happens to be blessed.

In this respect, early postwar Japan was fortunate, since the US decided to help rebuild war-damaged Japan as a bastion against the rise of communism, thereby providing a very favorable trade environment. Furthermore, internally Japan had a superb institutional capability of its own – and plenty of prewar experience – to organize labor-intensive manufacturing as the catapult for export expansion. The existence of *jiba-sangyo* in the form of Smithian – rather than Marshallian – industrial clusters, along with a large number of trading firms as facilitators of financial and commercial transactions, was clearly a godsend. In short, the development of comparative advantage is *embedded in* both *time* (i.e., path-dependent on the past experiences of the nation as well as those of other nations with which it interacts in commerce) and *space* (i.e., where production is localized and how it is organized and governed in a location-specific milieu). Thus, the history (historical specificity) and geography (locational specificity) of institutional setups both matter – and matter a lot – in activating and capitalizing on the opportunities for labor-driven exports and growth.

Furthermore, trade itself causes – and interacts with – structural change and economic growth. To be specific, the labor-driven 'Heckscher–Ohlin' type of industrialization lasts only as long as wages are kept low. But wages will eventually rise, as an initially abundant factor is mobilized for production through the familiar 'factor-price magnification' effect. Once shortages of unskilled/semi-skilled labor emerge and a profit squeeze occurs, the firms engaged in labor-intensive production are compelled to transplant such production to low-wage countries as a way of economizing on labor costs. This thus initiates the phenomenon of the labor-seeking type of FDI. In the meantime, a process of industrial upgrading away from the labor-driven phase and toward the next higher value-added phase, is set in motion as wages and savings rapidly rise at home.

NOTES

1. 'The labor has come from a high rate of natural increase (the Netherlands), from transfers from agriculture to services and industry (Germany, France, Italy), from the immigration of refugees (Germany), and from the immigration of unemployed and underemployed workers from the Mediterranean countries (France, Germany, and Switzerland). Those countries with no substantial increase in the labor supply – Britain, Belgium, and the Scandinavian nations – on the whole have grown more slowly than the others' (Kindleberger, 1967: 30).
2. Okazaki (1954: 113–17).
3. It is interesting to note in passing that the current dramatic rise of China is now altering America's transpacific relations as 'Japan slips in power and relevance' (Abramowitz and Bosworth, 2003). Indeed, America's diplomatic focus has been first on Japan, then on the NIEs (Korea and Taiwan in particular), and now on China.
4. Cited in Berri and Ozawa (1997).
5. There are four major types of clusters. Smith's model can be classified as 'proto-industrial', while Marshall's is 'industrial'. Furthermore, we have 'late-industrial' and 'post-industrial' types of agglomeration. See Phelps and Ozawa (2003).
6. Economic Planning Agency (1971:104).
7. Ozawa, 1979b: 104.
8. Interestingly enough, some of these small- and medium-sized firms first sought low-cost labor in Okinawa, Japan's southernmost island, then still under occupation by the United States as a military base.
9. United Nations (1970: 538–46).
10. The fundamental assumption of the monopolistic theory of foreign direct investment as introduced by Stephen Hymer (1960/1976) is that the firm that invests for direct local production in a foreign market is at a disadvantage compared to local firms because of its unfamiliarity with local market conditions and that it inevitably incurs higher information costs than do its local counterparts. The investing foreign firms, therefore, must possess some type of firm-specific, rent-yielding advantages to offset the higher information costs of their alien status. Because of this assumption the investing firms are necessarily found in oligopolistic markets in which only large-scale firms with some corporate advantages can survive. This also means that *until a firm reaches a relatively large scale of operation at home, it is likely to put off foreign investment.* Richard Caves (1974: 130) explained, 'Because information costs associated with undertaking a foreign investment are both heavy and relatively fixed, small but rising firms that might someday find direct investment profitable may rationally postpone it until their penetration of the home market is more advanced'.
11. It should be noted that overseas investment is merely one of several adjustments necessitated by labor shortages and rising labor costs. Yamawaki (1992), for example, examines the different adjustment approaches employed by Japan's textiles and clothing producers and summarizes: 'Companies in the industry have adjusted their production processes, investment strategies and products to the changing conditions in domestic and foreign markets. The adjustments have included shedding excess labour and capital equipment; closing inefficiently small plants; investing in new labour-saving equipment; undertaking more research and development; specializing in production of commodities with high value-added per worker; and shifting production abroad'. His careful statistical study bears out some important links between these domestic adjustments and the changing pattern of Japan's trade competitiveness. 'In particular', he concludes, 'the productivity-raising adjustments, rather than protection increases, were a major force in slowing the decline in Japan's international competitiveness' (p. 111).

3. Scale-driven stage – and logic – of modernizing heavy and chemical industries: a high growth period

3.1. PUSH FOR *JU-KO-CHO-DAI*

In Japan, the heavy and chemical industries such as steel, heavy machinery, ships and basic chemicals are popularly called *Ju-ko-cho-dai* [heavy-thick-long-big] because of such physical characteristics of their goods produced – in sharp contrast to, say, consumer electronics goods which are identified as *kei-haku-tan-sho* [light-thin-short-small]. In the prewar period Japan's push for heavy and chemical industrialization was motivated to produce armaments and infrastructure goods for industrial development under the twin policy of *Fukoku Kyohei* (rich nation, strong army), a national policy that had been established at the start of the Meiji government in 1868.

On the other hand, Japan's postwar efforts to reconstruct and modernize its war-shattered heavy and chemical industries were driven by the desire to raise its standard of living beyond the level achievable during the immediate postwar phase of labor-driven industrialization centered on light industry manufacturing. The modernized heavy and chemical industries would naturally be higher value-added in production, requiring far more human capital than labor-intensive light industry (hence, more suitable for educated and skilled labor which was unemployed or underemployed in the immediate postwar days). Furthermore, they are more generative of linkage economies for other industries through input supplies – and most of all, conducive to increasing returns to scale. Japan's initial reliance on low value-added light industries such as textiles and clothing as an export-competitive sector should be only a *transitory* step, since they are the dead-end industries from a perspective of long-term industrial upgrading.

In other words, Japan would not remain a happy toy-maker for long – that is, it would not be satisfied with the *static* doctrine of comparative advantage, because it knew that such an advantage would be ephemeral, soon to be lost to other Asian countries that were far more labor-abundant and had much lower wages. Besides, such labor-based advantage is self-destructive, as stressed in the previous chapter. As a national economic goal, therefore, Japan was fully determined and bent on reconstructing and modernizing its heavy and chemical industries, the industries whose many physical facilities were left damaged by air raids or remained largely inoperative because of lack of replacement equipment, parts and raw materials at war's end. This chapter explores how Japan went about reconstructing and modernizing the prewar-built – but war-damaged – heavy and chemical industries.

3.2.   'VISIBLE' HAND OF ASSISTANCE–AND PRODDING

The above new policy focus for heavy and chemical industrialization is nicely explained by Yoshihisa Ojimi, a former Vice-Minister for International Trade and Industry:

> After the war Japan's first exports consisted of such things as toys or other miscellaneous merchandise and low-quality textile products. Should Japan have entrusted its future, according to the theory of comparative advantage, to these industries characterised by intensive use of labour? That would perhaps be rational advice for a country with a small population of 5 or 10 million. But Japan has a *large* population. *If the Japanese economy had adopted the simple doctrine of free trade and had chosen to specialise in this kind of industry, it would almost permanently have been unable to break away from the Asian pattern of stagnation and poverty*, and would have remained the weakest link in the free world, thereby becoming a problem area in the Far East. (cited in OECD, 1970: 15–16, emphases added)

Ojimi's observations epitomized the prevailing thinking of Japanese policy makers in the early successful days of industrial reconstruction. He clearly enunciated the direction of Japan's industrial policy toward the production of high income-elastic, technology-intensive, and high-productivity manufactures. Ojimi continued to argue:

> [MITI] *decided* to establish in Japan industries which require *intensive employment of capital and technology*, industries that in consideration of comparative costs should be the most inappropriate for Japan, industries such as steel, oil refining, petro-chemicals, automobiles, aircraft, industrial machinery of all sorts, and electronics, including electronic computers. From a short-run, static viewpoint, encouragement of such industries would seem to conflict with economic rationalism. But from a long-range viewpoint, these are precisely the industries *where income elasticity of demand is high, technological progress is rapid, and labour productivity rises fast.* (cited in OECD, 1972: 16, emphasis added)

It was a powerful future *vision* that was constructed out of the consensus among industry, the government, and academia for the purpose of mobilizing a concerted national effort. In fact, the Industrial Structural Council organized by MITI issued a series of visions for each new decade – for example, 'Policy Visions for the 1970s' and 'Policy Visions for the 1980s'. These visions were of the nature of *consensual affirmation* rather than of indicative planning. These visions were not unilaterally created and handed top-down by MITI. They were in many ways the synopses of the prevailing opinions of the private businessmen (corporate executives), the bureaucrats (economic technocrats), and intellectuals (university professors and pundits in the media), the consensus-based perspectives that indicated the future direction in which the Japanese economy ought to be heading in the subsequent stages of growth. In short, what MITI advocated was an *unconventional* departure from the conventional wisdom of static comparative advantage. *For the very reason that Japan was then a labor-abundant economy, it was reasoned that it needed capital-intensive industries all the more in order to go beyond the labor-driven phase.*

MITI's sagacity should not be overplayed, however. In a sense, such a progressive plan was the natural course for Japan to purse as a catching-up economy under the aegis of the Pax Americana, since this was a course already mapped out by the logic and track records of global capitalism, as detailed in Chapter 1. Moreover, the United States itself began to encourage Japan to modernize its war-torn heavy and chemical industries so that Japan would be capable of standing against communism as an industrially strong ally. The nature and internal logic of the American hegemony were such that Japanese industry was encouraged to move up the ladder of industrialization already built and demonstrated by the West.

3.2.1. Trade-Driven Logic of Factor Price Magnification

The pursuit of such a path to more capital-intensive industrialization did cause more labor shortages and more rising wages, yet it simultaneously *prepared* Japanese industry for the next higher tier of industrialization (assembly-based 'differentiated Smithian' industries). In other words, given the success of labor-driven industrialization, it was actually impossible that Japan 'would almost permanently have been unable to break away from the Asian pattern of stagnation and poverty', as Ojimi feared. On the contrary, Japan *did* begin very quickly to break away from the Asian pattern of stagnation and poverty, because it followed the 'factor-price-magnification' logic of the Heckscher–Ohlin trade theory early on by focusing on the activation of its most abundant factor, labor.

Japan's economy could not, therefore, remain labor-abundant for long, because its very push for labor-driven growth ineluctably eroded its trade competitiveness based on low-cost labor. This is in line with the principle of 'increasing factor incongruity' (to be explained in Chapter 7). While the market mechanism automatically weakened the competitiveness in labor-intensive goods, there was nevertheless no guarantee that the next stage of higher value-added growth would be autonomously achieved. In other words, the market mechanism *alone* was certainly incapable of directing and driving the process of industrial upgrading because there were so many hindrances to the smooth functioning of the market, particularly in a war-torn economy. Thus, market imperfections and failures were rampant and the order of the day. Hence, some government involvement was needed as an organizing catalyst.

As a consequence, industrial policy was deployed. MITI, however, did not apply industrial policy to all industries indiscriminately; labor-intensive industries were actually left largely to market forces (apart from finance to help promote exports in the early postwar period), since all the necessary institutional arrangements were already in place (as discussed in Chapter 2). Yamazawa (1988) even argues that Japan's trade policy for textiles, for example, adhered to the free trade system and stood in strong contrast to the import restrictions widely imposed by the Western countries. The light industries were after all overcrowded with a large number of small- and mid-sized firms and fiercely competitive with a high rate of entry and exit, a market structure itself not too distant from a textbook description of a perfectly competitive market in which fierce competition prevailed. The Japanese industrial policies were actively formulated and adopted to build up capital-intensive, higher value-added higher-echelon industries, especially the heavy and chemical industries, under protection.

How, then, did Japanese industry proceed to institutionally organize production in heavy and chemical industries? Although Japan had already developed the basic traditional segments of heavy and chemical industries before WWII, it again found itself far behind the West in its more advanced modern segments such as specialty steel, petrochemicals, and plastics. These industries were not only resource-intensive but also technology-based. How could resource-indigent Japan develop resource-based competitiveness in such resource-intensive modern industries? How was it possible that Japan soon emerged as the world's most efficient and largest producer of steel, for example?

3.3.   GEOGRAPHY AND *KEIRETSU*

Japan's postwar heavy and chemical industries were jump-started by the military procurements of the United Nations for the Korean War. The rate of growth in iron and steel production, for example, jumped 5.4 per cent in 1949 to 30 per cent in 1951 (Tsuru, 1993). The huge amounts of excess profits earned under the 'price is secondary' policy of the UN forces were then quickly poured into the modernization of plants and equipment in those industries.

Japan's latecomer status turned out to be a blessing in many respects. Japanese industry chose and secured the latest and best possible technologies from the available stock of industrial knowledge accumulated in the advanced West and from which Japan was cut off during the war. For example, Japan's steel industry promptly adopted the basic oxygen furnace technology ahead of the United States, which was stuck with the obsolete steel mills built a century earlier (Lynn, 1982). Japan thus acquired competitiveness on the world market exploiting the latest technology and building large steel plants to exploit scale economies under the 'three-stage Rationalization Plans 1951–55, 1956–60, and 1961–65' pushed by MITI (Yamawaki, 1988). Japan's petrochemical industry likewise depended heavily on the government's import-substitution policy and subsidies, as well as on technology absorption from the West (Peck, 1976).

In this respect, MITI clearly played the major role of industrial developer in collaboration with the *keiretsu* groups. Johnson (1982: 236–7) gives a detailed account:

> In its fully elaborated form, the late 1950's MITI system of nurturing (*ikusei*) a new industry (for example, petrochemicals) included the following types of measures: First, an investigation was made and a basic policy statement was drafted within the ministry on the need for the industry and on its prospects – an example is the Petrochemical Industry Nurturing Policy adopted by a MITI ministerial conference on July 11, 1955. Second, foreign currency allocations were authorized by MITI and funding was provided for the industry by the Development Bank. Third, licenses were granted for the import of foreign technology (every item of petrochemical technology was obtained on license from abroad). Fourth, the nascent industry was designated as 'strategic' in order to give it special and accelerated depreciation on its investments. Fifth, it was provided with improved land on which to build its installations, either free of charge or at nominal cost. (In August 1955, MITI ... approved the sale of the old military fuel facilities at Yokkaichi, Iwakuni, and Tokuyama to four newly created petrochemical companies ...). Sixth, the industry was given key tax breaks – in the case of petrochemicals, exemption from customs duties on imported catalytic agents and special machinery, the refund of duties collected on refined petroleum products used as raw materials for petrochemicals, and special laws exempting certain users form gasoline taxes. Seventh, MITI created an 'administrative guidance cartel' to regulate competition and coordinate investment among the firms in the industry – in this case, the 'Petrochemical Cooperation Discussion Group,' established by MITI on December 19, 1964. (pp. 236–7)

In addition to absorbing state-of-the-art technologies from the West, along with the modern plant equipment and machinery, the postwar modernization of Japan's heavy and chemical industries consciously took advantage of the

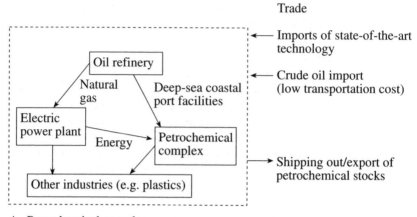

A. Petrochemical complex

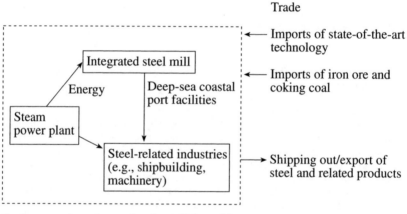

B. Integrated steel complex (e.g., Kawasaki)

Figure 3.1 Konbinato *clusters*

economies of *spatial clustering* in those pieces of industrial property sold at subsidized prices. The spatial/geography-driven source of Japanese competitiveness in the heavy and chemical industries is illustrated in Figure 3.1.

As pointed out in the above quote from Johnson (1982), the government improved and provided large tracts of land (industrial sites) on which to build new steel mills and petrochemical complexes, 'either free of charge or at nominal cost'. These sites were prepared in the coastal areas right on the water front with new port facilities in such a way that low-cost sea transportation could be taken full advantage of in importing and unloading bulky raw materials and loading and shipping out processed goods of heavy weight. Moreover, in those new industrial sites, a petroleum refinery, a set of adjunct petrochemical plants, and a power-generating plant were simultaneously arranged to be located in close proximity to each other so as to achieve efficient flows of energy, inputs, and outputs. Since the key plant facilities were placed in an optimal spatial and functional combination, they were called *konbinato* in Japanese.

> ... During the late 1950s, the petroleum industry established refining facilities near port facilities in combination (*konbinato*) with steam-powered electric generating facilities. The concept mushroomed into a much more complex type of *konbinato* in which the large volume of exhaust gas produced during the oil refining process was utilized by the electric power industry, and petrochemicals facilities came to be located in the same *konbinato* near oil refinery plants, which provided their raw materials. Moreover, since the *konbinato* themselves were located near major new ports, all the industries involved benefited from the lower transportation costs, especially of oil. (Uchino, 1983: 93)

This highly compact type of industrial clustering also occurred in integrated steel-making complexes where electric power plants and steel mills stood side by side. They proved to be space-saving in design and efficient in energy use and cost reduction; for example, the Kawasaki and Chiba steel *konbinato* were only about one fifth of the usual plant space used by US Steel and Bethlehem Steel in the United States, yet the Japanese mills produced more steel.

All these *konbinato* were designed to exploit internal, as well as external, scale economies at the same time. Large volumes of output were made possible by Japan's rapidly grown domestic demand as well as successful exports – that is to say, expanding markets made it possible for Japanese firms to capitalize on scale economies in a fashion as stressed by Adam Smith's adage: 'the division of labor is limited by the extent of the market'. This Smithian dynamic effect of cumulative causation in market expansion and productivity growth was built on, and reinforced by, the cluster efficiency of *konbinato*.

Another form of industrial clustering at the industrial organization level was created in the form of Japan's unique system of *keiretsu* groups (closely-knit industrial conglomerates). Mitsui, Mitsubishi, and Sumitomo were the most representative of these *keiretsu* and were globally known, since their prewar counterparts once existed as *zaibatsu* (holding-company-controlled financial combines). And these *zaibatsu*-turned *keiretsu* vied vigorously with each other in setting up a new set of capital-intensive growth industries (such as petrochemicals, specialty steel, alloys, and plastics) within their own business circles by way of importing state-of-the-art technologies from the West and making investments in productive capacities, a phenomenon that came to be known as the 'one-set' principle of industrial development.

This headlong modernization of the heavy and chemical industries was the major engine of Japan's investment-driven ('investment-led-by-investment') high growth at an average annual rate of more than 10 per cent from 1959 to 1973. In fact, investment in physical capital (tangible assets) was especially critical during this high growth, when as much as 60 per cent of growth – compared with 40 per cent of growth in the US – is said to have been attributable to such investment, though human capital formation through the education and training of the Japanese labor force was also a significantly contributor (Jorgenson, 1995).

Interestingly, furthermore, each major *keiretsu* was assigned separate subsidized land on which to establish its own new *konbinato*. In petrochemicals, for example, the Mitsui Group would operate at Iwakuni; the Mitsubishi Group at Yokkaichi; the Sumitomo at Niihama; the Nippon Oil Group at Kawasaki, and the Idemitsu Kosan at Tokuyama (Miyazaki, 1980). Thus, the geographically concentrated and *keiretsu*-organized clustering is double-layered to take advantage of dynamic external economies of scale and special institutional arrangements. And the resultant oligopolistic rivalry was fierce, resulting in what the Japanese called 'excessive competition'.

It was not long before Japan emerged as the world's largest and most competitive exporter of steel, although Japan's petrochemical industry, on the other hand, lagged far behind in attaining competitiveness on the world market for a variety of reasons (Itami, 1991). Be that as it may, the upshot of such an intensive heavy and chemical industrialization was the irony that a resource-scarce economy like Japan would end up with such resource-intensive growth.

3.4.   'RESERVED COMPETITION'

As a latecomer seeking to catch up with the advanced West, especially after WWII, Japan pursued an import-substituting but simultaneously export-focused approach of nurturing domestic industries and their export competitiveness, an approach that can be conceptualized as, in an ex post sense, a 'reserved domestic market' or 'reserved competition' paradigm of industrial development (Ozawa, 1997a). MITI was the major protector and promoter of import-competing industries. It should be emphasized, however, that MITI itself did not perceive the effectiveness of its protection policy in the way conceptualized in this section. (In fact, as will be demonstrated in Chapter 4, on a couple of occasions MITI tried to weaken the efficacy of reserved competition.)

What MITI once pursued was a dynamic version of the infant industry protection model. This approach was not always applied across the board, but it was witnessed in the experience of those industries considered 'strategic' – and hence worth protection – by the Japanese government, such as steel, petrochemicals, automobiles, and computers.

Protection is usually said to breed inefficiency, since it reduces competition. Many initially protected, but later successful Japanese industries, however, did not become growth-stunted juveniles. On the contrary and paradoxically, protection ended up generating more – rather than less – intense competition at home than might have occurred without protection. In fact, many protected industries soon grew to be more efficient and strongly export-focused. Exporting itself in turn stimulated further technological improvements because of the necessity to compete with more technologically advanced Western producers. Why and how did certain types of protected Japanese manufacturing turn out to be success stories?

The key feature of this catching-up approach is that a selected new industry was initially heavily protected from both imports and inward FDI, but that, within that protected industry, a large number of domestic entrants were attracted to enter the same industry and compete vigorously with each other in a fierce market-share-grabbing contest. This multi-entrant formula is diametrically opposite to the 'national champion' strategy deployed by Europe, especially by France.

The effectiveness of this dynamic 'infant industry' approach depended on the conditions under which a fostered increase in the intensity of domestic competition needs to be greater in absolute terms than the reduction in foreign competition caused by protection so that a net competitive effect would be positive; otherwise, the surviving domestic firms would never be able to compete in the global markets:

Fostered domestic   Suppressed foreign   Net competitive effect
competition (FDC)   –   competition (SFC)   =   (NCE) > 0

There is no doubt that competition is the mother of efficiency and technological progress. In a sense, what is protected by the reserved competition formula is not only an industry, but more importantly, the *efficiency-inducing* effect of competition itself – that is, the outcome of the 'survival of the fittest' process – that can nurture world-class producers, instead of letting only a few privileged firms effortlessly enjoy 'protection rents'. The winners from this unique brand of protection are *always* national firms and not foreign firms.

Here it is worth contrasting this 'reserved competition' model with the so-called 'national champion' approach. The latter is well conceptualized at the policy level and popularly known as such. By contrast, 'reserved competition' is only an *a posteriori* notion – that is to say, Japan's policy makers themselves – or for that matter, captains of industry themselves – did not have such a clear-cut idea as is detailed here about the coincidental efficacy of their protectionist approach. Its efficacy owed much more to the private-sector dynamism than to MITI's interventionism, though the latter was certainly a necessary component of this unique phenomenon. No doubt, competition is the mother of efficiency and technological progress.

Interestingly enough, what Krugman (1986) describes about Japanese protectionism is actually relevant to the 'national champion' model but *not* to the Japanese reality:

> When businessmen try to explain the success of Japanese firms in export markets, they often mention the advantage of a protected home market. Firms with a secure home market, the argument runs, have a number of advantages; they are assured of the economies of large-scale production, of selling enough over time to move down the learning curve, of earning enough to recover the costs of R&D. While charging high prices in the domestic market, they can 'incrementally price' and flood foreign markets with low-cost products ...
>
> *By giving a domestic firm a privileged position in some one market, a country gives it an advantage in scale over foreign rivals.* This scale advantage translates into lower marginal costs and higher market share even in unprotected markets. (Krugman, 1986: 180–1, emphasis added)

On the contrary, the reserved competition model deprives entrants of 'a privileged position in some one market'.

Furthermore, protection is usually said to encourage rent seeking – hence, inefficient. Rent seeking is thus theorized as an efficiency-reducing activity. For example, Bhagwati and Srinivasan (1983) label it 'directly unproductive profit-seeking activities'. Yet the dynamic (technology-focused) type of rent seeking demonstrated in the reserved competition model is actually efficiency-enhancing and productive in the long-run, since it can generate *more* – not less – competition and technological progress.

3.5. THE PARADOX OF 'RESOURCE-DRIVEN GROWTH IN A RESOURCE-SCARCE ECONOMY'

Because Japan is poorly endowed with natural resources, its push for the *ju-ko-cho-dai* meant an ever-growing dependence on foreign supplies. Japan, in fact, soon became the world's largest importer of many vital mineral resources. For example, during the stage of heavy and chemical modernization, its share of trade in coking coal among the OECD member countries climbed from 15.8 per cent in 1964 to 41.6 per cent in 1969; in iron ore from 23.7 to 39.3 per cent; in copper from 9.5 per cent to 19.1 per cent;

and in crude oil from 12.6 per cent to 15.6 per cent. By the end of the 1960s, Japan's dependency on overseas sources for bauxite, nickel ore, and uranium had already reached 100 per cent; about 90 per cent for iron ore; 83 per cent for copper; 73 per cent for natural gas; and 50 per cent for lead and zinc (Ozawa, 1979b). All these developments clearly reflected a rapid shift of orientation in Japan's industrial structure from light industry to heavy and chemical sectors that are both resource-intensive and more energy-consuming.

Indeed, the resource requirements (intensity) of Japan's industrial structure in 1970 ironically became the world's highest, despite the fact that it is one of the world's most resource-indigent countries. Japan came to exhibit the highest concentration of industry in the sectors consuming the most resources (21.6 per cent) and the lowest concentration in the sectors consuming the least resources (14.7 per cent), compared with West Germany (19.4 per cent and 18.1 per cent) and the United States (15.0 per cent and 22.3 per cent) (Ozawa, 1979b).

Japan's industrial strategy for resource-based industrialization was, for the most part, accommodated by fortuitous economic conditions prevailing overseas at that time. In the first place, Japan was initially allowed to have free access to the supplies of resources-producing countries such as Australia and Canada, as well as of those Western multinationals that operated and traded globally in oil, natural gas, and minerals. Soon afterwards, when the Western majors' grip on the global resources market was loosened in the wake of a wave of expropriations of their operations in the Third World, the market became fluid, providing Japan with fresh opportunities to secure the basic materials directly from new independent sellers in the developing countries such as India, Brazil, Chile, Peru, and Zambia (Vernon, 1983).

Paradoxically enough, one may even argue that the exiguity of domestic natural resources turned out to be an unexpected boon – the key source of competitiveness – for resource-scarce Japan compared to the resource-abundant Western countries, which often had to maintain artificially high prices for domestically available resources. This was, for instance, the case with Australia in newly discovered oil at home:

> ...Japanese industry is not compelled to buy expensive and/or inferior domestic materials but can buy from *the cheapest source in the whole world* ... with respect to a country that discovers some natural resource which for reasons of its quality, location or domestic factor costs is not the cheapest in the world ... this has happened in Australia, where the recent discoveries of oil (which for various reasons will be substantially dearer than the imported oil) will tend to impoverish the country for many years because the oil could be obtained at a lower 'opportunity cost' from abroad, but the government compels the country to use the dearer domestic oil. (Bieda, 1970: 45)

Thus, the meagerness of Japan's domestic resources did allow its buyers to shop around in the world market and secure raw materials at the most economical prices, enabling them to escape the burden of supporting a continued production of costly domestic supplies.

It should be noted, however, that actually the Japanese government initially imposed a tariff on oil and gave domestic coal price subsidies to make it competitive with petroleum. But in the early 1960s, the government moved away from protecting the coal industry and instead acted to directly mitigate the social and economic dislocations caused by mine closure. As a result, a shift to imported coal and then increasingly to imported petroleum quickly occurred. For example, in 1953, no less than 46.8 per cent of Japan's national energy requirements was met by domestic coal, only 6.0 per cent was accounted for by imported coal, and 17.7 per cent by petroleum. Twenty years later, however, the weight of domestic coal declined to a minuscule 3.8 per cent, while that of imported coal nearly doubled to 11.7 per cent and that of petroleum more than quadrupled to 77.6 per cent (Ozawa, 1979b). Furthermore, not only did the supply of overseas resources become favorable but also demand for processed resources grew strongly on the world market, especially during the Vietnam War. (How a relatively capital-scarce Japan was able to finance this phase of capital-intensive industrialization will be discussed in Chapter 9.)

3.6.   HOUSE-CLEANING TYPE OF FDI

Such a headlong rush to expand heavy and chemical industries in a small island economy, however, inevitably led to the malignancies of pollution, congestion, and ecological destruction. *Konbinato* was efficient, but its extremely high density of production per unit of space, easily a few times the norm of the West, had its flip side; it caused serious pollution problems in a concentrated manner at the peak of heavy and chemical industrialization in the late 1960s. For example, mercury poisoning (via poisoned fish in the bay) occurred at Niigata, and asthma (via air pollution) at Yokkaichi. The high capital–labor ratio required in these industries also led to a continuous rise in wages, further weakening the already-declining labor-intensive industries, a phenomenon akin to the so-called 'Dutch disease' (intersectoral diseconomy via the wage mechanism).

A serious shortage of land as industrial and living space soon became apparent. The Japanese economy, confined to a small mountainous archipelago, was clearly pushing its meager physical limit for industrial expansion. By the end of the 1960s, the Pacific coastal regions of Japan's mainland, known as Tokaido, were literally cluttered with factories, with continuous urban industrial sprawls obliterating the rural intervals that had once existed.

The 1973–4 oil crisis and rising economic nationalism in resource-exporting countries suddenly made the vulnerability of Japan's dependency on overseas industrial resources critical. For many years, Japan had been fortunate in its ability to import the necessary energy and mineral resources at attractively low prices. The conventional trade mechanism was sufficiently reliable to ameliorate the situation resulting from Japan's exiguous natural endowments, a handicap that otherwise would have stultified any budding industrialization in that island economy (Ozawa, 1979a).

The postwar Japanese economy was redesigned to operate essentially, as it had in prewar days, as a *processing workshop* that imports raw materials, processes, and fabricates them into finished products, and then exports them. Such processing activities came to be centered, as they had not in prewar days, around heavy machinery, chemicals, and petrochemical products, instead of light manufactures, as seen above. In the early postwar period, trade was initially the sole link with the outside world, a means Japan had to escape from the scantiness of natural resources at home. In the early 1970s it became evident that access to overseas resources through trade was no longer as secure and as dependable as before. There was a sharp rise in worldwide demands for natural resources, and the resource-exporting countries also became more interested in extracting as many economic and political concessions as possible from the resource-importing countries.

Although scarcities of labor and land became quite serious at the start of the 1970s, nevertheless, Japan fortunately had succeeded in making another key factor, capital, both financial and human, relatively abundant. The abundance of financial capital came in part in the form of foreign exchange reserves as a result of Japan's rising trade surpluses. In order to remove the uncertainties of foreign supplies of industrial resources and to cope with shortages of labor and land at home, surplus capital began to be exported to other countries. This culminated in the first wave of outward investments from Japan in the early 1970s.

The suddenly swollen coffers of international reserves and the steep appreciation of the yen triggered by the successive devaluations of the dollar in the early 1970s also compelled the Japanese government to go through a series of yen defense programs to reduce an embarrassingly large stock of reserves and to prevent the yen from further appreciation. The first program was introduced in June 1971, the second in May 1972, and the third in October 1972. Various measures were taken to encourage imports and capital outflows, each time more progressively than before, and to discourage exports and capital inflows on a temporary basis. All overseas investments were in principle completely liberalized in June 1972.

Given the strong macroeconomic forces that pushed for overseas investment, especially in increasingly comparatively disadvantaged, labor-intensive industries, and the institutional rigidities that still hindered imports and portfolio capital outflows, the yen defense promotional measures discussed above ended up exerting an unprecedented push effect on overseas investments. The yen's appreciation itself brought about a subsidy effect on investing Japanese enterprises. On top of liberalizing capital outflows, the government instituted a special loan program for overseas investment which included a lower rate of interest and expanded availability of long-term funds in foreign exchange. This led to a heavy dependence of investing Japanese firms on external loans (loans from state agencies and banks), one of the distinctive characteristics of Japan's overseas investments.

In the face of the uncertain supplies of overseas resources, the irremediable scarcities of labor and industrial sites at home, and the deteriorating environmental conditions, the Japanese government adopted an epoch-making policy to restructure Japan's industry, a proposal made by the Industrial Structural Council, which was a consultative organ for MITI. The policy emphasized a shift from *pollution-prone* and *resource-consuming* heavy and chemical industries to *clean and knowledge-intensive* industries, and assigned overseas investment a new role to serve as a catalyst to spring-clean the economy. It also meant the *ju-ko-cho-dai* (heavy-thick-long-big) features of Japanese industry had to be reoriented to the *kei-haku-tan-sho* (light-thin-short-small) ones best exemplified by electronics.

In the end, this new structural upgrading strategy proved successful, since the Japanese economy was already bumping against the limits of heavy and chemical industrialization, while newer growth industries had luckily started to bear fruit. The new policy was a confirmation of the direction of change in which the economy had already been inexorably compelled to move under the socio-political economic forces generated in the course of resource-based industrialization.

3.6.1.   Theoretical Implications

Japan resorted to an internal structural adjustment and overseas investment essentially to escape from the threatening *macroeconomic* organizational bottlenecks into which it was relentlessly being led by its own high-powered economic growth. This way of looking at the uniqueness of Japan's overseas investment activities helps explain why such activities suddenly expanded in the late 1960s and continued to grow in the early 1970s at a rate faster than that of any other country. Classical growth stagnation theory, especially what may be called 'the Ricardian trap of growth bottlenecks' (see Chapter 7), conveniently provides a relevant framework for interpreting the basic forces that underlay Japan's overseas investment in those days (Ozawa, 1979a). Japan's overseas investment was initially concentrated in labor-intensive manufacturing, as examined in Chapter 2 – but now quickly shifted to resource-extractive and resource-processing activities.

By way of contrast, the Western (notably American) type of FDI in the 1960s and 1970s was largely designed to exploit individual firms' superior corporate assets abroad and could therefore be explained by the so-called 'monopolistic' theory of international investment, a theory that is micro-theoretic. It implies that with or without the macroeconomic shortages of key productive factors, any successful firm will naturally evolve into a multinational enterprise as it grows in size and technological/organizational sophistication in an age of modern communications and transportation. Such a pattern of evolution appropriately represented the experiences of Western multinational enterprises, notably those of US-based firms. US multinationals moved outward more or less as an organic growth of individual business organizations, displaying an oligopolistic discrete behavior of the Galbraithian technostructure (Galbraith, 1973) or the product-life-cycle firm (Vernon, 1966).

Such a view is, however, not quite appropriate to explain the early postwar Japanese experience. It does not help explain why Japanese enterprises in resource-processing industries had to go overseas; it does not help explain either why Japanese firms, especially the small- and medium-sized, suddenly and simultaneously took on multinational characteristics in the late 1960s, even though they had not yet, by Western criteria, quite reached the stage at which they would have evolved naturally into multinational enterprises. As emphasized above, Japanese firms in those days were driven overseas by the macroeconomic forces of newly emerged factor scarcities at home, growing environmental constraints, and increasing uncertainties about the supply of key industrial resources, rather than by the growth of their internal capacities to operate on a global scale (Ozawa, 1979b).

The very weakness of their capacity to go overseas as individual units led, in part, to Japan's unique pattern of government-supported and group-oriented multi-firm investment abroad and to a heavy reliance on external funds, much of which were generated directly or indirectly by the government.

The driving forces for outward FDI and for the next phase of structural upgrading in Japanese industry are schematically summarized in Figure 3.2. Japan's second surge of FDI was generated by the market forces associated with the phenomenal growth of heavy and chemical industries in the spatially constrained island economy. Japan is indigent in the very natural resources its heavy and chemical industries require. As Japan emerged as the world's leading producer and exporter of resource- and energy-intensive goods, such as steel, aluminum, ships, heavy machinery, and chemicals, the security of resource supplies from overseas became a high priority in policy considerations.

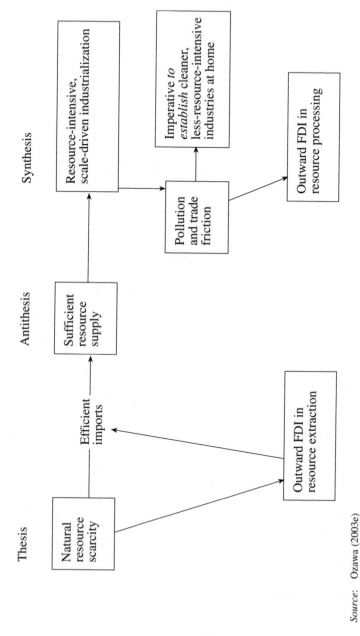

Thesis

Antithesis

Synthesis

Natural resource scarcity

Efficient imports

Sufficient resource supply

Resource-intensive, scale-driven industrialization

Imperative *to establish* cleaner, less-resource-intensive industries at home

Pollution and trade friction

Outward FDI in resource processing

Outward FDI in resource extraction

Source: Ozawa (2003e)

Figure 3.2   Paradox of resource-driven industrialization in resource-poor Japan – and its outcome

Early on, Japan relied on trade for importing vital resources but soon began to secure the supply sources by foreign investment. Those investments took two basic approaches: (i) the *invest-and-import* format in which equity ownership, mostly partial and minority, of foreign resources was sought in order to endure import supplies, and (ii) the *loan-and-import* format in which direct loans were extended in exchange for long-term supply contracts. These resource-seeking investments were made in large quantities for minerals and energy resources such as iron and copper ores, bauxite, oil, and natural gas, especially in the early 1970s and immediately after the 1974 oil crisis, although Japan had initiated such investment projects as early as the mid-1950s.

3.7. SUMMING UP

Japan's postwar high growth was spawned from assimilating advanced Western technologies, which sparked a high rate of investment in physical capital such as machinery, equipment, plant facilities, and industrial infrastructure. Investment-led growth was the core of Japan's high growth period (up to the first oil crisis of 1974). The government played the key role of assisting the private sector to modernize the prewar-built heavy and chemical industries. The use of industrial policy was the hallmark of this 'non-differentiated Smithian' stage of catch-up growth. Japan's *dirigisme* was largely tolerated by the US, which wanted to see Japan emerge as a strong industrialized economy, serving as the major bulwark against the spread of communism in the Asian Pacific.

The *keiretsu* groups were organized and engaged in the 'one-set' principle of establishing a full range of basic heavy and chemical industries (such as steel, non-ferrous metals, and petrochemicals) within each group. The government-subsidized, coastal *konbinato* proved to be highly efficient and cost-effective in energy use, sea transportation, and handling of both bulky inputs and outputs (unloading imported raw materials and loading finished goods at the dockside). Resource-intensive industrialization, however, made Japan ever more dependent on overseas natural resources. And paradoxically, resource-indigent Japan became one of the most resource-intensive producers in the world. Japan's abnormally high dependence on resources resulted in the resource-seeking (extractive) type of outward FDI in order to secure stable sources of supply abroad.

Furthermore, the rising environmental cost of heavy and chemical industrialization at home due to the air and water pollution caused by resource-processing activities, became intolerably high at the height of heavy and chemical industrialization. This problem grew all the more serious because Japan is a mountainous country with a small part of its total area in flat land along the coastlines. In fact, pollution was among the primary reasons leading the Japanese government to adopt a new industrial policy to promote less pollution-prone, knowledge-based, high-value-added industries (mostly of the *kei-haku-tan-sho* type). Toward the end of the high-growth period, environmental problems also led to the house-cleaning type of overseas investment by Japanese industry. (When all the social costs, environmental as well as foreign-relational, of resource-based industrialization are taken into account, the 'price-knowledge/industry-flow' theory *à la* Hume holds equally for Japan's outward FDI and technology exports in the course of resource-based industrialization.)

4. Assembly-driven stage – and logic – of industrial upgrading

4.1. COMPONENTS-INTENSIVE, ASSEMBLY-BASED INDUSTRIES

The components-intensive, assembly-based industries that manufacture high-income-elastic consumer durables, notably automobiles and consumer electronics, soon came to replace the heavy and chemical industries as Japan's leading growth sector from the mid-1970s onward (i.e., shortly after the first oil crisis of 1974). Japan's success in building higher value-added, high-quality, and energy-efficient goods in the assembly-based industries has been spectacular by any standards ever since.

Throughout the industrial world, automobiles and electronics have grown very rapidly after WWII, but the growth of these industries was particularly pronounced in Japan during the 1970s and 1980s. The growth index of the electric/electronics goods industry over the period 1970–82, with 1970 as the base year (100), for example, reached 292 in Japan, compared to 156 in the US and 139 in West Germany. The transport equipment industry (automobiles and ships) was the second fastest growth sector in both Japan and West Germany, but its output rose much faster in Japan (177) than in the latter (127). In contrast, the US experienced rather slow growth (112). General machinery (such as motors and machine tools) was another industry that experienced a rapid expansion in both Japan and the US, but again Japan's general machinery industry grew at a faster pace (151) than that of the US (145) (MITI, 1986). This reflected in part the fact that Japan was a latecomer, catching up to the West in these higher value-added industries – and in part Japan's own technological contributions.

Furthermore, these three groups of industries soon became Japan's star exporters. In 1983, for example, they represented as much as 63.8 per cent of Japan's manufactured exports as against 42.3 per cent for the United States and 45.6 per cent for West Germany (MITI, 1986). As will be discussed below, the very success of Japanese exports in these new growth industries would later inevitably force Japan to transfer these newly acquired comparative advantages overseas via outward FDI. In other words, these home-based exporters would quickly transform themselves into overseas investors (multinational manufacturers) to produce locally in their overseas markets.

The assembly-based industries are high value-added, product-differentiated, and knowledge-intensive on the supply side, and high income-elastic on the demand side. Their competitiveness emanates not from national endowment-specific advantages but from individual firms' ownership-specific advantages in product development, manufacturing, and marketing. Besides, as indicated by the nomenclature given to this group of industries, they are intensive in the use of parts, components, and accessories (PCAs), many of which are outsourced. They are vertically integrated with a deep division of labor between assemblers and suppliers of PCAs, and this vertical division of labor can occur easily across borders.

Automobiles were most representative of this assembly-driven stage of growth (the 'differentiated Smithian' phase), although early-generation consumer electronics (e.g., transistor radios and black-and-white TV sets) made its debut at about the same time when domestic passenger cars began to be produced for post-war Japan's protected home market. The electronics industry as a whole, however, actually came of age during the subsequent stage of R&D-driven growth (the 'Schumpeterian' phase) when further technological progress in semiconductors was made, leading to the innovation of a great variety of sophisticated electronics goods (including computers).

There is, furthermore, a fundamental difference in the role played by the Japanese government in the growth of domestic automobiles and consumer electronics. Automobiles did benefit from the 'reserved competition' model discussed in the previous chapter, but consumer electronics was on its own from the very beginning (as will be seen in Chapter 5). In addition, Japan's automobile industry made a truly significant innovation in making assembly operations dramatically efficient and cost-effective, a new manufacturing paradigm that would out-compete and soon replace Detroit-style mass production. Hence, this chapter analyzes the assembly-driven stage of catch-up mainly in terms of the automobile industry's experience as the primary focus. The development of electronics in Japan will be examined in detail in the next chapter.

4.2.   THE PARADOX OF 'MULTIPLE ENTRANTS IN A SMALL MARKET'

The components-intensive, assembly-based industries, particularly automobiles, require a large amount of fixed capital. They also must constantly introduce different models by differentiating products to cater for the changing tastes of consumers. Consequently, the overhead-cost problem (how to reduce per unit cost by exploiting *both* scale and scope economies) is of paramount importance, and the size of the market is the most crucial determinant of production costs.

When Japan moved into production of automobiles in earnest in the early 1950s by adopting mass production techniques, the domestic market was not only small, but there was demand for all sorts of vehicles, each in small quantity. Farmers, shop owners, and wholesale merchants usually used small one-ton trucks, while long-distance hauliers required large-size trucks. Passenger cars, taxies, and buses were also needed. Many of these vehicles had to be compact enough in size for narrow Japanese streets and alleys – and be economical in fuel consumption. It was, therefore, imperative for the Japanese automobile industry to come up with a new method of 'multi-variety and small-lot production' in order to meet the diversified needs of the Japanese market. *But how could such a manufacturing method be invented?*

The first thing the Japanese automobile manufacturers had to do after the war was to learn the basics of assembly operations from their Western counterparts. Hence, the government allocated then scarce foreign exchange to permit the Japanese firms (i) to secure from Western carmakers the knockdown-assembly contracts under which they would put together foreign car kits and (ii) to import all the necessary machinery and equipment (which they would soon adapt for their own use through modification and improvement). Four short-term ventures therefore came into existence: a Nissan–Austin (UK) tie-up in 1952; an Isuzu–Rootes (UK) contract in 1953; a Hino–Renault (France) tie-up in 1953; and a venture between Shin-Mitsubishi Heavy Industries and Willy's Overland (US) in 1953. The fact that all these ventures were arranged with European and America's relatively small carmakers reflected the Japanese realization that since the Detroit production system was, after all, designed for the huge and affluent American market, it was totally inappropriate for the small and low-income Japanese market in the early postwar period.

To protect what little domestic market they had at that time, the government imposed restrictions on imports of vehicles and began to modernize Japan's automobile industry under the 'Basic Automobile Industry Policy' (which was introduced as early as 1948). Shortly after, the Law on Temporary Measures for Promoting the Machinery Industries (Machine Industry Law) was introduced in 1956, and 17 machinery industries (including auto-parts) were targeted for promotion. The Law was designed to build a streamlined production system by upgrading and rationalizing manufacturing facilities (e.g., via special depreciation measures and subsidized funding from the Japan Development Bank), promoting exports, assisting technological absorption and progress, and formulating overall raw materials policies.

This policy created some protection rents, but as seen in Chapter 3, the dynamics of *keiretsu* was such that this promising new growth industry inevitably attracted multiple entrants and sparked fierce competition, thus quickly dissipating any rents (as posited in the 'reserved competition' model of infant-industry protection). At the start, Toyota, Nissan, Prince, Isuzu and Hino were the first entry group that began to assemble vehicles, but were quickly followed by the second entry group of other carmakers: Mitsubishi, Toyo Kogyo (Mazda), Honda, Daihatsu, Fuji Heavy Industries (Subaru), and Suzuki. Thus, as many as *11* automobile producers soon crowded the Japanese market, although Nissan soon absorbed Prince (in 1966), thereby reducing the number to ten. The intensified continuous rivalries among the ten local competitors forced them to lower the break-even level of production for survival. They vied relentlessly with each other in expanding productive facilities, cutting costs, and raising output at a phenomenal pace. But *how did so many entrants manage to operate in Japan's small domestic market which provided only a very limited basis for scale and scope economies, and eventually to succeed in growing into world-class carmakers?*

Before we proceed to examine Japan's unique manufacturing revolution, it is worth noting how fast its automobile industry expanded during the 'differentiated Smithian' stage of growth, a phenomenal catch-up and surging ahead which is vividly shown in Figure 4.1. From 1960 to 1965, output expanded by 322 per cent (from 165000 passenger cars to 696000); from 1965 to 1970, it expanded by 357 per cent (from 696000 to 3179000), first overtaking European carmakers and emerging as the second largest passenger carmaker after the United States; from 1970 to 1975, there was a 43.7 percent jump (from 3179000 to 4568000), with Japan finally catching up with and then unseating the United States as the world's largest car manufacturer in the late 1970s.

At the same time, Japan became the world's largest exporter of passenger cars. Its dependency ratio on exports rose from 4.2 per cent in 1960 to 14.5 per cent in 1965, 22.8 percent in 1970, 40.0 per cent in 1975 and to 56.1 per cent in 1980.

It should be noted, however, that during the precipitous growth of car production, MITI ironically tried to curb what it perceived as 'an excessive competition' among the multiple entrants in terms of two policy proposals: (i) the 'People's Car' concept in 1955, and (ii) the 'three-producer group' concept in 1961. The People's Car program aimed at introducing a low-priced minicar for both domestic and export markets with its production concentrated in one firm so as to reap scale economies, a plan modeled on Germany's VW. But all the entrants produced small sub-compacts anyway, and MITI's attempt to force production concentration did not work because of fierce rivalries among the domestic carmakers.

The three-producer group plan of 1961 was introduced as a way of

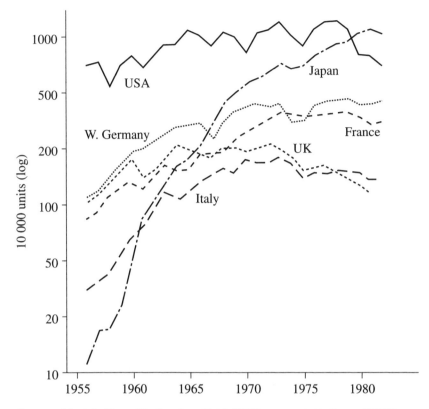

Source: Adopted with modifications from Mutoh (1988), as presented in Ozawa (1977d)

Figure 4.1 Passenger car production by major countries

strengthening the competitiveness of the Japanese automobile industry, since Japan was forced to liberalize car imports, for commercial vehicles in 1961 and for passenger cars in 1965. The government scheme would divide the domestic carmakers into groups of two to three firms each, with one group specializing in mid-sized passenger cars (with a monthly output of at least 7000 vehicles), with a second group producing high-end specialty vehicles (a monthly output of 3000 luxury and sports cars) and a final group manufacturing minicars. The industry strongly resisted this administrative interference and the plan was scratched.

It was against the intense competition at home that Mitsubishi Motors, a newcomer, maneuvered to tie up with Chrysler, then a powerful American carmaker, in 1971, despite MITI's opposition. In the same year, Isuzu concluded a similar capital link-up with GM, which acquired a 32 per cent equity interest. Another new challenger, Toyo Kogyo (Mazda) established close relations with Ford, which culminated in the sale of 25 per cent equity to Ford in 1979. These Japanese carmakers were still in the learning stage (as well as in a weak competitive position vis-à-vis their larger domestic counterparts) and gained from partnerships with their American affiliates in their efforts to capture larger export market share in the United States.

The end result was the continuing existence of a relatively unconcentrated market structure, which has turned out to be quite opposite to the European 'national champion' model, where only one producer is chosen as a national champion to enjoy the privilege of monopolizing a small domestic market for the sake of attaining scale economies. The Japanese paradox of 'multiple entrants in a small domestic market' was a manifestation of the 'reserved competition' phenomenon.

4.3.   LEAN (OR FLEXIBLE) PRODUCTION

It was in the above competitive yet growth-conducive environment that Toyota Motor first succeeded in introducing the now well-known technique of 'lean (flexible) production' (also called 'the Toyota production system'), which other Japanese carmakers quickly and eagerly adopted. The upshot was a dramatic reduction in per unit production cost and an impressive improvement in quality (Shimada, 1988; Womack et al., 1990; Kenney and Florida, 1993; and Abo, 1994). In what follows, the key characteristics of the new paradigm of lean production are outlined.

4.3.1.   Smithian Specialization Efficiency vs. Veblenian Interstitial Efficiency

As mentioned earlier, the assembly-based industries are intensive in their use of PCAs to be assembled into final products. Hence they require precise coordination among the operating constituent sub-units if a myriad variety of PCAs are to be put together in the most efficient possible manner.

Although it is not widely known, Thorstein Veblen (1927) was the first economist who emphasized the significance of the notion of 'interstitial coordination' in modern manufacturing processes:

> By virtue of this concatenation of processes, the modern industrial system at large bears the character of a comprehensive, balanced mechanical progress. In order to [achieve] an efficient working of this industrial process at large, the various constituent sub-processes must work in due coordination throughout the whole. Any degree of maladjustment in the *interstitial coordinations* of this industrial process or any industrial plant will do its work to full advantage only when due

adjustment is had between its work and the work done by the rest. *The higher the degree of development reached by a given industrial community, the more comprehensive and urgent becomes this requirement of interstitial adjustment.* (p.16, emphasis added)[1]

Veblen is clearly referring to relational or transnational efficiency or what may alternatively be called 'interstitial efficiency' – in addition to the widely known concept of 'specialization efficiency' attainable from the division of labor. The latter was stressed as the key source of productivity gain – hence the major cause of the wealth of nations – by Adam Smith (1776/1908) in terms of task specialization in his proverbial 'pin factory'. Specialization efficiency, however, all the more necessitates a higher degree of interstitial coordination and efficiency.

In this regard, the notion of 'relational assets' introduced in John Dunning (2003) clearly fits in with that of Veblenian interstitial efficiency. Dunning defines firm-specific relational assets as:

The stock of a firm's willingness and capability to access, shape and engage in economically beneficial relationships; and to sustain and upgrade these relationships. Such relationships, though always conducted by and between individuals, may take place both within the confines of a particular firm, or between that firm and other organizations and individuals. (pp. 3–4)

He then identifies relational assets as facilitating value-added activities by observing that 'When properly deployed, they enhance – one way or another – virtually all functional activities of the possessing firm. These include R&D, production, sourcing, financial management, marketing, as well as the exchange [of] specific activities of firms' (Dunning, 2003: 5). In other words, the corporate chain of value-added is reinforced by the 'proper' use of the firm's relational assets.

No doubt, the components-intensive, assembly-based industries are exactly the kind of manufacturing where interstitial coordinations – that is, management and governance of relational assets – are most strongly called for, because their production processes are vertically integrated, involving the numerous stages of producing or procuring and then finally assembling a large number of intermediate goods (PCAs). Interstitial (inter-process) coordination gains are thus as important as, or even more critical than, the conventional gains that can be derived from the Smithian division of labor and specialization (which attained the highest level of job fragmentation and standardization under Fordism-cum-Taylorism in America's automobile industry).

In this regard, Japan's assembly-based industries have been pursuing through organizational means (via networking) *both* Veblenian interstitial efficiency and the Smithian scale-based division of labor in as synergistically optimal a combination as possible. In contrast, the American assembly-based industries (at least in the past) tended to focus mostly on Smithian efficiency through hierarchies, leaving outsourcing operations to the market mechanism (i.e., purchasing PCAs from independent suppliers in the open market).

In fact, two types of Veblenian interstitial efficiency are being actively exploited by Japan's assembly-based industries in the form of lean production. One may be called '*intra-shop* interstitial efficiency', the other '*intra-industry* interstitial efficiency'. The former refers to the efficiency of inter-process coordinations on the assembly line within a given plant, and the latter to that of inter-process coordinations between assemblers and their closely affiliated suppliers of inputs in the product development and delivery system of a given assembly-based industry. These two types of interstitial coordination can be best illustrated below in terms of Japanese carmakers' experiences, as they innovated ways of achieving interstitial efficiency.

4.3.2.   Intra-shop Interstitial (Inter-process) Coordination

As is already well known, Japan's carmakers, beginning with Toyota, which innovated the methods of lean production, adopted a so-called 'pull' system of assembly operations (Ohno, 1978; Abegglen and Stalk, 1985). As illustrated in Figure 4.2, the conventional Fordist-cum-Taylorist paradigm of mass production is characterized as a 'push' system. In the old Detroit system, work-in-process is pushed downstream from one station to the next, whether the latter needs a particular piece of work right away or not, since any work done at one station is forwarded downstream and piled up in an inventory at the next station.

Quality control is centrally implemented and exogenously exercised by inspectors (quality specialists), usually at the end of an assembly line, and is thus not the job assigned to assembly workers themselves (i.e., a clear-cut Smithian division of labor and specialization between assembling and inspecting). As a rule, therefore, a given tolerable rate of defect, say, 5 per cent, is set and considered 'good enough',[2] and workers can rely on the proportion of good parts available in the station's inventory. After all, inventories are meant to be for the 'just-in-case' contingencies. If the defective rate exceeds tolerance, specialist engineers try to figure out the problems.

In sharp contrast to Detroit's traditional 'push' process with the 'just-in-case' inventories, what Toyota eventually succeeded in creating is a diametrically opposite, new approach that can reduce inventories to the bare minimum or even eliminate them altogether. Work-in-process and parts are produced *as they are needed by a downstream station*, that is, 'just in time' for use as they are needed. The famous *kanban* (a piece of paper indicating a

A The 'push' system

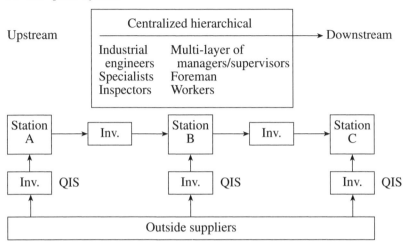

B The 'pull' system

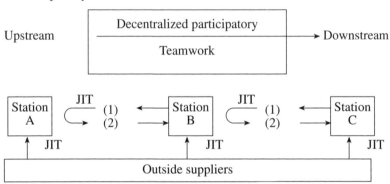

Notes: Inv.: inventory; QIS: quality inspection/sampling; JIT: just-in-time

Source: Ozawa (1977d)

Figure 4.2   Conventional mass production (a 'push' system) vs. Toyota's lean production (a 'pull' system)

'pull' order or a production order) was initially used as a communication device from a downstream to an upstream station.

The *kanban* (which is now entirely 'computer-programmed-online') is an instrument to achieve Veblenian interstitial coordinations along the assembly line, an instrument that has proved more efficient than the use of inventories. In its ultimate form, the 'just-in-time' approach can lead to a zero inventory for each work station. It saves physical space, time, and motion (no work is required for piling up and then pulling out inventories) and minimizes the cost of financing inventories, if all the sub-works of the entire production process are completely synchronized within the assembly plant, as well as with its multi-layered group of suppliers (to be described in detail below).

More importantly, as they strove to minimize inventories by way of the 'pull' method, they discovered that there was no allowance left for defective parts or work-in-process being passed on to a downstream operation; the line would stop if a defective work-in-process was found, since there was no longer an inventory to serve as a buffer. In fact, under the new system, each worker is assigned the task of inspecting each piece she receives ('pulls out') from upstream – in addition to making sure that what she produces at her station is defect-free. The worker is no longer a mere assembler (automaton), mindlessly putting and adding pieces together as instructed, a work practice that is appropriately depicted in Charlie Chaplin's *Modern Times*. She is now a quality inspector as well, *responsible* for the quality of what she produces and of what she receives from upstream stations – and from outside suppliers. Thus assembly workers have to do a lot of 'thinking' as well as 'doing' (whereas their only function is 'doing' under the Fordist-cum-Taylorist approach).

To prevent any defective work from being passed on downstream and assembled into a finished vehicle, therefore, each station is equipped with a stop button on the assembly line. When the stop button is pushed at a particular station and the assembly line stops, the entire factory floor is able to tell where the trouble has occurred by looking at a huge work flow chart displayed on a factory-ceiling board above the workers' heads. This stoppage of work flow appears costly but is actually much cheaper than the more substantial costs to be later incurred if defects are assembled into the final products. (As will be discussed in Chapter 6, this practice has been translated into a so-called 'front-loading' technique with the use of information technologies.) In such a situation, the workers at the troubled station are compelled to solve the problem as a team as quickly as possible, helping each other. This teamwork also means that each worker needs to be familiar with – hence to be trained for – a multiple variety of related work in her station.

Furthermore, in order to prevent any recurrence of a given problem, the team will get together and find out its root causes. For this purpose, each station has a quality control (QC) circle. After a day's regular work, they discuss any problem they have encountered or expect to encounter and make suggestions as to the possible ways of improving their productivity. They usually receive pecuniary rewards for those suggestions if adopted by management.[3] These direct rewards are perhaps not of primary importance, however. As workers' productivity rises, thereby making their company more profitable, not only do their wages increase but they can also expect a larger bonus. Japanese companies pay bonuses twice a year as a profit-sharing custom, which as a rule results in an additional three-to-four-months of compensation. Thus the bonus system serves as an important incentive mechanism for workers' brain inputs.

As will be discussed below, when the above system of intra-shop interstitial coordinations needs to be transplanted to other countries, FDI under Japanese management is the most effective approach for a variety of reasons.

4.3.3. Intra-industry Interstitial (Inter-firm) Coordination: the Pyramidal Structure

The automobile industry is vertically deep in the structure of manufacturing activities (the chain of value-added operations). Accordingly, as will be seen below, the pattern of industrial retention and relocation in this phase of economic growth is shaped along the vertical characteristics of integrated production. In organizing and managing such vertically integrated production, the industry has formed an *externalized* pattern of a vertical division of labor along the lines of different wage levels, factor intensities, and technological sophistications; that is, a vertical division of labor among (i) several major assemblers (large-sized oligopolistic firms) at the top, (ii) their closely affiliated primary suppliers of sub-assemblies, parts and components (mid-sized firms) in the middle, and (iii) a large number of secondary and tertiary subcontractors (small-sized firms) operating in a highly competitive market further down the hierarchy and at the bottom. Thus Japan's automobile industry cannot be classified merely as oligopolistic; it covers practically the whole range of market structure from a highly concentrated to an almost perfectly competitive market.

Toyota, Nissan, Honda, Mazda, and other Japanese carmakers reign as the main assemblers, each thus constituting its own *keiretsu* (closely knit industrial group). About 70 to 80 per cent of car parts and components are normally 'outsourced' to their primary suppliers (about 10 to 15 in number for each *keiretsu*, totaling 168 shops in 1985), which in turn farm out some portion of work to their own secondary subcontractors (4700 shops for the automobile industry as a whole), which again in turn depend on the lower-echelon producers, and so on, down to the bottom of the hierarchy (such lower-echelon shops number as many as 31 600 in the entire industry) (Shimokawa, 1985). (By comparison, Detroit carmakers used to produce about 70 per cent of parts and components internally, the exact reverse to the Japanese practice. Their in-house production has come down considerably, however, as they have adopted a Japanese-style subcontracting approach.)

Associated with firm size are significant wage disparities along the pyramid. At the bottom, the wage is about 40 per cent of the average rate at the top. This reflects the relatively unskilled labor-intensive nature of work performed at the bottom. Capital intensity is lowest at the bottom, while highest at the top. Vertical specialization takes place along the lines of different factor intensities and technological sophistication, resulting in a high degree of vertical social division of labor.

The industrial pyramid thus formed by the *keiretsu* is schematically illustrated in stylized form in Figure 4.3. In reality, this multi-layered organization has many more layers than three. The top segment is highly capital (both physical and human)-intensive and large-scale-based (that is, exploiting scale economies) in market structure, its intermediate segment less capital-intensive and medium scale-based, and its bottom segment labor-intensive, with the lowest wage scale. Hence the relative capital–labor ratios largely determine the relative wage (w) and rental (r) ratios: $(w/r)a > (w/r)b > (w/r)c > \ldots (w/r)n$. In other words, the whole organization of vertically linked production is hierarchically built on what is popularly known as the 'dual' structure (though 'multitudinous' is a more appropriate adjective).

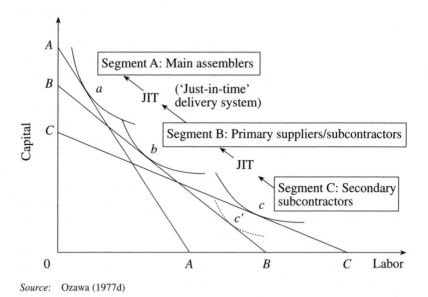

Source: Ozawa (1977d)

Figure 4.3   A multiple division of labor in the vertically integrated stages of production

The top-echelon firms (main assemblers) are able to employ large-scale, capital-intensive methods of production, thereby exploiting internal scale economies, *which may otherwise be impossible to do, if scarce capital is evenly distributed throughout the industry.*

The workers in the final assembly sector are elite employees who can enjoy lifetime employment (guaranteed) and high wages; they are usually recruited directly from college. On the other hand, the lower-echelon firms specializing in labor-intensive PCAs can remain price-competitive by employing low-wage workers (who are usually graduates from high school) in an 'open' labor market and using labor-intensive methods of production.

4.3.4. The Economics of Pyramidal Organization

The logic of wage differentials can be explained as follows. For instance, assume that an economy has a given overall capital–labor ratio, but a certain sector needs to be more capital-intensive than the overall ratio to be economically viable, and a certain other sector happens to be more labor-intensive than the overall ratio. If available factors are all proportionately allocated at the same factor prices for the two sectors, they will not be able to produce efficiently, since such a factor allocation does not match the optimum factor intensity of each sector. Consequently, more capital should be allocated to the capital-intensive sector at a relatively low interest rate and more labor to the labor-intensive sector at a lower wage rate. Each sector, then, can exploit its comparative efficiency in factor use. This argument matches the notion of 'optimum factor-price differentials' (Kojima, 1996), where 'factor price differentials among industries are helpful, as in the case of the Japanese economic development, in transferring resources during periods of structural change and in making stronger the international competitive power of the industries which are intended for expansion' (p.13).

This vertical social division of labor is designed to exploit *an intra-industry pattern of comparative advantages* along the lines of both the Heckscher–Ohlin theory of factor proportions and the Ricardian model of different technological (labor productivity) levels, since all these sectors *trade* in PCAs within the *keiretsu* pyramid. Such an intra-industry (intra-*keiretsu*) cultivation of comparative advantages through *networked trade* in PCAs is then translated into – and reinforces – Japanese carmakers' competitive (or comparative) advantages in the world markets. Thus, this type of magnified competitive advantage emanates from the intra-*keiretsu* interstitial coordination and efficiency. (In other words, there exists a 'flying-geese' modality of industrial organization within Japan's assembly-based industries.)

Furthermore, the transactions between the assembler/procurers and subcontractors are based on long-term, trust-based, and reciprocal relationships. As might be expected, the 'terms of trade' between them tend to favor the higher-echelon firms that place orders, but the relationship is, on the whole, mutually beneficial. In fact, the large firms usually give managerial and technical guidance and assist their subcontractors financially, whenever necessary, so that the latter are able to continually improve quality and productivity. After all, the existence of stable, reliable, and efficient suppliers is a must for the 'just-in-time' delivery system. (It should be noted, however, that such a delivery system is mainly between the main assemblers and their primary suppliers, and that it tends to decline as subcontracting moves down the hierarchy, since the lower-echelon producers are engaged more in standardized work).

It is not unusual for the main assemblers to demand a cut in price for parts, say, by as much as 10 per cent, at times of intensified competition. This is, however, not a totally one-sided exploitation of smaller firms, since whatever help is necessary is usually provided to raise efficiency and cut costs. The so-called *kyoryoku kai* (cooperative supplier associations) are critical as an institution through which technical knowledge and information flows are channeled and controlled. Each major assembler has its own association; Toyota has the *Kyoho Kai*, Nissan the *Takara Kai*, Mitsubishi Motors the *Kashiwa-kai*, and so on.[4]

Moreover, a final assembler and its cohort of key suppliers are usually clustered in close geographical proximity for 'just-in-time' delivery. Toyota Motor is the most famous in this respect. All the major suppliers of critical sub-assemblies, parts, and components are located within a radius of approximately 30 minutes' driving time in Toyota City, Nagoya. The whole area, approximately 530 square kilometers, became a self-contained 'virtual factory floor'. The way it is organized, therefore, the *keiretsu*-based cluster is *sui generis* – quite distinct in organizational structure from the conventional structure of the conventional type of Marshallian industrial district (discussed in Chapter 2).

Positive externalities in the Marshallian district remain 'externalized', benefiting all the firms congregated in the district. The clustered firms transact and compete with each other at arm's length. The price mechanism and competition rule the market. In comparison, Toyota City or any other *keiretsu*-governed industrial clusters are 'internalized' ('monopolized') *within* the group; hence, no intra-group competition exists. It is governed by the principle of cooperation and reciprocity.

Operating in such a closely collaborative – and exclusive – business environment within each *keiretsu*, Japan's automobile industry also adopted a so-called 'design-in' or 'black box parts' system (Fujimoto, 1995) in which the major assemblers work closely with their parts suppliers from the very beginning of a new model change in developing engineering drawings and prototypes. (As will be detailed in Chapter 6, this systems approach has developed into 'concurrent engineering' with the information technology revolution.) Such a product development practice has led to Japanese carmakers – and other assembly-based industries, notably consumer electronics – having enormous strengths in *time-based* competition for introducing new products on the market ahead of competitors (Stalk and Hout, 1990).

In sum, the *keiretsu*-based pyramidal organization and industrial clusters have proved to be major sources of competitiveness for Japanese industry at the assembly-driven stage of growth. Nevertheless, as will be analyzed below, their very competitive prowess (emanating from the lean production methods) has ironically resulted in a self-dismantling (self-dissolution) of this cooperative structure, especially at the bottom of the pyramid through overseas investments.

4.4. TRADE FRICTION, YEN APPRECIATION, AND TRANSPLANTS ABROAD

The combination of Veblenian interstitial efficiencies at both plant and industry levels crystallized into Japanese-style lean production and gave Japan's carmakers a formidable competitive strength, not only in price but also in quality and the speed of product development, and delivery. As already seen in Figure 4.1, Japanese production and exports of cars recorded an explosive growth in the global market.

This led inevitably to two dramatic changes in the market conditions that began to affect Japanese corporate decisions as to the location of production in the 1980s. One was the rising incidence of trade conflicts with the countries at whose markets Japanese exports were aimed, notably, the United States and Europe; the second was the sharp appreciation of the yen that started after the Plaza Accord of 1985. This was caused by Japan's huge trade surplus, especially with the United States, about 60 per cent of which was accounted for by the export of cars and auto parts in the 1980s. An appreciated yen weakened Japanese carmakers' price competitiveness and the profitability of their exports. Indeed, Japan's domestic output of cars leveled out in the mid-1980s as production had increasingly to be transplanted abroad. Hence these two adverse developments were self-induced and self-inflicted, in the sense that the very effectiveness of Japan-born lean production was basically responsible for this production shift.

The above paradoxical evolutionary outcome matches the Humean 'price-knowledge/industry-flow' mechanism of rapid successful catch-up growth and is schematically illustrated in Figure 4.4.

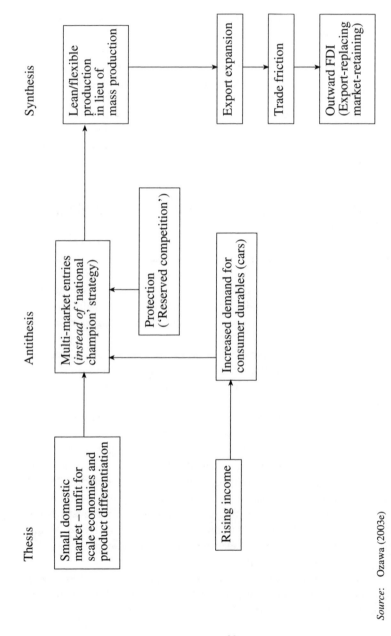

Source: Ozawa (2003e)

Figure 4.4 The paradox of 'multiple entrants in a small market', reserved competition, and outward FDI

In response to trade conflicts and the ever-rising yen, Japanese carmakers began to establish assembly operations ('transplants') in North America and Europe in the mid-1980s. These are the markets Japanese carmakers captured by initially exporting small-sized, fuel-efficient compacts (for which demand was also increasing rapidly at home as Japan entered the stage of motorization with a sharp rise in per capita income, that is, the Rostowan stage of 'high mass consumption'). Hence the assembly segment of Japan's pyramidal structure (segment A in Figure 4.3) began, in part, to be transplanted abroad.

However, to counter the criticism that these transplants were merely the 'screwdriver plants' designed to assemble imported kits in the local markets and to meet the demand for local content requirements, Japanese parts makers quickly followed suit by setting up parts-manufacturing ventures, in many cases as joint ventures with local interests (that is, segment B in Figure 4.3 started to be transplanted overseas in tandem with segment A). Consequently, fears of the 'hollowing out' of Japanese industry began to be expressed at home. But the establishment of overseas outposts, at least initially, contributed to Japan's exports of plant equipment, machinery (especially industrial robots) and tools that had been specifically developed in-house by the carmakers in connection with their innovation of lean production techniques – hence the 'hollowing-out' effect tended to be cancelled out by the 'new export-creating' effect of FDI.

Given the intra-*keiretsu* internalization of interstitial coordinations between the main assemblers and their key parts suppliers, it is easy to understand why Japan's carmakers (main assemblers) initially could not depend on local parts producers. In fact, the quality of locally produced parts was early on unacceptably low, with a high defective rate and unsuitable for their highly differentiated models. As pointed out above, Japanese carmakers at home developed a system of 'design-in production' in which parts producers work closely with their carmakers from the very beginning of a product development. Hence it has taken a considerable amount of time to recruit and mold some local suppliers into Japanese-style design-in parts manufacturing and 'just-in-time' delivery.

Whenever the yen appreciates, overseas-produced parts become cheaper for Japanese carmakers. While some parts are produced at home and exported, increased imports of parts are creating new trade: *inter-parts* trade. Japan exports higher value-added, more sophisticated components and parts, while it imports low value-added, standardized (hence, more price-sensitive) components, particularly from its neighboring developing countries. Now that many parts have been increasingly transferred to overseas production to be imported back to Japan, a yen appreciation brings back the benefits of exchange gains – that is, Japanese carmakers are able to procure at lower prices. This is one important reason why Japanese carmakers (and, for that matter, other components-intensive producers) are not so much victimized whenever the yen rises in value. (Theoretically speaking, they don't need to ask their suppliers to make price cuts, since such cuts are now automatically granted through the currency exchange mechanism.)

4.5.   TRANSPLANTATION OF LEAN PRODUCTION ABROAD

4.5.1.   Effectiveness

Given the fact that the paradigm of lean production originated under Japan's enterprise unionism, which resulted in relatively cooperative industrial relations between management and workers at the individual company level, how well can it be adopted overseas? As seen above, lean production is not so much a technical (*technocentric*) paradigm but rather an organizational and human-interactive and -relational (*anthropocentric*) paradigm requiring team work within an assembly plant, as well as between assemblers and suppliers. Although it is possible to export some lean-production-related equipment and tools (artifacts), the essential techniques of this paradigm are both 'know-how and know-why'[5] and cannot be so easily sold or effectively transferred in a contractual form such as licensing and a technical assistance agreement, since they are simply not codifiable. Know-how and know-why are tacit instead of explicit. Moreover, it takes time to learn, since learning takes place on the shop floor via 'learning-by-doing' (Arrow, 1962) – or more appropriately 'learning-by-*working together*' in the case of the Japanese system, because newly hired workers must learn from working together with their mentors (experienced workers) through on-the-job training. This human-interactive mode of tacit knowledge transfer on the shop floor is emphasized by Koike (1996), who even argues that the more and the longer Japanese skilled expatriates stay as mentors for local workers in Japan's overseas ventures, the more effective the transfer of tacit knowledge. Thus, these characteristics make FDI the only way of replicating the Japanese production system overseas effectively.

By choosing this route, however, Japanese assemblers need to set up overseas both an intra-plant system of lean production by hiring those local managers and workers who are compatible and sympathetic with the philosophy of the paradigm and an inter-firm supply chain of PCAs, by recruiting those local suppliers, if any, who can meet the required standard of quality and the speed of delivery. These are not easy tasks.

It is said, however, that local managers and workers in the developing Asian countries are considerably amenable to being trained for lean production.

Several important studies have been made on the efficiencies of manufacturing at Japanese-owned plants in East Asia (Ichimura, 1988; Koike and Inoki, 1990). The most comprehensive study is a research project on the 'application and adaptation' abroad of the Japanese production system by Japanese multinationals in automobiles and electronics, a project led by Tetsuo Abo and his associates (Abo, 1994; Itagaki and Abo, 1993). This group's study reveals that the East Asian hosts exhibit a relatively high degree of 'application' (a fairly good straightforward application), especially in the areas of workshop organization, multi-skilling, wage and promotion structures (all related to human-relations-interfaced operations). In sharp contrast, these are the very areas in which America and Europe show a relatively low degree of application, therefore necessitating a strongly 'hybridized' form of 'adaptation' (Abo, 1994).

It is also generally known that local workers at Japanese plants throughout East Asia have experienced little resistance to such group-centered activities as morning calisthenics and singing company songs. Japanese ventures in the region have frequently adopted Japanese managerial practices such as a seniority wage system (for example, 68 per cent of Japanese ventures in Thailand, and 50 per cent of those in Indonesia, according to a survey by Japan's Ministry of Labor in 1996[6]). Another survey found that Asian managers consider 'hard work, respect for learning, and honesty' among the six most important values, whereas their North American counterparts identify 'freedom of expression, personal freedom and self-reliance' as their most important values, followed by 'individual rights, hard work, personal achievement and thinking for oneself'.[7] Thus, the intra-plant industrial relations in East Asia seem suitable for lean production at least so far as the organizational dimension is concerned. It is another matter, however, how effectively local managers and workers can acquire both the necessary 'know-how' and 'know-why' of the Japanese paradigm, particularly about its high-quality requirements. In this regard, the Malaysian government's effort to raise 'quality awareness' among local managers and workers through such measures as the establishment of 'Quality Month' (each October) and 'National Quality Awards' (Kondo, 1996) is certainly encouraging.

4.5.2. Issues

Japanese assemblers obviously have difficulty finding local suppliers in those developing countries that are yet to develop a supporting industry. The initial solution is to import all the necessary parts. In fact, knockdown kits are usually the first step to local assembly operations. Eventually, however, Japanese assemblers are compelled to assist the host countries to develop the requisite supporting industry, normally under the pressure of import-substitution policy. In this regard, a successful transplantation of Japan's assembly-based operations involves an intricate process of nurturing and fostering a local industry capable of supplying PCAs.

Another problem in developing countries is small market size. Parts makers need a large output to reduce costs through scale economies. Hence, the recent formation of a regional trade bloc is a blessing, as seen in ASEAN's 'Brand-to-Brand-Complementation' program, which gives preferential treatment to parts and components produced among the signatory countries.

As a rule, the governments of the developing host countries are understandably impatient about the pace of localization by Japan's assembly-based ventures. The local pressure for the creation of upstream linkages usually comes in the form of local content requirements, which are an expression of economic nationalism. There is a danger of being 'politicized', in the sense that some localization goals become out of step with the host countries' own capabilities and economic realities. It should be noted that even in advanced host countries where the necessary supporting industry already exists, it takes time for Japanese assemblers to organize an effective network of relations with local suppliers in order to implement Japanese-style lean production practices such as the 'design-in' procurement of parts and the 'just-in-time' delivery of supplies.

Four major complaints about Japan's assembly-based ventures in developing countries can be summarized as follows:

1. the ever-rising imports of key parts and components and other capital goods from Japan, leading to a deterioration in the host countries' trade deficits with Japan;
2. 'follow-the-leader' investment ventures by Japanese parts suppliers to meet the needs of their assemblers, dominating the local supporting industry (much of which, however, may hardly have existed before the arrival of Japanese ventures);
3. the high ratios of expatriate managers and technical staff members to their local counterparts in Japanese ventures, and;
4. the transfer of only obsolete technology and the reluctance to use state-of-the-art technology – that is, an accusation of 'technology hoarding' on the part of Japan's parent companies.

All these 'notorious' features of Japanese FDI pertain mostly to their assembly-based ventures and are perceived as 'problems' on the side of the host governments – an unfortunate indictment that Japanese industry, along with its government, conspires to control technological progress and knowledge-based production throughout Asia by establishing a 'regional *keiretsu*' or still worse, '*keiretsu* colonialism'. The notion of 'Asia in Japan's embrace' (Hatch and Yamamura, 1996) encapsulates this perspective:

> ... We argue that Japanese capital and technology are stitching together the disparate economies of Asia, integrating them into a multilevel production alliance ... These networks, promoted and nurtured by the Japanese government, are based on a division of labor; the parent firm in Japan generally supplies the most technology-intensive components used in production, while affiliates in Asia contribute less sophisticated parts ... Like subcontractors in a vertical keiretsu, [affiliates in Asia] enjoy the benefits of quasi integration, including access to capital and technology. To varying extents, all Asian economies have used this Japanese production alliance to expand their manufacturing exports. On the other hand, they have *become embraced by, or dependent on, Japanese capital and technology* ... local firms integrated into the lower strata of these coordinated networks are denied the opportunity to understand the overall production process or the underlying technology. (pp. x–xi and 108)

These descriptions, though somewhat hyperbolic, are nevertheless largely true. But the whole development should be kept in perspective. In the first place, local firms are naturally 'integrated into the lower strata of these coordinated networks', for the simple reason that they have a *comparative* advantage in 'less sophisticated parts', while the Japanese parent firms have an advantage in 'sophisticated parts'. This pattern of specialization is nothing unnatural or sinister. Even without Japanese FDI, this pattern of trade would occur by the logic of the Heckscher–Ohlin factor proportions theory, assuming that local firms are independently capable of producing and exporting their endowments-compatible products.

It should be recalled that, as examined in Chapter 2, Japan, too, once specialized in labor-intensive, standardized light industry goods (such as apparel, toys, and sundries) and *benefited* from the wage magnification effect of the Heckscher–Ohlin stage of catch-up growth. In those days, the country-of-origin label 'made in Japan' meant shoddy and cheap ('lower strata') manufactures. Of course, Japan by choice pursued a rather neo-mercantilist policy of discriminating and minimizing inward FDI, absorbing Western technologies mostly under license, and building up its own technological capability – not to become dependent on foreign industries. Indeed, the NIEs, notably Korea and Taiwan, have largely replicated the Japanese experience of industrial upgrading (though with their own different macro-organizational policies suitable to the prevailing politico-economic conditions in the world market) and have already spawned their own world-class enterprises such as Posco (Korea), Samsung (Korea), Hyundai (Korea), Acer (Taiwan), and TSMC (Taiwan), just to name a few. And most notable of all is China's current rise as the world's workshop and its nascent national enterprises such as TCL (TV sets), Galanz Group (microwaves), Konka Group (TV sets), and

Haier Group (compact refrigerator). All of a sudden, the effectiveness of Japanese firms' 'flying-geese' strategy of 'high-end goods at home, mid-end in the NIEs, and low-end in ASEAN and China' has been considerably eroded, especially in high-tech sectors such as electronics.

On their own volition, nowadays, the developing countries are *opting for* an inward-FDI-driven strategy of industrialization – that is, to utilize the corporate ('created') assets of foreign multinationals as key inputs for building their own assembly-based industries. Even though a local economy has not yet developed its capacity to produce the parts and components required, say, for automobiles, it can still instantly 'manufacture' automobiles starting out with the most downstream activity – that is, assembling cars with imported kits. In other words, these developing host countries need not wait until they can produce all the necessary – and sophisticated – inputs locally. But obviously there is a price to pay for this 'dependence' strategy of capitalizing on inward direct investment. Of course, they could choose a more autonomous (self-reliant) path of industrial development. The final choice boils down to a strategic choice that each sovereign country must ultimately make as part of its macro-organizational development policy.

4.6.   SUMMING UP

In the latter half of the 1970, automobiles emerged as Japan's major exports, along with electronics (to be examined in Chapter 5). The *keiretsu*-based pyramidal organization, combined with the innovation of lean production, became the major sources of Japanese automobile makers' competitiveness during Japan's assembly-driven stage of growth. These outcomes are ascribable to Japanese industry's ability to focus on and cultivate not only Smithian specialization efficiency but also – and more importantly, Veblenian coordination efficiency.

Because of this new success, however, Japan continued to pile up trade surpluses, and the yen began its steep ascent on the foreign exchange market as soon as the Bretton Woods system of pegged rates collapsed in the early 1970s. In response to this newly emerged handicap imposed on exporting – and the rising clamor for protection against Japanese exports – Japan came to witness its automobile producers increasingly transplant production overseas, thereby sharing the newly acquired comparative advantage with the host countries. That is, home-based exporters in the assembly-driven stage, too, were again forced to transform themselves into multinational firms over a very short span of time. In other words, as at the earlier stages of catch-up growth, Japanese automobile makers were similarly 'pushed' out of their countries and had to produce locally in overseas markets earlier captured by their exports.

Thus, the Humean 'price-knowledge/industry-flow' mechanism was once again at work during the assembly-driven stage of growth.

NOTES

1. The author is indebted to his colleague, Dennis Black, for pointing out Veblen's writings on this topic. For an analysis of the relevance of Veblenian economics to Japan's economic growth, see Ozawa and Phillips (1994).
2. Womack et al. (1990) observe: 'perhaps the most striking difference between mass production and lean production lies in their ultimate objectives. Mass-producers set a limited goal for themselves – "good enough" – which translates into an acceptable number of defects, a maximum acceptable level of inventories, a narrow range of standardized products. To do better, they argue, would cost too much or exceed inherent human capabilities. Lean producers, on the other hand, set their sights explicitly on perfection; continually declining costs, zero defects, zero inventories, and endless product variety. Of course, no lean producer has ever reached this promised land – and perhaps none ever will, but the endless quest for perfection continues to generate surprising twists' (pp. 13–14).
3. Toyota's records indicate that the number of suggestions (ideas) submitted by workers in 1980 alone totaled no fewer than 859 000 and 94 per cent of them were adopted for implementation. Toyota gave 88 344 000 yen ($389 181 at the 1980 average exchange rate of 227 yen to the dollar) (Ikari, 1981: 217).
4. For an excellent study of Japan's automotive parts industry published in English, see Smitka (1991). It contains a historical description of the development of this industry in Japan and the functions and activities of supplier associations.
5. Soriano (1996: 12) makes the following distinction: 'Know How has to do with "doing things right" (i.e., appropriate technology, efficient process, high productivity, etc.). Know Why has to do with "doing the right things" (i.e., ethics, organizational purpose, core values, a guiding philosophy, a healthy sense of priorities)'. His definitions are all related to management capability. Here, for the Japanese production system, know-how is defined in the same way, but know-why means the intellectual capacity of *understanding why things work the way they do* on the part of shop-floor workers.
6. As reported in *Nihon Keizai Shimbun*, November 25, 1996.
7. This survey on Asia was conducted by Whirthlin and McLean (US research firm), while the North American survey by the Center for Strategic and International Studies, Washington, D.C. These comparative results are reported in *Wall Street Journal*, March 8, 1996.

5. Knowledge-driven stage – and logic – of catch-up growth

5.1. 'CREATED' RESOURCES

As early as the 1960s, the Japanese government launched major efforts to scale the ladder of industrial upgrading toward the next rung of knowledge-driven growth (the 'Schumpeterian' phase). It seeded new growth industries through a variety of measures, such as stepped-up efforts to acquire cutting-edge technology from overseas under license, setting up cooperative research programs between government and industry, and cajoling those foreign multinationals (for example, IBM) then already operating in Japan to disseminate new technology to local firms. Government–industry research collaboration in particular was instrumental in enabling Japan to emerge as a dominant producer of high-quality semiconductors (microchips) before long. Semiconductors were considered so vital that they came to be regarded as '*sangyo no kome*' (the rice/staple of industry) in Japan. No effort was, therefore, spared to develop through industrial policy semiconductor electronics, simultaneously with the domestic computer industry that needed the semiconductors. Both of these would become the key foundations for knowledge-driven, high-tech industries. (In fact, Japan's semiconductor industry would celebrate its coming of age in the early 1980s with its dominance in the field of LSI semiconductors surpassing the United States.)

In the meantime, consumer electronics, which was developed by Japanese entrepreneurs practically without any help from the government, spearheaded the growth of Japan's electronics production and exports. Early on, transistor radios and television sets were the major initiators of this industry in the late 1950s and the early 1960s. They served as catapults for a host of related electronics goods. Japan's consumer electronics in particular best exemplified the industrial trend of miniaturization in the innovative commercialization of those new products that were characterized by the features of what the Japanese called '*kei-haku-tan-sho*' (light-thin-short-small)'.[1]

This chapter examines the birth and subsequent evolution of this stellar industry as the best exemplifier of Japan's early-generation, knowledge-driven industries, beginning with its early days and tracing the track of its technological and industrial development. The government's involvement in fostering and nurturing Japan's high-tech industries will then be discussed with the focus on the development of home-grown computers and semiconductors.

5.2. TRANSPLANTATION OF CONSUMER ELECTRONICS FROM THE US[2]

Japan's electronics industry originated with the production of radios before WWII. In 1925, radio broadcasting began for the first time in Japan, and the first 'made-in-Japan' radios were introduced by Hayakawa Electric (presently Sharp Corporation) under a licensing agreement with RCA (US). Other electric appliance makers, including Matsushita Electric, soon joined in radio production. Its annual output had reached the level of 876 000 units in 1941 on the eve of WWII. During the war these companies continued to produce radios and other communications equipment to meet the needs of the Japanese military.

At war's end, however, this nascent communications equipment industry was in shambles due to air-raid destruction of plant facilities. Nevertheless, the wartime procurements – and military research activities – had resulted in an accumulation of industrial knowledge and skills which would prove to be valuable assets for its postwar reconstruction. Fortunately, the General Headquarters (GHQ) of the Allied Forces instructed the Japanese government to jump-start the industry, along with a restart of extensive radio-broadcasting services designed to keep the public informed about the GHQ's democratization policy. Four million radios were immediately ordered for the purpose of facilitating civil communications – and for broadcasting the 'Free Radio/ Voice of America'. Before long radio production zoomed from Y1.7 million in 1950 to Y11.5 million in 1954. By the end of the 1950s, it reached Y56.4 million – that is, a 33-fold jump from 1950.

Then, another shot in the arm came with the outbreak of the Korean War, as the United Nations forces used Japan as the key supply base of military goods and services, almost instantly boosting Japanese manufacturing and triggering a so-called 'Korean War boom'. The quickly improving economic conditions soon ushered in a new age of mass consumption of household electric appliances. TV sets (then black and white), washers, and refrigerators were coveted and eagerly snapped up by Japanese consumers, who dubbed these appliances as their 'three divine treasures'.

A phenomenal expansion of the consumer electronics industry was further propelled in no small measure by the innovation of transistor ratios in 1955 by a then-unknown small company, Tokyo Tsushin (the present-day Sony Corporation). Others quickly followed suit in manufacturing and exporting transistor radios. For example, as much as 90 per cent of the 12 million units of transistor radios produced in 1959 were then exported to the United States. This indicated how quickly such radios became popular overseas and how important the US market was as the key buyer of Japan's new exports.

What really fostered and drove to prominence Japan's consumer electrics industry, however, was the industry's quick adoption of TV production. NHK (Japan's public broadcasting corporation) began the first TV broadcasting in February 1953, and the first 'made-in-Japan' TV set appeared – again at the hands of Hayakawa Electric under RCA's licenses in the same year. TV production stood at 240 000 units in 1955, but soon soared to reach 2 850 000 units in 1959, only four years later – nearly a 12-fold increase over four years. Output continued to rise by about 1 million units each year. In 1962, Sony 'transistorized' TV sets; 'micro-TV sets' (initially black and white), were marketed in Japan in 1960 and swiftly caught the fancy of overseas consumers, especially American ones, in the years immediately following. And in 1965, the first shipment of 'made-in-Japan' color TV sets arrived in the US market, where TV viewers at that time were switching from monochrome to color TVs.

In the meantime, Japan's domestic demand for consumer electronics continued to soar *pari passu* with a sharp increase in household incomes. Between 1955 and 1969 (during the so-called 'high growth' period), the average real income of farmers and urban workers approximately doubled. The popular consumer durables in the early 1950s were relatively low-income products such as radios, fluorescent lamps, electric fans, bicycles, and sewing machines. The domestic demand for more sophisticated goods such as color TVs and air conditioners expanded throughout the 1960s.

Whether it was transistor radios or TV sets, however, it is crystal clear that the US market played a critical role in granting Japanese producers a huge open market, thereby enabling them to reap economies of scale and learning. *Why is it, however, that the US so willingly transferred to Japan all the necessary technologies and imported Japanese-made TV sets in those days?*

5.2.1.   RCA's Push for Licensing Overseas

Although not widely known, RCA initially provided Japan with all the necessary technologies to produce TV sets, thus putting the latter's emerging consumer electronics industry firmly on a growth track. Some argue that this marked the first step toward the eventual decline – and near demise – of consumer electronics in the United States. For example, a fascinating account of this episode is presented in two books, *The Fall of the U.S. Consumer Electronics Industry: An American Trade Tragedy* (Curtis, 1994) and *Inventing the Electronic Century: The Epic Story of the Consumer Electronics and Computer Industries* (Chandler, 2001). These studies both explain why the US consumer electronics industry suddenly declined in the 1960s and soon all but vanished. Curtis takes the standpoint of Zenith Electronics, an initial rival with RCA in color TV set production, and blames RCA for the death of America's TV set industry. In contrast, Chandler examines the century-long vicissitudes of electronics development in the US, Europe, and Japan on a comparative basis and from a historical point of view.

Curtis (1994) points out that in the early postwar period, RCA actively 'pooled' patents on television transmitters and receivers to monopolize the industry. It used a 'package license' scheme and forced any potential TV producers to become members of the patent pool; otherwise RCA threatened infringement lawsuits. This practice was designed to extract monopoly profits and further to gain any additional improvement patents from the licensees under the 'grant back of patent rights' agreement, thereby strengthening the patent cartelization. It was, however, Zenith that 'considered the package license scheme to be no different than garden-variety extortion' (Curtis, 1994: 33). Zenith legally challenged, and ultimately won, the litigation originally filed by RCA because the defendant refused to renew its licensing agreement after it had expired in 1946.

In the mid-1950s, despite its premature technology RCA rushed to mass produce color TV sets and dismally failed, since the color tubes RCA produced were found to be usable in only one out of every three. Ever after that, RCA decided not to manufacture color TV sets on its own but to license its patents worldwide. In the meantime, Zenith succeeded in establishing a dominant position in both monochrome and color TV sets: 'By 1961, Zenith's development work in color TV reached a point that permitted mass production of a greatly improved and simplified color receiver, which was reliable and easy to repair. Zenith entered the color TV market, and sales took off like a rocket' (Curtis, 1994: 104).

Then, RCA quickly found in Japan a potentially lucrative production base for its patent pool – and an effective tool of revenge against Zenith:

> RCA's lucrative patent licensing scheme in the United States was facing destruction through Zenith's Chicago litigation, its settlement, and the subsequent criminal and civil antitrust prosecutions by the government. *In a brilliant and cynical move, Sarnoff [RCA's boss] more than replaced the threatened patent licensing fees extracted from American manufacturers with a generous percentage of the entire production of the new, super-efficient Japanese cartel, which had a protected monopoly in Japan and was successfully beginning to prey on the markets of the United States and other nations.* This operation would produce for RCA as much as $200 million in licensing revenue yearly by the time GE reacquired RCA in 1985. (Curtis, 1994: 107, emphasis added)

Sarnoff was invited to Japan in 1960 by the Japanese Federation of

Economic Organization and received a hero's welcome (as 'the hero of the new Japanese television industry' according to *The Japan Times* at that time). Even Emperor Hirohito received him in private audience and honored him with the Order of the Rising Sun, the highest decoration that could be conferred on foreigners (Curtis, 1994; Chandler, 2001).

5.2.2.   SONY's Challenge

The postwar growth of Japan's consumer electronics industry has been all but synonymous with the legendary growth of Sony Corporation, which has innovated many of the world's firsts. Indeed, Sony's success also originated from its efforts to *learn* from the US electronics industry in the immediate postwar years. It is a well-known story that one of the company's co-founders, Masaru Ibuka, had a chance to see an American-made tape recorder in the Occupation forces' broadcasting office and succeeded in persuading an American officer to bring it to Ibuka's factory and demonstrate how it worked to a group of his fellow workers. Impressed by the quality of the tape recorder, Ibuka dropped his research on the wire recorders which he had been trying to commercialize and plunged into building a new recorder with a magnetic tape (Morita, 1986). In late 1949, Sony managed to produce the first type of tape recorder (code-named G-type), which was, however, too bulky and too expensive to be sold widely – and then in 1951 a second type (H-I), which was portable and reasonably priced (Morita, 1986; Lyons, 1976). Sony's endeavor of tape-recorder commercialization was truly the 'break or make' event for the then small startup's fate – and Sony finally succeeded.

Another legendary innovation was the commercialization of transistors in the form of portable radios which were small enough to be fit into listeners' pockets. When Sony signed a licensing contract to use Western Electric's patent on the transistor, they were advised that 'the hearing aid was the only product [they] should expect to make with it' (Morita, 1986: 71). Disregarding such a suggestion, Sony went on improving the power of the transistor via phosphorus doping (which the Bell Labs once tried but discarded prematurely) and developing its own high-frequency type suitable for the radio. It is said that the initial size of the transistor radio actually turned out to be a little larger than a standard men's shirt pocket so that Sony had some shirts made for its 'salesmen with slightly larger than normal pockets, just big enough to slip the radio into' for demonstration (Morita, 1986: 79). The rest of the company's success was history.

Sony's subsequent record of innovative products includes the world's first transistor TV (1960), the world's first transistorized compact-size VCR (1963), 'Trinitron' color TV (1968), 'Betamax' VCR (1975), 'Walkman' headphone stereo (1979), CD player and 'Betacam' broadcast use camera

(1982), single-unit, 8 mm video camera (1985), 'Mavica' electronic camera (1988), HD-Trinitron color TV (1990), the world's first high-brightness green light-emitting diode (1994), DVD video player (1997), entertainment robot 'AIBO' (1999), and the world's largest full-color organic EL display (2001) (Sony, 2003). And Sony's PlayStation game consoles became a blockbuster product. Thus Sony's achievements represented the rise of Japan's consumer electronics. There was no hubris or exaggeration when Ibuka reportedly once said that without Sony, the birth and growth of Japan's consumer electronics industry would have been slower by several years (Kibi, 1980).

Be that as it may, it needs to be noted that if it had not been for America's open consumer markets, Sony's success would have been impossible. It is a well-known story that Morita, a marketing genius, moved his family to New York and strove to learn American English and ways of life in the world's most mass-affluent economy – and similarly encouraged company executives to do the same – in order to develop and cultivate the market for Sony's products. (Yet, as will be explored in Chapter 6, Japan's consumer electronics companies, including Sony, began to encounter stiff competition from the NIEs – notably Samsung of Korea – and China toward the end of the 1990s, eroding their incomes. Consequently they have been forced to restructure their business operations to prevent profits from plummeting. In this sense, Sony's malaise or a so-called 'Sony shock' was emblematic of the challenge Japan's electronics industry as a whole has recently faced.)

5.3. INDUSTRIAL POLICY FOR HIGH-TECH INDUSTRIES

5.3.1. Government–Business Cooperative R&D Program

Starting in the mid-1960s, the Japanese government began to organize – and subsidize – the so-called cooperative R&D programs (often called large-scale national projects) among local competitors under government sponsorship. Because of the ambitious technological goals pursued by the Japanese government and industry in collaboration, this type of high-profile project generated a mixed reaction of concern and admiration abroad: concern from market-oriented economies to which such nationally designed projects posed threats of unfair tactics – and admiration from the developing countries that were interested in promoting their own high-tech industries.

The effectiveness of large-scale R&D projects was witnessed in the rapid growth of Japan's computer industry, which was initially dominated by IBM. The company was able to set up a wholly owned subsidiary in Japan under the so-called yen provision despite the government's restrictive policy for inward FDI at that time. How firmly and eagerly the Japanese government was determined to deter IBM from monopolizing the domestic market is well illustrated in the following 1950s episode as described by Johnson (1982):

> Sahashi (MITI's vice minister) wanted IBM's patents and made no bones about it. In as forthright a manner as possible, he made his position clear to IBM-Japan: 'We will take every measure possible to obstruct the success of your business unless you license IMB patents to Japanese firms and charge them no more than a 5 percent royalty.' In one of his negotiating sessions, Sahashi proudly recalls, he said that 'we do not have an inferiority complex toward you; we only need time and money to compete effectively.' IBM ultimately had to come to terms. *It sold its patents and accepted MITI's administrative guidance over the number of computers it could market domestically as conditions for manufacturing in Japan.* (p. 247, emphasis added)

Once Japan secured basic technologies through licensing, it went on to develop and manufacture its own computers under cooperative R&D programs. For example, in order to catch up on IBM's System 360 series (the 'third-generation' computers based on LSI (large scale integration)), three large-scale projects were organized by the MITI: first, the 'Project for Developing an Ultra-High Performance Electronic Computer System 360 series' (1966–72); second, the 'Project for Developing Information Processing System' (1968–75); and third, the 'Project for Developing Pattern Recognition System' (1971–81).

Since there were fierce rivalries among six domestic computer manufacturers at that time, they were divided up into three groups so as to promote *cooperation* in pre-competitive research, while still retaining a high degree of *competition* in product development. The three groups consisted of three pairs of Japanese producers: Fujitsu and Hitachi, NEC and Toshiba, and Mitsubishi and Oki. These nationally mobilized efforts under the 'cooperation-cum-competition' formula proved to be effective in narrowing the technological gap relative to IBM on the hardware: 'Each group was as a result successful in developing new series in line with the liberalization schedule, with the announcement starting in 1974 by the Fujitsu-Hitachi group of the M series, followed by the ACOS series of the NEC-Toshiba group and the COSMO series of the Mitsubishi-Oki group, with complete lines of machines in these series by 1978' (Shinjo, 1988: 352). And the same catch-up success was repeated when IBM introduced the 'fourth-generation' computer in 1979 (Sano and Degawa, 1993).

It should be noted that since the 'fourth-generation' computer required VLSI, the domestic semiconductor manufacturers were likewise organized, again under the 'cooperation-cum-competition' formula, into two groups: Fujitsu, Hitachi, and Mitsubishi as one group, and NEC and Toshiba as the second. Each group formed a four-year subsidized VLSI research project (1976–80). This program similarly proved successful, since over 1000 patents on the high-precision processes of manufacturing VLSIs were secured.

Subsequently, exactly the same approach was again adopted for the 'fifth-generation' computer development program (1982–93) and the 'supercomputer' project (1980–89) with equally effective results as before, achieving technological parity or even superiority vis-à-vis the United States in high-speed computing and image data recognition (Tatsuno, 1990).[3] And several more cooperative R&D projects have been initiated in a multitude of other high-tech areas such as robotics, biotechnology, superconductivity, biocomputing, and nanotechnology.

One interesting question raised about these government-coordinated research projects is whether or not the fiercely competing Japanese companies willingly followed MITI's leadership in the joint research programs. Okimoto (1989) says no and points out their reluctance and even their objections:

> The government's willingness to underwrite the full cost of a number of the frontier R&D projects, however, should not be misinterpreted. It does not mean that all private companies are eager to jump on the bandwagon and reap the benefits of the government's free ride. Consider the case of the Fifth Generation project; several firms had to be coaxed into participating, and several groused openly about it ... On top of the bureaucratic red tape [paperwork, regulations, government monitoring, etc.], contracting companies in Japan are usually not allowed to retain proprietary rights over the research results. Patents automatically revert to the sponsoring government agency, which makes them available on a nondiscriminatory basis to all nonparticipating companies for the cost of a patent license fee. Despite full financial coverage, therefore, *itaku* [contract research] is not as attractive to private companies as the term *free ride* might suggest. The administrative costs alone are hardly trivial. (p. 81)

Two important aspects of MITI's role are thus hinted at; (1) the cost coverage of some frontier R&D projects by the government, and (2) the government's control of patents and the non-discriminatory dissemination of created knowledge to all non-participating companies. Although this type of project was normally financed half by the government and half by the private firms, some large projects were so risky that the private firms were not willing to participate without full financial support from the government. Even when a full footing of the bill covered the financial risk of precompetitive (pre-product development) research, however, the government policy to disseminate the fruits of joint research to all non-participating firms would still raise the risks associated with commercialization.

It is important to keep in mind, however, that the government policy was after all *intended* to stir up, and resulted in, a high degree of competition in *product development*. Indeed, the corporative research program worked because it forced the competing firms to collaborate in precompetitive research activities so as to create and make commonly available basic technology, but to compete vigorously in commercializing new products, thereby accelerating the industry-wide pace of product innovation.

There is also another important reason why the government had to cajole firms into getting together for collaborative research. Saxonhouse (1986) explains:

> … Cooperative R&D projects are important in Japan only because in Japan, relative to other industrialized countries and particularly the United States, there is *much less* informal communication and cooperation among scientists and engineers working at different firms. As Japanese government survey after survey shows, *Japanese firms rarely look to other firms and individuals in their own industry as a source of new technological information* … In the United States, the diffusion of useful research results across firms is possible because of the high degree of professional orientation among firm scientists and engineers. This pattern has developed in the United States because of the strong, common theoretical background of university-trained R&D staff, which not only facilitates communication but also creates labor market related incentives for communicating effectively with R&D workers at other firms. (p.125, emphasis added)

What is observed here indicates that inter-firm flows of knowledge and information, one of the major sources of positive externalities for the industry, are very weak – indeed, too weak to create *information externalities* for each other in Japan's high-tech industry. Hence, this necessitated government involvement in bringing them together for a joint research effort at some competition-free, 'neutral' facilities (usually at a government laboratory). But why are Japan's inter-firm flows of information so weak in the first place? This deficiency is due mainly to the *keiretsu*-based structure of networking, and will be theorized in Chapter 8 (terms of 'knowledge/information creation vs. knowledge/information diversion').

5.4. THE 'TECHNOPOLIS' AND 'REGIONAL RESEARCH CORE' PROGRAMS

Another government-sponsored program to push Japan's technological frontier was the 'technopolis' project that was initiated in 1984 under the Technopolis Law of 1983. It was designed to set up twenty 'technopolises' across Japan's archipelago corridor. Each technopolis is an integrated complex of high-tech industries, research universities, local supporting industries, housing, and communications and transportation facilities, a high-tech cluster that engenders economies of linkage and agglomeration. Therefore, the idea of '*konbinato*' or the Silicon Valley genre of industrial clustering was behind the scheme. MITI was given the authority to act as the program coordinator, but the actual planning and financing of individual technopolises was delegated to the local governments.

This program had a multitude of objectives, explicit and implicit. To start with, it would promote a nationwide building of high-tech supportive infrastructure, thus encouraging regional economic development. It would disperse industrial concentration away from the overcrowded Tokyo and Osaka mega-metropolises toward the yet uncongested outliers of Japan – with better allocation of industrial activities throughout the country for both environmental and economic efficiency reasons as a result. Moreover, MITI, whose administrative purview had been considerably reduced as Japanese industry gained autonomy, wanted to regain its turf of political influence:

> ... one reason for the alacrity with which MITI has grabbed hold of the issue [of industrial location] is that it presents an opportunity to extend MITI's influence beyond Tokyo, where it tends to be concentrated, into the farthest reaches of the countryside. To help prefectural governors formulate and implement plans for industrial development, MITI now sends a number of its bright young bureaucrats to serve for short periods as special assistants. This has put MITI in a position to expand its influence in local areas (a position the Construction and Finance ministries have enjoyed for years). It is possible that the establishment of regional influence will serve as a local base for former MITI bureaucrats to run for election to the national Diet, just as the local tax offices serve as a springboard for former MOF [Ministry of Finance] officials to run for elective office. For MITI, the extension of its influence into the outlying regions has softened the blow of losing many of the key powers it once possessed. (Okimoto, 1989: 96)

Yet the program proved to be a failure. The technopolises were soon found to be incapable of attaining the critical mass needed to generate the agglomeration effect for a variety of reasons, as explained by Tatsuno (1990):

> The infrastructure to support a future generation of researchers is gradually taking shape in the technopolises. But global economic shifts have undermined the assumptions behind the technopolis program. Since the yen shock of 1985, Japanese manufacturing plants have moved offshore to less expensive sites in Asia, Europe, and the United States, reducing the flow of technology from Tokyo and Osaka. In 1986 plant siting in the technopolises took a sharp nosedive, though it recovered somewhat in 1988. Another setback was that regional governments initially focused their efforts on 'hard' infrastructure projects, such as roads, airports, and highways, and underestimated the difficulty of developing the 'soft' infrastructure of R&D consortia, venture capital funds, and university research needed to drive the technopolises. Most technopolises are still empty shells, and top-flight Japanese engineers still prefer to live and work in the Tokyo area, whose wealth of educational and cultural resources attracts 80 percent of the nation's researchers. Unlike Tokyo or Silicon Valley, the technopolises are not beneficiaries of a natural flow of people and jobs. (p. 97)

To buttress the technopolis program that was originally more or less manufacturing-focused, in 1986 the MITI introduced another program, the 'regional research core' program that was more sharply aimed at fostering R&D to supplement the technopolises, as indicated by its official name. Twenty-eight such core clusters were set up at the end of the 1980s. Yet the 'regional research core' program too failed to create the intended viable research clusters for nurturing new industrial knowledge.

5.4.1. Economic Logic of Clustering and Strategic Alliances

In the meantime, the 'Silicon Valley' genre of high-tech clusters began *spontaneously* to spring up outside the government-initiated programs. For example, 'Bit Valley' (Internet-based information service cluster) in the fashionable Shibuya (literally translated as 'Bitter Valley') district of Tokyo and a high-tech manufacturing cluster in Kyoto (with Kyoto University, Kyocera and other mid-sized high-tech firms as its axes) are the prime examples. The Akihabara district, Tokyo's famous cluster of electronics retailers, is morphing into the capital of 'anime culture'. They are clustered in those urban areas where information density (hence, information externalities) is high and where creative entrepreneurs are naturally attracted and congregate because of the availabilities of business services and amenities – that is, definitely not in those isolated rural locations chosen by the MITI's technopolis or 'regional research core' project. The regionally dispersed '*konbinato*' model (in which advanced foreign technologies were once eagerly absorbed and assimilated in heavy and chemical industries) would clearly no longer be applicable for high-tech industries, which required entrepreneurship and new knowledge as key inputs in product/service development, production and marketing.

Furthermore, Japan's high-tech firms are by nature more outwardly (i.e., globally) than inwardly (i.e., parochially) focused. To tap R&D resources, they have set up new corporate research centers in such places as Silicon Valley, Route 127 (near MIT and Harvard), Cambridge (UK), Dublin (Ireland), and many other 'brain clusters' in the West. In addition to establishing these networks of their own research facilities overseas, Japan's high-tech firms began to engage actively in strategic alliances with foreign high-tech firms in order to organize joint project-based R&D. In fact, strategic alliances in research became rampant in the semiconductor industry. In 1992, for example, such an alliance – a tripartite mega-alliance – was organized for the first time among the world's electronics giants (IBM, Toshiba, and Siemens) to design and develop 256-megabit dynamic random access memory chips. The philosophy behind this was that they had complementary strengths and weaknesses in different areas.

Stated differently, this type of alliance in new product development is aimed at exploiting each partner's *comparative* advantage in a particular technological strength at the corporate level – akin to a trade-induced pattern of specialization (i.e., a trade-induced exploitation of comparative advantage) at the national level, as envisaged in the Ricardian theory of international trade. Thus, a micro-micro (*intra*-firm) specialization in core competences came to be pursued under *inter*-firm alliances among knowledge-based firms. That is to say, *alliances are an effective organizational framework within which corporate-level comparative advantages between firms can be capitalized on.* This approach represents a new 'spatial' (across border) and 'geography-free' way of creating brain-intensive clusters for specific research projects on a highly flexible short-term basis. Strategic alliances are most prevalent in high-tech sectors among the advanced countries (Table 5.1).

5.5. R&D AND ECONOMIC GROWTH

The Schumpeterian stage is characterized by a large sum of expenditures / investment in corporate R&D, whose outcome results in total factor productivity (TFP) growth. It is therefore expected that the more intensive the investment in R&D, the higher the growth rate of TFP. This relationship can be found in a simple correlation analysis between a change in R&D stock (a change over the previous five years in R&D expenditures) as a ratio of gross value-added and the growth rate of TFP (Figure 5.1). The more R&D intensive a given industry, the higher the growth of TFP (Science and Technology Agency, 1998).

Since industries are interconnected with each other in varying degrees through input-output relations, TFP growth in a given industry reflects a composite TFP effect comprised of its own TFP increase and an indirect benefit it receives from other industries' TFP improvement. No doubt, the latter's contribution is expected to rise as manufacturing becomes increasingly 'fragmented (input-output-oriented)' with the use of parts, components, sub-assemblies, and accessories. It is interesting to note that the TFP growth rate was as high as more than 2 per cent per year over the 1970–75 period, but declined to less than 1 per cent by mid-1980. It recovered somewhat over the 1985–90 period (due to an active investment in stepped up R&D and new productive facilities during the bubble) but again registered a secular decline over the 1990–95 period (Science and Technology Agency, 1998). This long-term trend of a slowdown in TFP growth mirrored in part the closing of a technology gap vis-à-vis the West; initially Japanese industry was able to adopt advanced foreign technologies at relatively low cost in connection with its investments in new productive facilities. By the mid-1980s, however, such a stock of borrowable technologies had either diminished or become harder to tap into because of the increased unwillingness on the part of

Table 5.1 Strategic technical tie-ups among the Triad companies, 1980–1989 and 1990–1999

	Japan–US technical tie-ups				Japan–Europe technical tie-ups				US–Europe technical tie-ups			
	IT	BT	Other	Total	IT	BT	Other	Total	IT	BT	Other	Total
1980	211	83	262	556	82	24	128	234	293	152	363	808
–89	(37.9)	(14.9)	(47.1)	(100.0)	(35.0)	(10.3)	(54.7)	(100.0)	(36.3)	(18.8)	(44.9)	(100.0)
1990	277	75	126	478	84	36	101	221	484	468	531	1483
–99	(57.9)	(15.7)	(26.4)	(100.0)	(38.0)	(16.3)	(45.7)	(100.0)	(32.6)	(31.6)	(35.8)	(100.0)

Note: IT = information technology; BT = biotechnology

Source: Based on data from US-NSF, *Science & Engineering Indicators 2002*, as cited in Ministry of Education, Culture, Sports, Science and Technology (2002)

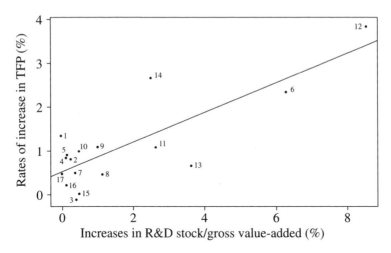

Notes:
1. Agr. forestry and fishery
2. Mining
3. Food and beverage
4. Textiles and apparel
5. Pulp and paper
6. Chemicals
7. Petroleum and coal prod.
8. Glass, clay and stone prod.

9. Primary metals
10. Metal products
11. General machinery
12. Electric machinery
13. Transport equipment
14. Precision equipment
15. Civil engineering
16. Construction
17. Public transportation

Source: Science and Technology Agency (1998: 24)

Figure 5.1 Changes in R&D stock and changes in total factor productivity (TFP), 1970–1994

Western firms to sell cutting-edge technologies for fear of creating fierce competitors.

5.6. COMING OF AGE

Contrary to the once widely held image of Japanese manufacturers as copy cats in the early postwar period, Japan's electronics industry, in particular, introduced a slew of sleek and wondrous electronics gadgets on their own, one after another, which were much admired by consumers around the world. It is true that Japanese innovators became successful at *commercializing* into new products certain inventions and basic ideas, many of which initially originated in the West (as seen earlier in Sony's development of transistor radios using the patent from Bell Labs). In the very course of commercialization, however,

Japanese entrepreneurs came to exhibit extraordinary creativity and originality in improving on, and successfully introducing, mass-merchandisable products.

Johnstone (1999) made a comprehensive study of the technology-commercialization processes initiated by particular individual engineers at Japanese companies such as Sharp, Seiko, Casio, Sony, and Citizen, involving a wide range of products – from pocket calculators and the quartz watch to liquid crystal displays (LCDs), to semiconductor lasers, and light-emitting diodes (LEDs). He argues:

> ... technologies were not transferred fully developed for Japanese corporations to copy. Rather, they were often adopted, after they had been abandoned by their originators, by visionary and highly motivated Japanese entrepreneurs, for very specific reasons, at small and medium-size firms, when there was still much research and development work remaining to be done. For the technologies they licensed, these firms paid the asking price – often sizable sums. And from their government, they received little encouragement or financial support. In no sense was this, as is often charged, a 'free ride' on other people's ideas. (Johnstone, 1999: xxii)

Johnstone's aim is to dispel 'the myth of MITI' in consumer electronics – and additionally the widely held myth that the Japanese lack originality and entrepreneurship because they are not individualistic, so much so that 'the very expression "Japanese entrepreneurs" sounds to our ears like a contradiction in terms' (Johnstone, 1999: xvi).

In fact, Japanese corporations steadily raised their investment in R&D with a much greater focus on basic research, and this was reflected in the rising ratio of R&D expenditure to GNP. The upshot was a phenomenal rise in the number of US patents granted to Japanese corporations. For example, according to a study made by *Business Week* (August 3, 1992), in the early 1990s the world's 25 top companies ranked in terms of the number of US patents granted in 1991 included 11 Japanese companies, 11 American companies, two German companies, and one Dutch company (Table 5.2). The top four positions were captured by Japanese companies. Furthermore, the world's top 15 companies with 'high-impact patents' (i.e., most frequently cited as building blocks in other companies' new patents) listed ten American companies, four of which took the first four rankings, and five Japanese companies (Table 5.3). Nevertheless, the world's top 15 companies that were 'closest to the cutting edge' (i.e., those with the shortest technology cycle time measured by the median age in years of patents cited in other companies' new patents) consisted almost entirely of Japanese companies – with the sole exception of one American company, Intel, which ranked ninth. Thus, the emergence of Japan as a technological superpower became undeniably evident in the early 1990s.

Not only on the technology (supply) side but also on the demand side, furthermore, Japan's domestic market had by then expanded and come of age,

Table 5.2   Top 25 corporations by number of US patents granted (1991)

	No. of US patents	Current impact index	Technological strength	Technology cycle time
1. Toshiba (Japan)	1156	1.45	1677	5.4
2. Hitachi (Japan)	1139	1.43	1633	5.7
3. Canon (Japan)	828	1.45	1201	6.0
4. Mitsubishi Elec. (Japan)	959	1.24	1190	5.1
5. Eastman Kodak (USA)	887	1.34	1186	7.8
6. IBM (USA)	680	1.71	1161	5.9
7. General Motors (USA)	863	1.32	1139	7.9
8. General Electric (USA)	923	1.16	1069	8.8
9. Fuji Photo Film (Japan)	742	1.42	1056	5.8
10. Motorola (USA)	631	1.54	969	5.5
11. AT&T (USA)	487	1.84	895	5.3
12. Philips (Netherlands)	768	1.02	781	6.0
13. Nissan Motor (Japan)	385	1.91	736	4.7
14. Texas Instruments (USA)	380	1.87	709	6.2
15. NEC (Japan)	483	1.46	706	5.0
16. Matsushita Elec. (Japan)	561	1.24	694	5.6
17. Du Pont (USA)	631	1.06	669	9.7
18. Xerox (USA)	353	1.75	619	6.8
19. Fujitsu (Japan)	382	1.56	596	5.3
20. Siemens (Germany)	610	0.97	589	6.6
21. 3M (USA)	374	1.39	519	10.9
22. Hoechst (Germany)	575	0.88	507	8.6
23. Minolta Camera (Japan)	315	1.61	506	5.1
24. AMP (USA)	275	1.84	505	7.1
25. Sharp (Japan)	388	1.27	493	5.4

Note: The number of patents granted by the US government is a traditional test of high-tech strength. But CHI Research Inc. has come up with more sophisticated measures, based on earlier patents cited as building blocks in new patents. The current impact index measures how often a company's patents are cited relative to those of all other companies. The 1.45 for Toshiba, for example, means its patents are cited 45 per cent more than average. CHI multiplies the index by number of patents to get technological strength, the basis for this ranking. Technology cycle time is the median age in years of patents cited in a company's new patents. The shorter the cycle time, the faster the company is developing new technology

Source: 'Global Innovation: Who's in the Lead', *Business Week* (August 3, 1992: 68)

especially for high-income products, with the fast-rising disposable incomes of Japanese consumers and their ever-diversifying and increasingly sophisticated tastes. Japanese companies began to innovate inward, that is, first for domestic consumers, and once a new product was successfully test-marketed at home, it would then be exported. They thus became major

Table 5.3 *High-impact versus cutting-edge patents (1991)*

A. High-impact patents	Current impact index	B. Cutting-edge patents	Technology cycle time
Cordis (USA)	2.25	Fuji Heavy Ind. (Japan)	4.1
Intel (USA)	2.16	Mazda Motor (Japan)	4.5
Proctor & Gamble (USA)	2.08	Pioneer Electronic (Japan)	4.5
Alza (USA)	1.96	Mitsubishi Motor (Japan)	4.6
Nissan Motor (Japan)	1.91	Ricoh (Japan)	4.6
Texas Instruments (USA)	1.87	Nissan Motor (Japan)	4.7
AT&T (USA)	1.84	Olympus Optical (Japan)	4.8
Nippon Telephone (Japan)	1.84	Nikon (Japan)	4.8
AMP (USA)	1.84	Intel (USA)	4.9
Fuji Heavy Ind. (Japan)	1.83	Aisin Seiki (Japan)	5.0
Mazda Motor (Japan)	1.81	NEC (Japan)	5.0
Mitsubishi Motor (Japan)	1.78	Sony (Japan)	5.0
Xerox (USA)	1.75	Mitsubishi Electric (Japan)	5.1
Colgate-Palmolive (USA)	1.72	Minolta Camera (Japan)	5.1
IBM (USA)	1.71	Toyota Motor (Japan)	5.2

Source: 'Global Innovation: Who's in the Lead', *Business Week* (August 3, 1992: 69). Original data are from CHI Research, Inc.

initiators of the product life cycle of many new products, particularly in consumer electronics – for the first time in corporate Japan's history.

5.7. SUMMING UP

Japan made a successful climb to the knowledge-driven stage of economic growth, initially developing both the semiconductor and computer industries by dint of its joint R&D efforts between the government and the private sector. This national focus was instrumental in developing early generations of microchips and computers. The real vitality of Japan's electronics industry, however, owed much to the entrepreneurial activities of its private sector in consumer electronics. Market forces – better still, *international* market forces, as seen in the transplantation of TV-set production from, and electronics exports to, the US – were crucial for the rapid growth of Japan's electronics industry. The production of transistor radios, TV sets, computers, and semiconductors examined in this chapter represented only early-generation electronics. The subsequent rapid scientific and technological progress would eventually lead to the IT revolution with an entirely new set of industries such as camera phones, electronic tags, music-downloading/playing devices, and other Internet-enabled goods, a topic to be discussed in Chapter 6.

The modern economic activities are now increasingly dependent on, and shaped by, *international learning* as the pace of knowledge creation and dissemination across national borders gathers momentum. FDI and other vehicles/modalities of international business are nothing but the channels through which knowledge and information are transmitted, assimilated, and exploited as key inputs in production and marketing. In this regard, Japan's stages of industrial upgrading are equivalent to the milestones of *sequential emulation and learning* over time. This is further elaborated below in an appendix to this chapter in terms of what may be called the 'Technology Development Path' to paraphrasing John Dunning's notion of the 'Investment Development Path'.

APPENDIX: THE MACRO-IDP (INVESTMENT DEVELOPMENT PATH), MESO-IDPS, AND THE TECHNOLOGY DEVELOPMENT PATH (TDP)[4]

A5.1.   A Hierarchical World and the Ladder of Development

This appendix will examine how the Japanese experience of industrial upgrading fits with the 'investment development path (IDP)' model introduced by Dunning (1981, 1991). This model explains the relationship between the net outward investment (NOI) position of a country (i.e., the gross outward FDI stock minus the gross inward FDI stock) and its path of economic development.

The IDP is framed in terms of Dunning's eclectic paradigm of international production:

> The IDP suggests that countries tend to go through five main stages of development and that these stages can be usefully classified according to the propensity of those countries to be outward/or inward direct investors. In turn, this propensity will rest on the extent and pattern of the competitive or ownership specific (O) advantages of the indigenous firms of the countries concerned, relative to those of firms of other countries; the competitiveness of the location-bound resources and capabilities of that country relative to those of other countries (the L specific advantages of that country); and the extent to which indigenous and foreign firms choose to utilize their O specific advantages jointly with the location-bound endowments of home or foreign countries through internalizing the cross-border market for these advantages, rather than by some other organizational route (i.e. their perceived I advantages). (Dunning and Narula, 1996: 1)

As illustrated in Figure A5.1, the IDP traces a J-curve for the first four stages plus a wiggle or a 'random walk' for the fifth stage in which 'Beyond a certain point in the IDP, the absolute size of GNP is no longer a reliable guide of a country's competitiveness; neither, indeed, is its NOI position' (Narula, 1996: 11).

The IDP is implicitly built on the notion that the global economy is necessarily hierarchical in terms of the various stages of economic development in which its diverse constituent nations are situated. In this respect, the IDP theory is clearly in the genre of hierarchical theory as stressed in Chapter 1. When a number of nations with lower per capita incomes experience net negative investment positions, there are necessarily a certain number of nations with higher per capita incomes whose net positive investment positions exactly correspond in value, given the fact that the global economy is a closed system.

What does such a path demonstrate? It should be construed that the IDP essentially traces out the net cross-border flows of industrial knowledge, the flows that are internalized in FDI and that restructure and upgrade the global economy, although there is also the non-equity type of knowledge transfer such as licensing, subcontracting, turnkey operations, and the like. In this respect, the IDP can thus be interpreted as a *cross-border net learning curve* exhibited by a nation that successfully moves up the stages of development by acquiring industrial knowledge from its more advanced 'neighbors'. A move from the J-shaped bottom or the negative NOI segment to the 'wiggle'

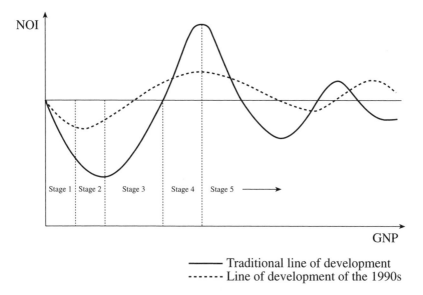

NOI

Stage 1 | Stage 2 | Stage 3 | Stage 4 | Stage 5 ──────▶

GNP

─────── Traditional line of development
------- Line of development of the 1990s

Note: Not drawn to scale – for illustrative purposes only

Source: Dunning and Narula (1996: 2)

Figure A5.1   The pattern of the investment development path

segment of the IDP indicates an equilibrium in knowledge dissemination – that is, a *narrowing* of the industrial knowledge gap between the advanced and the catching-up countries. Indeed, the IDP theory is quite similar to the FG paradigm, since they both emphasize the hierarchical nature of external commercial relations, especially when the IDP theory is viewed from the perspective of developing countries.

How perfectly, then, does the Japanese path explored within the 'flying-geese' (FG) framework fit the IDP pattern of catch-up growth? And if it does not, why is this? In general, it should be expected that *the smaller the technological gap, the greater a catching-up nation's capability of absorbing technology and skills (both technical and organizational), and the more involved its government is in promoting locally controlled industries, the flatter, and the shorter, the U-shaped portion of the IDP.* In fact, the U-shaped segment may entirely disappear if inward FDI is restricted by the government but non-equity (externalized) channels of knowledge absorption are used instead. Thus, the IDP curve conceptualized by Dunning is an idealized pattern based on free-market exchanges of knowledge among countries.

This way of interpreting the IDP is useful in analyzing the experiences of

Japan as a latecomer to the scene of modern industrialization. The Japanese government actively orchestrated the catching-up strategy of its industry on a rather nationalistic basis; it minimized inward FDI through which foreign interests directly control the ownership of local productive capacities, but instead encouraged the maximum use of licensing and other non-equity forms of acquiring advanced industrial knowledge from the West. Furthermore, Japanese industry itself had a well-developed capacity to seek, assimilate, and even improve on, state-of-the-art technology from the West. Hence, the Japanese experience does not really follow the typical pattern of the IDP. Yet, if other forms of knowledge acquisition are taken into account, the main idea of knowledge transfers and equilibration propounded in the IDP paradigm still holds and can be attested to in the context of Japan's catching-up development.

In analyzing the Japanese experience, it is important to keep in mind that the process of industrialization is *not* a smooth, continuous, and simultaneous expansion of all the segments of domestic industry, but *a sequence of stages* in each of which a certain industrial sector serves as the main engine (the 'leading' sector) for structural upgrading. As will be seen below, the idea that a successful process of development is punctuated by stages in a step-like fashion gives an important analytical supplement to Dunning's IDP.

A5.2.   FG Paradigm and Meso-IDPs

The stage idea is also the crux of the FG paradigm. In fact, the FG paradigm places the sequential pattern of development in a global context in which the economic development of a latecomer nation is interpreted as a *derived* process, a process that involves *interactions* with richer 'neighbors' (in the Smithian sense) through trade, FDI, and other forms of economic engagement. This interactive mode of growth is in line with the IDP, which is a locus of cross-border interactive learning or emulation and leading or tutorship.

Akamatsu's original work (illustrated in Figure 5.1) focused on how a given manufacturing industry (e.g. textiles) developed in a follower-goose country (such as Japan used to be). Figure A5.2(a) depicts what he identified as the 'fundamental FG formation', *the sequential triple-step appearance of imports, domestic production, and exports over a long span of time* (as long as half a century), each with a wave-like trend curve: a curve initially rising, then cresting, and eventually declining. This appearance is observable first in finished goods, and later on in capital goods.

In fact, the developmental full-cycle process of some of the Japanese industries Akamatsu examined took more than half a century, a rather prolonged time period by today's standards. The imports of cotton yarn began right after the Meiji Restoration of 1868 (the official beginning of Japan as a

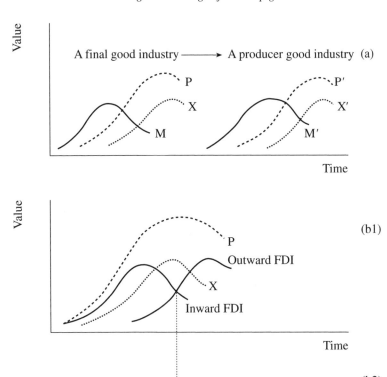

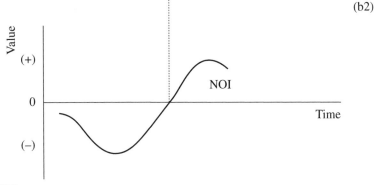

Notes:
(a)   Akamatsu's 'fundamental' FG pattern of industrial growth
(b1)   MNE-facilitated FG pattern of industrial growth
(b2)   Meso-IDP (in a particular industry)
M, M′: Imports
P, P′:   Production
E, E′:   Exports

Source: Ozawa (1996c: 145)

Figure A5.2   Flying-geese paradigm and the meso-IDP

modern state), but it was not until around 1887 (20 years later) that domestic production began to exceed imports, finally leading to the export phase, which in turn reached its peak at the turn of this century. On the other hand, the imports of capital goods, spinning and weaving machinery, started around 1883, but their domestic production and exports became significant only around 1903 and finally reached their respective peaks in 1939 (Akamatsu, 1962).

Why did it take so long for Japan to develop a vertically integrated cotton textile industry (inclusive of textile machinery)? Two important reasons are conceivable. First, in those days, FDI in textiles – that is, MNCs in cotton yarns, fabrics, and textile machinery – was rather rare, since the textile industry (especially its downstream segments) had a highly competitive market structure devoid of strong oligopolistic market power and without much extra organizational capacity to operate across national borders. Advanced Western countries – and their relatively small-sized textile manufacturers – were still interested in retaining and jealously guarding the textile industry at home, a dominant industrial employer at that time, although it was declining as a proportion of domestic industry in the face of emergent heavy industries, such as electric machinery, chemicals, and automobiles, at the turn of the twentieth century. (It is, indeed, in the latter types of industry that MNCs in manufacturing began to emerge as firm size increased and products became differentiated.)

More importantly, furthermore, the Japanese government in those days was pursuing an 'infant-industry' strategy, bent on developing domestic industries of its own through a variety of subsidies and protective measures. In short, the two sets of FG formation (one for final goods, the other for producer goods) thus exhibited rather prolonged secular curves, basically mirroring Japan's self-reliant (or anti-inward-FDI) stance of industrialization and the unavailability of MNCs, at that time, in textiles and textile machinery that could bring about industrialization practically 'overnight' (complete transfers of textile production facilities).

Nowadays, in sharp contrast, the governments of developing countries are interested in a much more speedy pace of industrial transformation by attracting MNCs as 'instant' transplanters of industrialization. The result is a considerably speeded-up (sharply accelerated) appearance for the FG formation of industrial development in a highly *time-compressed* fashion for both final goods and upstream producer goods.

One such possibility (what may be called an MNC/host-accelerated FG pattern of industrial growth) is illustrated in Figure A5.2(b1). Time compression occurs especially when MNCs' and host governments' strategic decisions coincide in establishing, as quickly as possible, vertically integrated local production (of final goods as well as producer goods) and in turning it into an export industry for the purpose of earning foreign exchange.

The conventional wisdom of FDI holds that the firm will first export to a particular overseas market, and then once a sufficient volume of sales is secured through exports, it will gingerly switch to local production – first, through licensing and then through FDI. These days, however, some MNCs may decide to set up local production from the very start without first exploring an overseas market via exports. In this case, local production necessarily precludes the import curve in the host country. In addition, the government of a developing host country is likely to impose, as is often the case, both *export and local content requirements.* If such an effort to domesticate/localize MNC-initiated ventures on the part of the host country is successful, both an export curve and a production curve for some (if not all) producer goods will appear almost simultaneously in the early stages of industrial growth without much time lag after the appearance of the local production curve for a final good. In other words, in the context of the FG paradigm of catching-up development, MNCs thus act as a compressor of the intertemporal length of Akamatsu's 'fundamental' pattern of industrial growth.

Suppose that a developing country has a potential comparative advantage in a labor-intensive light industry, say, apparel, and that it can attract MNCs in apparel to develop and exploit such comparative advantage. As illustrated in Figure 5.2(b1), the domestic productive capacity for apparel (curve P) will thus be developed by inward FDI (see curve labeled Inward FDI). These inward investments are likely to be highly export-oriented (curve X), although the domestic demand for apparel will also rise as local labor is fully employed by such export-led development policy. In fact, if such a policy for export-led, labor-driven development is successful, local wages will eventually rise and even shortages of low-skilled labor will occur (as experienced in early-postwar Japan and the Asian NIEs). In the end, then, the country will lose its comparative advantage in labor-intensive, low-skilled industries, thereby making the initial policy of labor-driven development no longer suitable.

The rising incomes, however, will in turn contribute to an increase in domestic savings (hence, needed funds will be available), enabling the country to have a more capital-intensive, sophisticated industry whose products can also be demanded at home because of increased domestic purchasing power. This self-altering process is the ineluctable result of labor-driven industrialization, as it is posited in, and explained by, the 'principle of increasing factor incongruity', a principle based on the 'Smithian vent-for-surplus' theory and the 'Stolper–Samuelson factor-price magnification' effect (Ozawa, 1992). To paraphrase the Schumpeterian notion of 'creative destruction', this self-upgrading process may be called 'creative structural destruction'.

As local wages rise, the host country starts to lose comparative advantages in labor-intensive industries. Consequently, inward FDI (of the labor-seeking type) begins to decline and eventually disappear, while outward FDI will appear in order to transplant the now comparatively disadvantaged activities onto lower-labor-cost countries in a manner that develops or augments the latter's comparative advantages. (Indeed, this is exactly what has happened in the Asian NIEs – and is about to happen in the ASEAN-4. The Asian NIEs are, in fact, the major manufacturing investors in the ASEAN-4's labor-intensive industries, notably apparel and sundries. Even the ASEAN-4 are now investing in China and Vietnam where wages are still lower than at home.) As shown in Figure A5.2(b2), this sequential process of FDI – first inward and then outward – can be depicted as a *meso*-IDP, an IDP distinct from Dunning's IDP, which can now be contrasted as a *macro*-IDP. This concept of the meso-IDP is useful to demonstrate the positive net outward investment positions of the Asian NIEs in labor-intensive industries, even though their macro-IDPs are still in the below-parity or negative NOI zone (i.e., around the bottom of the J-shaped portion of their macro-IDPs).

Assuming that a catching-up country develops step by step in line with its compatible factor endowments and its prevailing level of technological sophistication, a series of meso-IDP curves can be expected to appear, as illustrated in Figure A5.3(a). If this happens, they will trace out Dunning's macro-IDP as an *envelope* curve. This envelope curve will not stay flat but will turn up following a U-shaped path. For, since such a successful catching-up country is moving up the ladder of industrialization from low value-added, low-technology industries to higher value-added, higher-technology ones over time, the level of industrial knowledge accumulated in the process will rise steadily and will eventually be on a par with the advanced world. That is to say, as the knowledge gap narrows, the rate of outward FDI (cross-border knowledge dissemination) becomes greater than that of inward FDI (cross-border knowledge absorption). This is also reflected in the fact that each successive wave of the meso-IDPs (from, say, apparel to metal products to automobiles) necessarily becomes larger and larger, because higher value-added manufacturing is more knowledge intensive as well as capital intensive; hence, both inward and outward FDI will grow in value.

The series of meso-IDPs illustrated in Figure A5.3(a) assumes a stylized hypothetical situation in which both MNCs and the host country are interacting freely in an idealized fashion without any impediments to FDI flows, inward or outward. In contrast, if a catching-up country inhibits inward FDI but promotes outward FDI, such an asymmetry will equally be reflected in the shapes of the meso-IDP curves; while the net negative portions of all the

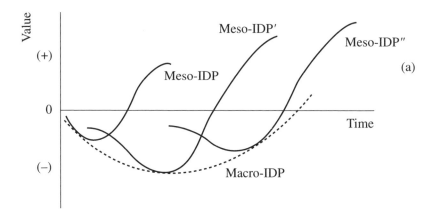

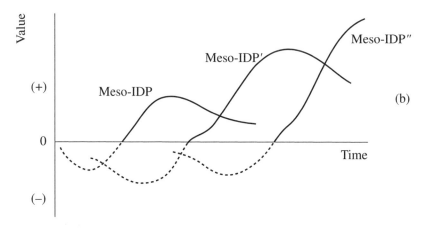

Notes:
(a) A macro-IDP as an envelope curve of meso-IDPs
(b) 'Distorted (inward-FDI-inhibiting)' meso-IDP

Source: Ozawa (1996c: 150)

Figure A5.3 Structural upgrading and meso-IDPs

meso-IDP curves disappear, their positive portions alone can be observed
(Figure A5.3(b)). Indeed, this modified model of the meso-IDP fits nicely with
the experiences of the Japanese economy after WWII, since Japan – early on,
intentionally at the policy level, and later, at the market structural level – came
to establish *an inward-FDI-inhibiting, but outward-FDI-fostering regime*
(although Japan is currently making efforts to redress such FDI imbalance).

This distorted or degenerate pattern of meso-IDPs is the inevitable outcome of its FG strategy of catching-up development. Japan did not exhibit the typical (normal) pattern of an IDP. Inward FDI was kept to a minimum, while technological absorption in unbundled form (i.e., licensing) was promoted. Consequently, ever since the end of the war, Japan's net outward FDI has never been negative; its NOI shows only positive values.

A5.3. Technology Development Path (TDP)

It was after WWII that Japan was able to devote practically all its national energy and resources (since it no longer needed to spend for military purposes) to catch up with the West in industrial endeavors by making the best use of its huge technology gap vis-à-vis the West, a gap that had widened during the war. Luckily, Japan could concentrate on industrial efforts under the benign tutelage of the United States in the context of the deepening Cold War. The United States largely tolerated Japan's protectionism, which enabled the latter to build up industries by importing technology through licensing agreements and restricting inward FDI to a minimum.

As a result, Japan's learning curve took the form of what may be called a 'technology development path' (TDP) via licensing rather than an IDP. In fact, if we measure the ratio of Japanese exports of technology to imports of technology (or net technology exports), a negative 'net technology receipt' pattern – akin to a negative NOI pattern – can be observed, as shown in Figure A5.4.

It is interesting to note that the ratio is still below parity (a ratio of one), but that it has been steadily increasing (from 0.05 in 1963 to 0.42 in 1992), indicating Japan's rising level of technological capacity. In 1992, Japan paid royalties and fees for industrial technology amounting to $4.7 billion, 34 times the amount ($136 million) it paid in 1963, partly reflecting the growth of its capacity to absorb and make use of imported technology. On the other hand, in 1992 Japan received about $2 billion, as much as 285 times the amount ($7 million) it received in 1963, another clear indication of the enormous technological progress it had made over the previous 30 years. All this attests to the fact that Japan has not become merely dependent on imported technology; rather, *because of* imported technology it has been able to raise its own technology development capacity. This is because imported technology was looked upon as a 'raw material', just like any other raw material, to be processed, assimilated, synthesized with local industrial knowledge, transformed into 'finished technologies', and exported back to the world (Ozawa, 1985).

Yet, the above aggregate statistics miss the vital changes that have occurred (i) in Japan's relations vis-à-vis technology trade partners, and (ii) in different

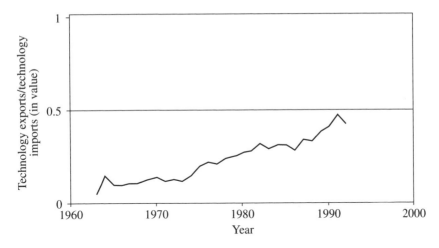

Source: Ozawa (1996c: 154)

*Figure A5.4   Japan's balance of technology trade as a technology
development path (TDP)*

industrial sectors as Japan climbed the ladder of industrialization stage by
stage, each stage led by a certain growth industry.

For example, as may well be expected, Japan has been exporting a
substantial amount of technology to the developing countries practically
without importing in return. In fact, East Asian countries are Japan's largest
customer for technology sales, accounting for 46 per cent (in 1994). Some
industrial technologies have begun to be imported from other Asian countries
in the recent past, but such imports are still insignificant in value. Japan thus
runs a totally one-sided surplus in technology trade with the developing
countries.

Another interesting picture emerges when one looks at Japan's technology
trade with four other major advanced countries: the United States, the United
Kingdom, Germany, and France (Figure A5.5). Japan began to experience a
surplus in technology trade with the United Kingdom in 1987, with technology
export receipts more than twice the payments in 1991. (This means that Japan
is already in the 'wiggle' stage of TDP vis-à-vis the UK). Japan still registers
technology trade deficits vis-à-vis the other three countries, but such deficits
have been declining (e.g., Japan's technology export receipts were only about
4 per cent of its technology import payments vis-à-vis Germany in 1975, but
grew to 53 per cent in 1991).

Similarly, disaggregation of Japan's technology trade balance by industry

Value of exports
──────────────
Value of imports

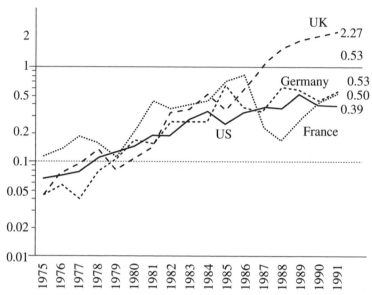

Source: Science and Technology Agency (1993: 141), as cited in Ozawa (1996c: 155)

Figure A5.5   Japan's technology trade with other major countries

reveals the differences in the sector patterns of such trade balance (Figure
A5.6). Japan's top net technology exporter is the construction industry,
followed by the steel industry, the stone, clay and glass industry, and the
automobile industry. Their appearances as net technology exporters occurred
in that order. The chemical industry is near parity, oscillating around the
balance line. Indeed, these curves may be called 'meso-TDPs'. The
differences in the timing of the appearance of surpluses are reflective of the
progressive stages of structural upgrading Japan has gone through.

   In short, Japan's learning curve of the past is better represented by the
macro-TDP than the macro-IDP. Now that Japan has joined the ranks of the
advanced economies, its macro-IDP is clearly visible and in the positive-
balance range, still at stage 4 of the macro-IDP, because of Japan's huge NOI
position.[5]

A5.4.   Concluding Remarks

This appendix has analyzed the linkage of the FG paradigm of intra-industry

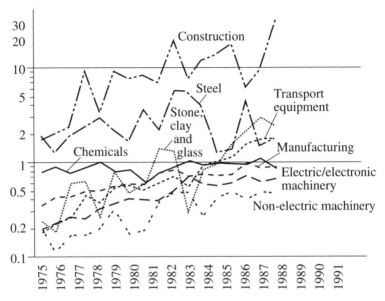

Source: Science and Technology Agency (1993: 141), as cited in Ozawa (1996c: 156)

Figure A5.6 Japan's balance of technology trade by manufacturing industry

structural evolution to the IDP paradigm. It has shown that the IDP path can be derived as an envelope curve of industry-specific meso-IDPs. Because of Japan's post-WWII policy and its social capability of maximizing emulative learning through licensing agreements while minimizing dependence on inward FDI, its macro-IDP exhibited a distortion in that the bottom of the curve was missing. In this respect, the TDP path is conceptualized to fill the gap left by the missing portion of Japan's past IDP.

However, to fully understand how Japan's economic development and its interactions with the West – and hence, with their MNCs – have proceeded since the end of World War II, the evolutionary stages perspective adopted is critical. In fact, the essential process of economic development, particularly when it occurs relatively smoothly and efficiently in an accelerated manner as it did in Japan, involves a ratchet-like upscaling of the industrial structure stage by stage, each stage being *compatible* with the prevailing factor endowments and overall technological sophistication at home. In addition, inflows of advanced technology (via licensing or FDI) become practically an *endogenous* variable of economic growth in the context of an open-economy, interactive, derived process of development, given the internal capacity to absorb technology from abroad. Similarly, outward FDI serves as a resource *reallocative* mechanism to assist structural upgrading at home, another endogenous variable of economic growth. In fact, this hints at a *new* growth theory, the theory of economic development as *endogenous growth,* that explicitly recognizes the existence of MNCs as the generators/disseminators of industrial knowledge across national borders – that is, as endogenous variables within the system of global capitalism.

NOTES

1. This zeitgeist was introduced and popularized in *Nikkei Business* (1982).
2. This section draws on Kanasaki (1982) and Koizumi (1990) for statistics and basic information.
3. For an excellent and detailed account of Japan's cooperative research programs under the MITI's guidance, see Tatsuno (1990).
4. This appendix is based on Ozawa (1996c).
5. Implicit in the TDP curve is the assumption that technology flows are substitutes for FDI flows. This is valid for Japan's technology imports (licensing) which were deliberately chosen as substitutes for inward FDI. But when it comes to Japan's technology exports, they often complement its outward FDI. This complementary relationship is statistically examined in Sekiguchi (1997). His regression analyses reveal that for Japan's manufacturing industry as a whole, technology exports (in value of sales) are positively related to outward FDI (a t-value of 12.3976 and significant at the 99 per cent level) with a regression coefficient of 0.1813 (i.e., $1 million of FDI is associated with $180,000 of technology exports). This complementarity is found to be about four times stronger in high-tech industries (chemicals, industrial machinery, electric and electronics machinery, and transport equipment) than in low-tech industries (food and beverage and textiles). Moreover, the relationship is even more pronounced for Japanese technology exports and FDI in Asia.

6. IT-driven stage – and logic – of new growth

6.1. THE IT REVOLUTION

The global economy is currently in the grip of the IT revolution, a communicational and organizational revolution that has been unleashed and has so far most successfully taken root in the United States. It is the driving force of the 'New Economy'. The recent phenomenal rise in US labor productivity (e.g., as high as 9.5 per cent in productivity growth in the third quarter of 2003, though 4.4 per cent for the entire year) can reportedly be ascribed to the application of IT, which makes flows and exchanges of information easier, faster, and cheaper – hence, making the benefits of the division of labor and specialization greater. (The 2003–4 'jobless recovery' of the US economy was blamed in part on such a rapid rise in labor productivity that corporate demand for manpower fell). Indeed, Adam Smith's famous maxim now can be aptly paraphrased to describe the productivity-boosting effect of the IT revolution: 'the division of labor is limited by the extent of the IT revolution'.

The advent of the IT revolution has driven Japan into the latest phase of growth that intensively employs intellectual capital. As pointed out in Chapter 1, this stage is characterized by production of 'abstract' or 'conceptual' goods (such as readily accessible information and transactions on the Internet), whereas in the earlier stages of catch-up growth more tangible inputs (e.g., cotton, steel, and chemicals) were intensively employed to produce 'physical' goods (e.g., apparel, machinery, cars, and TV sets). This chapter examines how the 'McLuhan' stage is impacting on the whole structure of Japanese industry and discusses the new opportunities, problems, and policy issues facing it.

6.2. BORN IN AMERICA

The present IT-driven economy is a creature of America's free-market system, its equally freewheeling stock market, and an abundant supply of venture capital and entrepreneurial talents. It is also a long-term outcome of deregulation, trade liberalization, a flexible labor market, and coalescing technological changes. Indeed, the US was able to spark a new revolution because the Golden Straitjacket was initially tailored and worn by the United States more willingly than by any other countries. It took the United States about two decades of deregulation to establish an IT-driven economy. In particular, liberalized capital markets (which spawned more venture capital, derivatives, equities, junk bonds, IPOs, and M&As) were an indispensable ingredient in the unprecedented long-lasting US economic boom of the latter half of the 1990s (a boom that ended in the bubble bursting in early 2000 but was followed by the robust rebound of 2004).

Because the IT revolution thus emerged as a result of drastic deregulations and free-market play in the United States, its spread to Japan has already been affecting the latter's economic institutions (especially those remnants of *dirigisme*) and policies very significantly. Along with rising FDI flows into Japan, the IT revolution is providing Japan with an autonomous, market-driven impetus for deregulating its business milieu so that entrepreneurial Internet-enabled ventures will flourish in the 'McLuhan' stage of structural transformation.

Most interestingly, the IT revolution has exerted its greatest impact on Japan's long-sheltered service industries, such as telecommunications, finance, and distribution (i.e., the erstwhile inward-dependent sector to be examined in Chapter 9) – mainly for two reasons. First, such a revolution necessitates deregulation and free-market transactions. Second, an application of IT enhances transactional efficiency and productivity. Therefore, *the more archaic, distorted, and inefficient an industry is, the greater the potential gains from IT applications* – and the faster the potential productivity growth. Japan has a huge backwater of still regulated and shielded industries that have only recently begun to open up gradually to global competition in trade and multinationals' investment and business activities.

6.3. GENESIS OF THE IT REVOLUTION

Thanks to this latest technological revolution, information and knowledge ('intellectual capital', as opposed to 'natural capital' and 'physical capital') have finally become *the* decisive input in economic activities. The Internet is sometimes described as 'an oil shock in reverse', since the former drastically reduces the cost of information in transactions, thereby boosting productivity and economic growth, whereas the oil shock of 1974 caused cost-push inflation and drove the world into recession.[1]

The origin of the present IT revolution can be traced back to the invention of the transistor, which ushered the world into the age of computers and information processing and transmission. (Some even trace the information age back as far as Gutenberg's removal-type printer.) The transistor rapidly developed into ever-more powerful and sophisticated microchips with declining costs of production through a dynamic learning curve. These microchips soon found their ways into personal computers (PCs), from desktops to laptops, and most recently to hand-held devices – all ever more flexible and more approachable than the mainframe computers which were once considered to be the major player in the world of computers.

The most important innovation for the IT revolution is, however, the Internet. The origin of this electronic networking is usually traced back to 1969 when Bolt Beranek and Newman (a computer-engineering firm) innovated a network, ARPANET, connecting computers at various research centers, under contract with the Advanced Research Project Agency (ARPA) in the US Defense Department. In 1972, the same firm developed an electronic mail software program that made it possible for geographically dispersed computers to be connected. In 1991, CERN (a European research laboratory) came up with the software for World Wide Web (www) servers and browsers (Hagel, 2002). Actually, Tim Berners-Lee, a British computer scientist at the lab, conceived the idea of the www, but decided not to patent it for the sake of making it free to anyone who could make use of it. (It is only in 2004 that his contribution has been finally recognized with the award of the World's most prestigious technology prize worth 1 million euros, the Millennium Technology Prize, from the Finnish Technology Award Foundation.[2])

The use of the Internet then spread quickly as it was linked up with computers, especially PCs. In the meanwhile, IT-based goods and services became cheaper and more manageable. And we were suddenly in the age of e-mail and www. As the inventor of the Internet, the United States now oversees the key technical coordination issues related to the global network through its semi-official governing body, the Internet Corporation for Assigned Names and Numbers (Icann).

In the meantime, telecommunications shifted from analog (electro-mechanical) to digital switching (computer-controlled and programmable exchanges), which is the nerve center of the telephone system, along with the use of fiber-optic cables for transmission. Telecom satellites, together with the global positioning system (GPS), and mobile phones came to serve as an alternative to fixed-line phone services. These technological developments, both artifacts and services, coalesced into one useful media package and began to spawn a new variety of information industries.

The IT revolution is often hyped as a 'third Industrial Revolution', the first being the 'Industrial Revolution' (of the early nineteenth century originated in England) represented by the innovation of the steam engine, and the second being the one delineated by the internal combustion engine and electricity. It is, however, still too early to assess the full impact of IT on economic activities, since this revolution is still in progress without yet revealing all its full potential effects and ramifications, though what has so far transpired is already far-reaching, especially through raising transactional efficiency and productivity.

It is clear, nevertheless, that the current revolution has to do with knowledge and information (intangibles embedded in human brains) – quite different in nature from steam engines, internal combustion engines, and electric power. It also basically has to do with the structuring of inter-agent relationships as a *network system* – not with certain new individual goods or energy sources per se. Since a variety of IT is impacting on the multifarious webs of transactions among billions of economic agents within and across countries, the world economy is changing in some fundamental ways.

6.4.   THE MCLUHAN STAGE AND ACROSS-THE-BOARD STRUCTURAL UPLIFTING

The IT-driven industries are a huge new media/information complex composed of telecommunications companies (e.g., AT&T, BT, Deutsche Telekom AG, Vodafone, and Nippon Telegraph and Telephone), networking gear makers (e.g., Lucent Technologies, Nortel Networks, and Cisco Systems), and PC makers (e.g., Apple, Dell, Toshiba, and IBM) as upstream operators; and operating system providers (notably Microsoft but also Linux) and portal providers (e.g., Yahoo! and America Online) as midstream operators; and e- (and m-) commerce (dotcom) companies (e.g., Amazon.com, ebay, Priceline, and hundreds of other online firms) and search engines (e.g., Google, Netscape, and Overture) as downstream operators. Most recently, cell phones are beginning to compete with PCs in some areas of service (such as e-mail, information searches, image transmission, and other 'information goods').

The arrival of the IT-based McLuhan industries represents the first most successful sibling born of the R&D-driven Schumpeterian industries. The salient features of this new phase, however, can be differentiated from, and contrasted to, the latter as follows:

- The McLuhan complex is composed of vertically linked industries, as seen above. Its upstream segments are highly intensive in R&D, straddling the Schumpeterian industries. On the other hand, its downstream operators (dotcoms) are not as R&D-intensive or as physical-capital-intensive as those in the Schumpeterian industries that are devoted to creating new 'physical goods' such as new drugs and new microchips. Internet-enabled dotcoms themselves require no such huge research expenditures in developing new services as in the Schumpeterian industries. They have no need for the formal research laboratories that are equipped with a variety of physical equipment. What is needed is basically imagination, ideas, and entrepreneurial spirits – and computer knowledge possessed by talented individuals.

- It is worth re-emphasizing, however, that the initial IT hardware took the form of microchips and computers in the crevices of the R&D-based Schumpeterian industries, information artifacts that are the indispensable physical tools of the Internet. In other words, some of the Schumpeterian industries are the input providers to the McLuhan stage of growth just as some non-differentiated Smithian industries (e.g., steel and plastics) are to the differentiated Smithian industries (e.g., automobiles and early-generation TV sets).

- The McLuhan stage of growth is currently evolving through the ongoing convergence of IT, both hardware and software, into an ever-growing coherent mass of interrelated businesses. However, unlike the previous *linear* and *sector-differentiating* progression of structural upgrading in which some new industry (say, automobiles) becomes a leading sector in the economy without much affecting yesteryear's leading sector (say, textiles), the McLuhan complex impacts on all the 'older generation' (Old Economy) industries in terms of the corporate value-added chain of knowledge creation (R&D), input procurement, production, warehousing, marketing, distribution, and customer services. The traditional non-manufacturing transactions, such as banking, finance, insurance, telecommunications, wholesale and retail businesses, telecommunications, and government services, are equally being overhauled. In other words, the IT revolution seeps through and permeates the entire economy. The Old Economy industries have to *upgrade* themselves by use of IT so as to attain higher levels of efficiency and productivity. In short, the McLuhan complex pulls up the entire existing economy. Put differently, the IT revolution raises total factor productivity in all the existing industries.

- The Schumpeterian industries augment the basis of trade competitiveness, since innovations in the advanced countries strengthen or create those higher value-added, knowledge-based industries in which their new comparative advantages lie. By contrast, the McLuhan industries may erode the basis for comparative advantage as they facilitate international factor movement (especially knowledge/information transmission by multinational corporations), thereby substituting international production for international trade, so long as such knowledge/information transfer is of the anti-trade type. At the same time, however, the IT revolution expands the basis of trade as the hitherto non-tradable sector (services) is turned into tradables – as is reflected in the debates on the offshoring (outsourcing overseas) of white-collar jobs. In addition, the time compression in catch-up growth (to be discussed in Chapter 7) is now being accelerated due to a rapid spread of knowledge in the McLuhan stage of global capitalism.

6.5.   IT-ENABLED INDUSTRY

The IT revolution is unfolding mainly in two types of technology: one in information *processing*, and the other in information *transmission*. The former derives from the ever-expanding capacities of semiconductors under Moore's Law (a doubling of the number of transistors on a microprocessor/silicon wafer every 18 to 24 months), which directly enhances computing functions. Information transmission is becoming ever faster due to the spread of the Internet and its fiber-optic technology called 'wavelength division multiplex (WDM)', both of which make it possible for a large number of people simultaneously to exchange information in real time at low cost and on a global scale (METI, 2001).

6.5.1.   Efficiency Gains from Information Processing Technology

How technological progress in information processing is leading to efficiency gains in manufacturing is vividly described below in terms of examples in the electrical machinery industry:

> ... substantial changes have taken place in the manufacturing process for electrical machinery, which once required adjustment of numerous parts. Replacing multiple parts with a handful of chips has reduced the number of parts and miniaturized products, and, in some extreme cases, the traditional belt-conveyor production method has been replaced with a *cell production* method whereby products can be finished by one person. In terms of in-house corporate organization too, many electrical machinery manufacturers once used the divisional organization method, with each product needing to be designed, tested and produced individually. IT has allowed this process to be shortened, or, in extreme cases, cut out altogether. Production sections are therefore being *integrated across projects*, allowing more flexible use of plant facilities. (METI, 2001: 48, emphasis added)

What is implied in this quote involves enhanced scale and scope economies. Parts reduction and miniaturization result in increased scale economies, while across-project integration (i.e., better coordination of the production of a variety of products) engenders more scope economies. Cell production is now a normal method widely used by Japanese electronics producers for high-tech goods such as sophisticated multi-functional cell phones.

6.6. DIFFERENCE IN IT SOFTWARE UTILIZATION

Although Japanese companies, notably in the electronics goods industry, are actively applying IT to reap efficiency gains in production, their appreciation of the effectiveness of IT utilization (via investment) in business administration is ironically said to be relatively low by international comparison. According to a survey made by Japan's Ministry of Economy, Trade, and Industry (METI) (2001), those responding Japanese companies that found IT investment 'very much more effective than expected' and 'somewhat more effective than expected' were only 4.0 per cent and 21.0 per cent respectively – in contrast to 9.0 per cent and 18.5 per cent for US companies, 13.0 per cent and 23.0 per cent for European companies, and 12.5 per cent and 31.5 per cent for Asian NIE companies. METI attributes this to the low rate of appointment of Chief Information Officers (CIO): 'Only 13 percent of Japanese companies have installed a dedicated CIO, around a fifth of the US level and a third of the European level, and even around half the level of the [NIEs]' (METI, 2002: 64). It is also pointed out that IT-related duties are not yet necessarily given high priority in Japanese management.

In fact, as summarized in Figure 6.1, so far as the introduction of major IT application managerial software is concerned, and when compared to the US, Europe, and the NIEs, Japan exhibits the highest usage of computer-aided design (CAD) (which is to be expected because of Japan's forte in product development and manufacturing), but it shows the lowest application ratios in enterprise resource planning (ERP), supply chain management (SCM), customer relationship management (CRM), and knowledge management (KM). Only in the area of electronic data interchange (EDI), is Japan neck and neck with the others. METI observes;

> Japanese companies appear to be relatively backward in terms of their *organizational* response to strategic IT utilization ... The low ratio of ERP introduction by Japanese companies is related to the large number of companies which do not use IT for management innovation but rather in support of their existing management systems. This would seem to indicate that top management in Japanese companies has been less interested than foreign companies in IT-based management innovation. (METI, 2001: 66, emphasis added)

The most interesting finding of the METI survey is, however, that Japanese companies are using *private online networks* more than the Internet, whereas their counterparts in the US, Europe, and the NIEs are far more actively

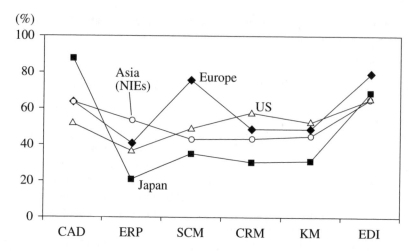

Note: CAD figures are for the manufacturing industry, SCM for the manufacturing, wholesale,
and retail industries

Source: METI (2001: 65)

*Figure 6.1   International comparison of rate of introduction of IT-related
applications*

engaged in open procurements through the Internet (Figure 6.2). This high
usage of private online networks in Japan mirrors the unique way Japan's
major assemblers interact with their suppliers in trust-based long-term
relationships:

> 'E-commerce' covers a range of transactions, but taking the example of materials
> procurement, survey results indicated that where US companies using IT to order
> materials are up in the tens of thousands, the same figure for Japanese companies is
> only in the hundreds to thousands. Procuring materials through the Internet helps to
> cut costs and uncover new sources. However, as whether or not a company engages
> in open procurement depends on a variety of factors such as differences in business
> architecture, *it is impossible to state as a rule that open procurement is superior in
> terms of business management.* In any case, even in the IT era, the same tendencies
> are still apparent in terms of the different management strategies, namely that
> Japanese companies favor long-term business relationships where foreign
> companies emphasize proactive cost-cutting through more open transactions.
> (METI, 2001: 68, emphasis added)

Actually, the relative superiority of a closed procurement architecture over
its open counterpart depends on the maturity of a product (i.e., the more
'commoditized', the more natural and effective the open procurement) and the

product development strategy of a company (i.e., the greater the emphasis on the 'design-in' or 'black box system' in which an assembler collaborates in R&D with its suppliers from the design stage of product development, the more necessary the closed procurement). It also depends on how much a company is oriented to the pursuit of Smithian specialization efficiency or Veblenian interstitial efficiency (the distinction between these two concepts is discussed in Chapter 4). Japanese companies are *more* conscious of the gains from Veblenian interstitial efficiency than companies in other countries. The 'design-in' method is expected to be more intensively practiced than before as we move up the ladder of product sophistication.

As may be expected from the close-knit transactional relationships that exist in Japanese industry, therefore, the outsourcing of business as a result of IT introduction by Japanese industry is found to be the lowest (about 10 per cent);

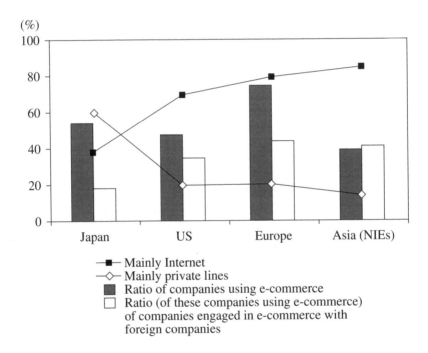

—■— Mainly Internet
—◇— Mainly private lines
▪ Ratio of companies using e-commerce
☐ Ratio (of these companies using e-commerce)
of companies engaged in e-commerce with
foreign companies

Note: Figures include all industries

Source: METI (2001: 67)

*Figure 6.2   International comparison of e-commerce use and main networks
used*

(%)

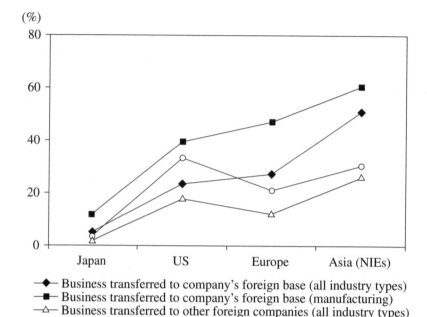

Source: METI (2001: 68)

*Figure 6.3   International comparison of foreign outsourcing of business as a
result of IT introduction*

by comparison, industries in the US, Europe, and the NIEs have much higher
ratios (Figure 6.3). No wonder, then, that outsourcing abroad ('offshoring') of
IT-related service jobs is not a hot issue in Japan as yet, though the hollowing
out of manufacturing is feared.

In fact, the Japanese companies in the assembly-driven, parts/components-
intensive industries (notably electronics and cars) have been paring down the
number of suppliers and making their stable long-term relations even more
closely 'connected', particularly when they practice 'design-in' procurement
and quality control. They are also concentrating on parts reduction and
miniaturization (resulting in savings on weight and size). For example, Sony
is striving to decrease the number of parts used in its products from 840000
down to 100000 by March 2006, thereby in turn reducing the current 4700
suppliers to about 1000. In the past two years, Matsushita has already
decreased the number of suppliers by as many as 2300 to about 4700 with an
eye to lowering procurement costs by dealing with more efficient remaining

suppliers.[3] Other producers are making the same streamlining efforts so that their procurements are made more cost-effective from the remaining suppliers, whose productivity and quality control can then be supported more strongly than before.

It should be noted, however, that all the major assemblers in Japan's electronics and automobile industries have been intensifying the crisscrossing networks of alliances in R&D, cross-licensing, product development, and marketing, particularly with foreign firms (as seen in Chapter 5) – and more recently with domestic firms, as well. (This strategy is designed to minimize the 'knowledge diversion' effect to be discussed in Chapter 7.)

6.6.1.   IT Investment at Macro-Level

METI's findings of relatively weak IT utilization by Japanese businesses is also in line with the general view that Japan lags behind the US in IT-related investment at the macro-level. However, one recent study reveals a much more sanguine assessment about Japan's deployment of IT throughout the 'lost decade' of the 1990s. Jorgenson and Motohashi (2004) argue that Japan was nearly identical to the US in terms of contribution of IT to economic growth when differences in statistical measurements for the national accounts are smoothed out. The differences are caused by (i) Japan's inclusion of only custom-made software, whereas the US counts both custom-made and pre-packaged software, and (ii) Japan's smaller rate of decline in the price deflators for IT equipment, which leads to an underestimation of the contribution of IT investment to its economic growth. Jorgenson and Motobashi conclude:

> We have corrected discrepancies between the price statistics for the two countries and used the harmonized prices to analyze the sources of economic growth. The contribution of IT capital to economic growth in the latter half of the 90s was similar – 0.78 percent per year for Japan versus 0.97 percent for the U.S. The growth in total factor productivity in IT-producing industries during the second half of the 90s was actually higher in Japan than in the U.S. – 0.61 percent versus 0.44 percent. The total contribution of IT was 1.39 percent per year in Japan and 1.41 percent in the U.S. Despite the enormous difference between the growth rates of the Japanese and U.S. economies after 1995, the contribution of IT was almost identical. (Jorgenson and Motobashi, 2004: 4)

This is encouraging news, indeed, since corporate Japan is *still* handicapped in IT application by all sorts of regulations and institutional barriers/practices, leaving ample room for a further unfolding of the IT revolution. Consequently, more IT-based productivity growth and IT-exploiting innovations are likely to be promoted in the near future.

6.7. HUME'S ENDOGENOUS RETROGRADATION SYNDROME?

Despite the current technological strength of Japanese manufacturing industry, there is concern that the young Japanese are increasingly 'shying away' (or 'departing') from science and engineering to less academically rigorous fields such as liberal arts and finance. Affluence has diminished the 'hungriness' of the young to better their lives by achieving degrees in the natural sciences and engineering. In catching-up countries engineering skills are in great demand, and science diplomas serve as tickets to high-income employment. In the advanced countries, notably in the US, on the other hand, affluence places a higher premium on leisure and the liberal arts/humanities (literature, music, visual arts, etc.) than hard work, both mental and physical, and technical skills. In this sense, science and engineering may be said to be *inferior goods*, in the sense that a rise in income leads to a decline in the public's interest in learning about the hard sciences.

Indeed, there has been a trend of steady decline in the interest of the Japanese public in science and technologies. This 'aversion' to hard sciences is particularly pronounced in the younger generation (below the age of 30). The 2004 annual survey conducted by Japan's Prime Minister's Office (2004) revealed that more than half (52.0 per cent) of the under-30 generation showed no interest in news or current developments related to science and technology. No doubt, Japan's rapidly aging demography also reinforces this trend. In 1985, for example, about 26 per cent of college applicants wanted to have degrees in the sciences and engineering, but this ratio has been steadily declining, now standing at around 18 per cent. Also, children's interest in science is quite high in elementary schools (more than 80 per cent find the sciences 'interesting'), but this ratio drops in junior high schools (down to 60 per cent) and even further in senior high schools (around 50 per cent) (Science and Technology Agency, 1997). Thus, the young generation is no longer as interested in science and engineering as they used to be.

This emerging Humean retrogradation in science and engineering is now increasingly mirrored in Japanese multinationals' overseas business activities, since a rapidly catching-up developing country like China produces school-trained engineers in abundance, thereby attracting FDI in the high-tech sector. Sharp Corporation, for instance, which now actively recruits Chinese engineers to staff its new R&D laboratories in the Pudong New Area, China, reportedly observes:

> The company's Japanese engineers are still better at designing the key components that distinguish electronic products. But Sharp's Chinese engineers, who are paid one-quarter as much, are rapidly closing the talent gap … Comparing Chinese and

Japanese on a cost-per engineer performance basis, Chinese are superior. They are hungrier. Most Japanese are no longer hungry.[4]

In addition, the Japanese government is concerned about the 'hollowing out of human resources', as Japanese researchers stay overseas for longer periods and take up jobs abroad. 'Having investigated the percentage of foreigners who have obtained Ph.Ds in the US and who plan to remain in the US after their study, although the percentage is still lower for Japan than for India, China and the UK, it has been increasing since 1994, particularly for the natural sciences (now about 70 per cent)' (Ministry of Education, Culture, Sports, Science and Technology, 2002).[5]

One weakness of Japanese-style corporate R&D is a strong team orientation to such an extent that individual researchers' contributions are largely ignored and usually not singled out for financial reward, though their companies may earn handsome profits out of individuals' inventions. This system has recently come to be challenged by those who made profitable discoveries or inventions as researchers for their companies. The first successful case of litigation was won by Shuji Nakamura, the inventor of the blue light-emitting diodo and a former employee of Nichia Corp. (now an engineering professor at the University of California, Santa Barbara, USA), when the Tokyo District Court awarded compensation of Y20 billion ($188.7 million) in January 2004. Since then, a number of similar lawsuits have come to be filed – and some won – by other former corporate researchers.

Asked about these developments in a survey by the *Nihon Keizai Shimbun*, Japan's leading business newspaper, 38.2 per cent of the company executives surveyed said that the court-ordered compensations for former employees would help motivate researchers and technicians in R&D activity at their firms. However 49.6 per cent said that they would send the wrong message – that individual achievement is more important than teamwork – making management more difficult. And 34.4 per cent observed such litigation could eventually erode earnings and impose a bigger burden on their companies.[6] On the whole, this indicates that teamwork is still considered a more effective way of raising efficiency and more of a desideratum than individual initiative and merit performance.

Although Japanese companies' emphasis on teamwork would surely make sense in manufacturing activities (as seen in Toyota's production system), R&D activity requires an optimal combination of teamwork and idiosyncratic individual performance. And for the first time, some Japanese companies are realizing this and realigning their corporate research operations:

In fiscal 2002, NEC reformed the way it decides on chief researchers. It now chooses them based on their *performance* instead of simply by *seniority* as in the past. 'We intend to motivate researchers by introducing merit-based promotion and increasing compensation for chief researchers'... This month NEC promoted a researcher still in her 30s to the post of chief researcher for the first time, underscoring its intention to rejuvenate the upper ranks.[7]

The fact that this type of development makes news in Japan, however, is indicative of how deeply Japanese-style management is still embedded in such world-class corporations as NEC and how they struggle to restructure R&D operations by balancing the imperatives of individualism-centered capitalism against the Japanese tradition of harmony and equality.

6.8.   E-JAPAN STRATEGY

Concerned about the recent trend of a diminishing scientific base in Japan, both the Industrial Structural Council and the Industrial Technology Council of the Japanese government urged a thorough structural overhaul of Japan's *socio-economic system* that hampers R&D performance in high-tech industries and a creation of the more attractive research environment at home:

> Amid an increasingly fierce competitive environment in the world, the superiority of Japanese manufacturing technologies, which has long been ensured, is now *declining*. And also *Japanese fundamental technologies such as information technology and biotechnology which lead to creation of new industries in the future, are comparatively inferior to major countries*. Furthermore, there is now rising anxiety about the 'hollowing out of R&D' with the increase of R&D investment abroad and outflow of R&D human resource because of *the lack of attractiveness of the Japanese R&D environment*. (MITI, 1996: 124, Emphasis added)

It was against such a background that, in January 2001, the government put into force the Basic Law on the Formation of an Advanced Information and Telecommunications Network Society (IT Basic Law), and established the IT Strategic Headquarters (headed by the Prime Minister) which is in charge of the 'e-Japan Strategy'. The specific goals and policies identified for this new initiative are (i) ultra high-speed network infrastructure development and competition policies, (ii) e-commerce rules and the development of a new environment, (iii) realization of electronic government, and (iv) nurturing of higher-quality human resources. The e-Japan Priority Policy Program was then initiated in March to achieve 'the swift and focused implementation of the necessary systemic reforms and measures over the five years from 2001' (JETRO, 2002: 49).

Actually, the passage of the IT Basic Law was preceded by the formation in September 2000 of a 20-member Information Technology Strategy Council, which was chaired by Sony's president and composed of other notable captains of industry such as Toyota Motor Corporation, Softbank, and IBM

(Japan). It announced an ambitious goal: to overtake and surpass the US in the Internet economy in five years. To this end, the Council urged the government to dismantle all institutional obstacles to the growth of a New Economy (i.e., burdensome regulations).

Be that as it may, a surprising but little-known fact is that the United States forced Japan to deregulate its mobile phone market in 1994 to support the advance of American telecom multinationals into the Japanese market. Motorola was once an early innovator in mobile phones. Until then, Japanese citizens were not even permitted to own personal cellular phones. Thanks to the US pressure to deregulate, Japan finally opened up this market and serendipitously leapfrogged to the forefront in the global race to a wireless Internet.

How effective e-Japan strategy will turn out to be remains to be seen. Nonetheless, some promising signs are emerging. According to a survey by OECD in October 2003, for instance, Japan was already ranked first in both the speed of broadband service and the prices of services.[8] Another study carried out shortly afterward by *Business Week* indicated, however, that Japan is now ahead of the US, yet overall, slightly behind Korea in the digital stakes:

> The U.S. lags far behind global leaders such as Korea and Japan, where broadband is far faster and cheaper, thanks to *more focused national policy, less cumbersome regulation*, and *more densely populated regions*...The world's broadband leader is South Korea, where 73% of households subscribe to high-speed Internet. Most Koreans pay $27 a month for a connection speed of up to 3 megabits. [In the U.S., a 3 megabit connection costs about $45.] But a few thousand choose to pay $52 a month for a 20-megabit advanced DSL connection, which is much faster and cheaper than anything available to Americans. Japanese can get some of the fastest and cheapest broadband service in the world – up to 26 megs for about $30 a month, using souped-up DSL. Europe's speeds and penetration are similar to those in the U.S.[9]

It is ironic that both Korea and Japan have achieved 'less cumbersome regulation' ahead of the US. And 'more focused national policy' has helped them outperform the US. In this regard at least the first goal of Japan's e-strategy, that is, to achieve ultra high-speed network infrastructure development, has already been attained.

6.9. ENTRY TO THE NEW ECONOMY: SUMMING UP

It is true that America's New Economy has lost its financial luster with the high-tech stock meltdown (which destroyed $5 trillion in paper wealth) of the early 2000s, the rampant failures of the dotcoms, and the shaky telecom industry. During the period 1996–2000, however, the US economy did enjoy considerable growth in labor productivity – a 2.5 per cent average rate, something unheard of since the 1960s. The New Economy was certainly not just a bubble that burst. The adoption of IT throughout the economy and the increased efficiency with which IT products are themselves produced are credited for this productivity growth. Japanese industry cannot expect to replicate a financial boom related to IT (a high-tech bubble it would like to avoid), but it is in a position to reap the benefits of real productivity improvement. And the vigorous growth of the US economy in 2004 again gave a much needed pull for Japanese exports and recovery.

Japan has long been known as a skilled emulator, as demonstrated by its successful industrial restructuring. Now, the advent of the Internet age is providing another unique opportunity to catch up. Sensing this opportunity, Japan has again begun to mobilize itself and to succeed in some important areas, as seen above in high-speed broadband services. Furthermore, Japan has a solid technological and production capability for IT-based products, including telecom equipment, fiber-optics, and digital goods. In fact, Japan's electronics industry is quickly shifting to the digitization and stepped-up upgrading of electronics appliances and cell phones with built-in chips, thereby pioneering a new digital consumer electronics sector. The Japanese manufacturers are concentrating on flat-panel TVs (both LCD and plasma-display), digital cameras, DVD recorders, camera phones, authentication systems ('smart tags'), wireless TV base stations, and music downloadable players. Japan is said to be turning into a 'ubiquitous networking society' (where anyone can access the Internet in any place at any time).

Reminiscent of the VCR format crush (Betamax vs. VHS) in the 1980s, a new technology battle over the DVD's high-definition successor has been raging recently between the blue-ray group (led by Sony and Matsushita) and the HD-DVD group (led by Toshiba and NEC) – with foreign multinationals backing the group of their choice. Another example is Japan's burgeoning cell phone (wireless telecom) market, which now boasts one of the world's largest numbers of subscribers to NTT DoCoMo's wireless Net access service (popularly known as 'i-mode', the world's most advanced mobile data service). This domestic advantage gave Japan a head start in the race to introduce third-generation (3G) cellular service. Japan thus clearly leads the way in this latest development in consumer electronics.

In addition, the recovery of Japan's consumer electronics driven by digitalization technology has led to such robust demand for semiconductors that the size of Japan's microchip market surpassed that of the US market for the first time in 2003. As the *Financial Times* nicely puts it, 'Second change: the digital revolution is reviving Japan's electronics industry'.[10] Furthermore, so as not to be copied and overtaken by Asia's formidable competitors so easily in newly pioneered products as has happened in the past, Japanese electronics firms are striving to innovate production process technologies and jealously guarding their plant operating know-how. In other words, they are finding new sources of competitiveness in technological fusions of picture making, digital compression, and small LSI chips (which, for example, are giving Japanese electronics firms a near monopoly position in the world market in digital still cameras).

Indeed, the age of information characterized by rising demand for abstract/ concept goods is providing Japan with more opportunities to develop and export fashion-focused Japanese-style goods than ever before – from toys, video games to *anime* (cartoons) and camera phones, all designed to meet the overseas craze for the 'Japanese cool' pop culture:

> In the last few years, Japan has become a rising force in a wide swath of fashion-focused industries, from kids' toys to entertainment, cell phones, and car racing ... Much of Japan's cultural output travels to other parts of Asia, but, increasingly, U.S. consumers are embracing Japanese style, too. The distinctive look of *anime* with its wide-eyed characters, is influencing toys, cartoons, comics, video games, even movies. And while U.S. kids have been enthralled with Japanese exports before – from Godzilla to Nintendo – the breadth of products has never been greater and their acceptance goes far beyond the Cartoon Network crowd.[11]

It is thus clear that in the McLuhan stage of IT-led growth, though certainly not without some structural problems such as the diminishing scientific infrastructure at home, Japanese industry has been given another God-sent opportunity to revitalize itself both technologically and organizationally after more than a decade's self-inflicted stagnation. In short, another round of catch-up effort is in the making as Japan strives to consolidate the McLuhan stage of economic growth and enter the New Economy.

NOTES

1. *The Economist*, April 1, 2000: 64.
2. Victoria Shannon, 'The father of "www" finally gets his due', *International Herald Tribune*, June 15, 2004: 23.
3. These numbers are cited in 'Electronics firms cut costs by upgrading suppliers', *Nikkei Weekly*, January 26, 2004.
4. Ken Belson, 'Japan's pride and joy gets a "Made in China" label', *New York Times*, February 17, 2004.
5. In this respect, it should be noted in passing that the US is enviably in a much better streamlined position, though it too has a similar problem with the declining enrollment by US-born citizens in the sciences and the engineering programs of higher institutions of learning. American universities are the powerful magnets for a large number of aspiring foreign students, who crave for the opportunities to learn and work in American society. The Silicon Valley – for that matter, its entire scientific community – also can count on foreign talents/immigrants. This capacity reflects the US's unique socio-economic, cultural flexibility and provides a huge advantage for America's high-tech industry. (Conversely, the

home countries of immigrants certainly suffer a 'brain drain' in the short run – but not necessarily in the long run, since a *reverse* brain drain is always a definite possibility eventually benefiting their home countries, as witnessed in rapidly caught-up economies such as Taiwan and Korea.)

6.   'Execs united on bullishness, divided on patent payouts', *Nikkei Weekly*, March 1, 2004.
7.   'NEC shakes up research to better compete globally', *Nikkei Weekly*, January 26, 2004.
8.   As reported in *Nihon Keizai Shimbun*, an evening edition, April 21, 2004.
9.   'High-Speed Internet: Broadband: What's the Holdup?', *BusinessWeek*, March 1, 2004: 38–9.
10. 'Comment & Analysis', *Financial Times*, August 6, 2004: 11.
11. 'Is Japanese Style Taking Over the World?', *BusinessWeek*, July 25, 2004: 56.

7. Analytics and stylized features of structural transformation: additional theoretical expositions

7.1. TIME COMPRESSION AND REGIONAL GROWTH CLUSTERING

We have so far mainly described how Japan went through each different stage of catch-up growth as it climbed up the ladder of industrial upgrading, one rung at a time. This stage-ratcheted progress is the very sequence of modern industry evolving under hegemon-led global capitalism, as emphasized in Chapter 1. It is nothing but the sequential path of industrial development trekked previously by *all* the advanced Western countries, albeit over a much longer span of time – more than two centuries following the Industrial Revolution. It is also the same path that Japan as a latecomer capitalist economy has successfully followed ever since the start of its modernization ('Westernization') orchestrated by the Meiji government in 1868, though temporarily disrupted by WWII.

It was in the post-WWII period, however, that Japan's task of a sequential catch-up, all the way from labor-intensive to knowledge-driven growth, has been accomplished, *all in one sweep*, at an astonishing pace. Japan telescoped the evolutionary path of capitalist development in a highly *time-compressed* fashion, taking only four decades to fully join the ranks of the advanced countries during its postwar catch-up – but about 100 years following the Meiji Restoration of 1868. (Now, the time-compression in catch-up growth is occurring in an even more condensed manner throughout East Asia.)

Japan was able to achieve a swift industrial transformation, because it had an excellent industrial flight map (a guiding perspective for climbing to the higher stages of growth), as it were – first, given by the hegemonic British industry and later, by the hegemonic American industry – that showed the image of Japan's own future. Postwar Japan revitalized industrial foundations already built in the prewar era as a launch pad for postwar modernization and build-up. Besides, Japan was given not only a flight map but also a variety of other flight instruments (i.e., technology, access to markets, and finance) to attain its century-old national goal to catch up with the West. (The same flight map and an even *better* and much *larger* set of flight instruments are now available to other Asian countries – for that matter, to any other developing countries that want to emulate and catch up.)

Japan's successful catch-up meant the incessant erosion (chipping away) of America's nearly self-sufficient, fully-established industrial structure at the end of the war. Europe's reconstruction, too, certainly contributed to this process of industrial diffusion as it absorbed American technology and capital (initially under the Marshall Plan), soon reviving its traditionally strong industries such as basic chemicals and pharmaceuticals. In this sense, both Japan and Europe enjoyed 'free rides' as the first beneficiaries of the forces of the Pax Americana-led growth clustering:

> The single best-known example of an upward spurt occurred during the so-called 'Golden Age' of the 1950s and 1960s in Japan and Europe (both East and West). In the two decades from the end of post-war reconstruction to 1973, growth rates nearly doubled in Europe [from 2.5% per year on average (1922–37) to 4.7% (1953–73) in Western Europe; from 2.7% to 4.8% in Eastern Europe] and more than trebled in Japan [from 2.8% to 9.1%], relative to their longer-term trends. (Boltho and Holtham, 1992: 4)

So far as Japan's catch-up is concerned, its rapid growth rates were in large measure the products of industrial upgrading from low value-added to higher value-added industries. As seen in the previous chapters, in the course of industrial upgrading Japan has actively shed comparatively disadvantaged industries (or goods) through the medium of FDI and other industrial transplantation activities overseas, starting with the labor-intensive light industries and then moving up the ladder of structural transformation.

This type of 'comparative advantage (or industry/market) recycling' (as discussed in Chapter 1) allowed Japan to develop and concentrate on higher value-added industries (or industrial segments) and simultaneously to capture gains from such 'discarded' industries in the form of profits from its overseas investments, profits that can be reinvested in new areas of advantage at home. In the meantime, those industries transplanted overseas, especially in the developing Asian countries, quickly grew as their new exporting industries, targeted mostly at the US markets – and to a lesser extent, to the European markets. This has resulted in a *triangular* trade pattern, in which Japan's newly emerged multinationals basically supply key intermediate goods and managerial expertise, while their Asian ventures, usually in joint operations with local interests, target Western markets. At the company level, this pattern of investment and trade means that these overseas investments 'were to be paid for by sharing revenues from export earnings which generated a pool of hard currency' (Dutta, 2000: 71). The upshot of such recycling of comparative advantages is the regionalized endogenous growth of East Asia (Ozawa, 2003a), as illustrated in Figure 7.1.

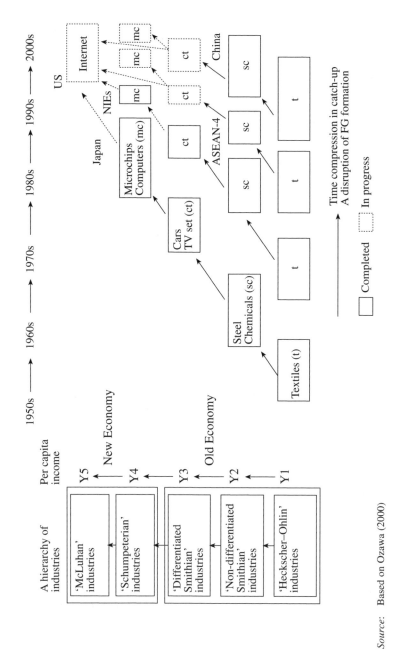

Source: Based on Ozawa (2000)

Figure 7.1 Industrial upgrading and growth clustering, flying-geese style, in East Asia (comparative-advantage-recycling cluster)

Such a dynamic, time-compressed process of industrial upgrading and recycling has been the major source of productivity improvement, hence accelerated high growth in Japan. This process continued to work, so long as Japan had not reached the top rung of the development ladder. As Japan successfully climbed the industrial hierarchy, however, it became increasingly more difficult to gain new advantages because of a shrinking technology gap vis-à-vis the West, while newly acquired advantages repeatedly proved ephemeral, since they were quickly snatched away by the even faster developing East Asian follower geese. Time compression is a phenomenon favorable to catching-up countries – but mostly deleterious to the advanced countries.   This result of growth convergence was clearly stressed when Akamatsu made a distinction between the two different periods of catch-up growth in terms of 'differentiation' and 'uniformization' in economic structures (as discussed in Chapter 1 and also related to the 'triumvirate pro-trade structural transformation' and the 'price-knowledge/industry-flow' theory to be presented below). Time compression is most likely to cause disruption of FG formation as it seems already to be doing in the Internet-based industries where South Korea races ahead of Japan – and even ahead of the United States – especially in broadband services (as seen in Chapter 6).

7.2.   FG CATCH-UP STRATEGY: FDI AS A CATALYST FOR INDUSTRIAL UPGRADING AND GROWTH

The stages-specific relationships between industrial upgrading and shedding (via FDI and other modalities of international business) are schematically illustrated in Fig. 7.2, which summarizes what has been described in the preceding chapters. The evolutionary sequence of industrial upgrading – (I) labor-driven ➔ (II) scale-driven ➔ (III) assembly-driven ➔ (IV) R&D-driven ➔ (V) IT-driven – has been accompanied by its corresponding sequence of outward FDI and other business operations: (I') the elementary stage of offshore production (or low-wage-seeking investment centered on labor-intensive light industries, such as toys and apparel), (II') resource-seeking and house-cleaning type of investment by heavy and chemical industries, (III') assembly-transplanting type of investment (*inclusive* of the low-cost-labor-seeking type in parts, components, accessories, and low-end lines of products) by manufacturers of electronics and automobiles, and (IV') alliance-seeking (strategically networking) type of business operations in production, marketing, and R&D (often and increasingly via M&As).

It should be noted that the motives for outward business operations are

(a) recycling of comparative advantages and earning investment incomes

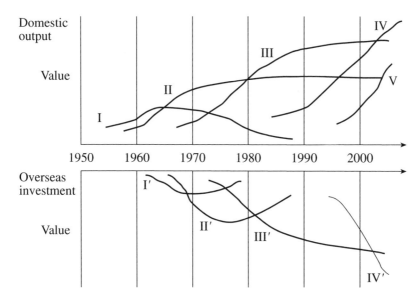

Source: Based on Ozawa (1993, 2001a)

Figure 7.2   Japan's stages of industrial upgrading and outward FDI

from overseas operations by making the best use of corporate assets no
longer suitable for the changed home business conditions (e.g., higher
wages and home currency appreciation),
(b) securing imports of natural resources abroad,
(c) avoiding a high concentration of pollution-prone economic activities at
home,
(d) averting trade conflicts and simultaneously retaining (and further
expanding) market share via direct local production and distribution,
(e) developing competitive advantages in cooperation with overseas 'rivals'
through strategic alliances in R&D and product development and
marketing, and
(f) escaping from the regulated high-cost home business environment in
search of better (freer) pro-business locations (which in turn compels
institutional reforms at home).

The motives (b) and (c) are becoming relatively less important because
Japan's industrial structure has moved away from heavy natural resource
dependence (per unit of output) and grown more and more knowledge-based.
On the other hand, motives (a), (d), (e), and (f) are becoming increasingly
critical in a mutually reinforcing manner, now that the Japanese economy has

reached the higher rungs of the development ladder. This is because new knowledge-based advantages now have to be created out of strategic alliances in innovations, as the product life cycle gets shortened and innovations are turned more quickly than ever before into 'commodities' that can be cost-effectively produced offshore – away from the high-cost advanced countries like Japan. In other words, recycling of comparative advantages is accelerated and even more time-compressed.

In essence, the core of Japan's FG catch-up – and surge ahead – development strategy has been emulation and learning: that is to say, *scaling of the ladder of industrial upgrading, rung by rung, by learning from higher-echelon countries as much – and fast – as possible (i.e., capitalizing on its latecomer status) – and passing on to lower-echelon countries those industries (activities) that have become disadvantageous at home.* Although Akamatsu himself did not specifically prescribe such a development strategy as a scheme, Japan's catch-up policy was formulated and pursued in the spirit of his original insight (Korhonen, 1994). More specifically, the FG strategy of building up national industries can be viewed as consisting of three critical types of industrial policy in terms of Akamatsu's original triumvirate FG patterns; the import → domestic production → export (M–P–M) sequence, the 'from crude/simple to complex/refined articles' sequence (i.e., a process of industrial upgrading), and the 'alignment of nations along the different stages of development' sequence':

1. a policy for continuous industrial upgrading from low value-added (low productivity) to higher value-added (higher productivity) industries;
2. a policy for import substitution-cum-export promotion (IS–EP), namely Akamatsu's M–P–M. In this trade-triggered development process of a given specific good or industry, vital technology was early on acquired mostly in an 'unpackaged' form (i.e., under licenses). Later on, however, the IS–EP process skipped the initial imports of finished and intermediate goods and quickly *shifted* to the sequence of imports of 'seed' technology → commercialization at home (i.e., domestic production) → exports. This is best represented by many of Japanese innovations in consumer electronics – such as transistor radios, pocket-sized calculators, quartz watches, and so on. In this later version, the government role declined or did not even matter, since private initiatives/entrepreneurship and corporate R&D came to play a decisive role in spotting the promising seed technologies or ideas and innovating new products and processes on their own;
3. A policy to transplant comparatively disadvantaged industries (such as toys, textiles, and sundries) or labor-intensive industrial segments of the higher echelon industries (e.g., standardized lines of products and parts in

electronics and automobiles) to other countries (mostly the nearby developing Asian countries) so as to retain higher value-added industries at home, a process of comparative advantage recycling and 'dynamic *adaptive* efficiency' (as opposed to 'static *allocative* efficiency') enhancement at home.[1]

Obviously, the outcomes of these policies have been closely and sequentially interrelated. Industrial upgrading is the *ultimate* objective of the FG catch-up strategy. Industrial upgrading can be accomplished by the IS–EP sequence and through the mechanism of comparative advantage recycling to achieve dynamic adaptive efficiency. Once a new comparative advantage (commensurate with Japan's factor endowments and technological conditions prevailing at a given point in time) was created out of formerly disadvantaged industries through the IS–EP policy, Japan continued to foster other future growth industries at home with an eye to reaching the higher rungs on the ladder of industrial upgrading. Once export industries (or industrial segments) began to lose competitiveness (i.e., became comparatively disadvantaged), they were then transplanted via overseas investment to other countries, especially those developing Asian countries where factor endowments and technological levels were still suitable for such industries.

What is more, those goods transferred and produced overseas are now being imported back home – hence, the IS–EP policy eventually turned to the full-circle sequence of 'import ➔ domestic output ➔ export ➔ overseas production via FDI ➔ import', thus going beyond Akamatsu's original M–P–E. In the meantime, the resources released from the contracting (now disadvantaged) sector were shifted to newly emerged competitive sectors at home. At the same time, overseas investments augmented and sparked new comparative advantages in the developing host countries where Japanese firms transplanted production via FDI. This represents an interactive and synergistic process of growth in both Japan and the host countries.

7.3.   SAGACITY OF THE JAPANESE GOVERNMENT

The above development process had its internal logic of orderly evolution, in the sense that new self-organizing and self-propelling market forces were generated in each phase, compelling Japan to move on to the higher and higher levels of industrial activity by discarding disadvantaged industries. In other words, a given economic situation in each time period 'bears the seeds of its condition in the following period' (Nelson and Winter, 1982: 19). As amply evidenced in the preceding chapters, however, Japan's catch-up growth has not been driven by market forces alone.

The catch-up regime Japan set up after WWII was undeniably a nationalistic *dirigiste* one, and the development policy used by the government was basically a dynamic 'infant industry' protection policy. Yet, Japan's industrial development policy was designed to foster and assist the private sector in such a way as to accelerate the pace of self-organizing market forces for the future growth of its economy. Gregory (1986) called it 'market-facilitating/creating', and Aoki et al. (1997) regarded it as 'market-enhancing'. Nevertheless, Japan's industrial development policy, early on, involved extensive restrictions on imports, technology transfers, and inward FDI – all for the purpose of building up national (*not* foreign-owned) domestic industries. Government involvement was quite significant, particularly when Japan reconstructed and modernized capital-intensive heavy and chemical industries and also when it built knowledge-based industries (as detailed in Chapters 3 and 4). Japan's postwar industrial policies have been explored elsewhere (*inter alia*, by Patrick and Rosovsky, 1976; Komiya et al., 1988) – hence, there is no need to dwell on them here.

It should be stressed, however, that there is nothing extraordinarily sagacious and perspicacious about the Japanese government's involvement in facilitating the stage-by-stage orderly sequence of Japan's industrial catch-up. Only in retrospect – and as a revealed historical pattern – does such an evolutionary sequence appear to give full credence to the foresight of the Japanese government as an industrial orchestral leader. What really made Japan's catch-up growth successful, however, were the forces of US-led growth clustering – that is, the forces of global capitalism disseminated by the Pax Americana. Of relevance here is Buckley's (1994) observation, made rather exasperatedly in his review of *World Investment Report 1994* (published by UNCTAD):

> ... particular attention is paid to the upgrading or restructuring of the Japanese economy. This reviewer cannot be alone in expressing regret that developments in the Japanese economy are always presented as planned (By whom? Is MITI's remit now global? Does it have the capacity of complete foresight in an increasingly global economy?), whereas the rest of the benighted human race is at the mercy of unmitigated uncontrolled (market) forces! (Buckley, 1994: 98–9)

True, if there were any elements of foresighted planning, it was, indeed, already spelled out in the thrust of global capitalism. MITI's only contribution was a mere tweaking of the way global capitalism works so as to fit Japan's unique postwar economic conditions – that is to say, it used an 'adaptive' industrial policy. In fact, the Japanese government quickly lost its capacity of foresight, thereby losing control of its economy, once the world economy became more integrated 'at the mercy of unmitigated uncontrolled (market) forces' (as will be evidenced in Chapter 9).

In this connection, there is a similar view that Japan's miraculous recovery and expansion was even engineered by the United States, the current leader of global capitalism, since the latter actually wanted to make Japan both a bulwark against communism and a supplier of low-cost goods and services to accommodate the hegemon's needs. For example, Arrighi (1994) argues,

> [The] explosive growth of Japanese exports to the wealthy US market as well as its trade surplus, was a critical ingredient in the simultaneous take-off of Japan's great leap forward in world-scale processes of capital accumulation. Nevertheless, *it was not due in any measure to an aggressive Japanese neo-mercantilist stance. Rather, it was due to the growing need of the US government to cheaper supplies essential to its power pursuits, both at home and abroad.* Were it not for the massive procurement of means of war and livelihood from Japanese sources at much lower costs than they could be obtained in the United States or anywhere else, the simultaneous escalation of US welfare expenditures at home and of warfare expenditures abroad of the 1960s would have been far more crippling financially than it already was. *Japan's trade surpluses were not the cause of the financial troubles of the US government. The increasing fiscal extravagance of the US warfare-welfare state was. The Japanese capitalist class promptly seized the chance to profit from US needs to economize in the procurement of means of war and livelihood.* But by so doing, it was servicing the power pursuits of the US government as effectively as any other capitalist class of the free world. (p. 341, emphasis added)

By the 'US warfare-welfare state', Arrighi means the stepped-up Vietnam war effort and the Great Society program simultaneously pursued by the Johnson administration in the mid-1960s. Nonetheless, the aggressive Japanese neomercantilist stance did matter, especially in fostering the domestic manufacturers of computers and semiconductors, as detailed in Chapter 5. Such Japanese policy was nevertheless tolerated because of the geopolitical need of the United States in those days. (Doesn't the same observation now apply to the present US situation encumbered by the rising trade deficits with China and the war against terrorism? *Déjà vu*?)

Besides, under the umbrella of America's military protection – and under Japan's new postwar constitution that specifically prohibits rearmament, Japan was relieved from the fiscal burden of defense spending and able to concentrate on building up its economy.

7.4.   STRUCTURAL TRANSFORMATION, TRADE, AND FDI: A STYLIZED FRAMEWORK

The stages-delineated concurrent trends of industrial upgrading and FDI we have observed are actually nothing but a reflection of the unfolding of global capitalism when a latecomer country adopts a capitalist process of economic development. Certainly, Japan has molded it to suit its own purpose (as seen earlier in Japan's FG catch-up strategy). We need, therefore, to understand the basic underlying patterns (undercurrents) of hegemon-led global capitalism, which have only been mirrored in the Japanese experiences, though in a somewhat 'contorted' way due to their molding interventions.

We can generalize the fundamental features of the open-economy capitalist process of economic development as follows. First of all, *a particular stage of economic development is associated with a particular pattern of export competitiveness*, as is empirically detected in many studies (*inter alia*, Chenery, 1960, 1979; Chenery and Taylor, 1968; and Balassa, 1965, 1989). That is to say, in terms of our FG industrial upgrading model, the labor-driven stage is related to labor-based trade advantages (in labor-intensive goods and services), the scale-driven stage to scale-based advantages (in large-scale, capital-intensive industries), the assembly-driven stage to assembly-based advantages (in components/parts-intensive goods), and the knowledge-driven stage to R&D-based advantages (in high-tech manufactures and services). Thus, structural transformation and its concomitant economic growth (growth in per capita income) are simultaneously accompanied by the corresponding changes in the patterns of dynamic comparative advantages in trade. And this is a well-received theory.

But, how about FDI (inclusive of other forms of cross-border business activities), now that international production (the global value of local outputs by multinational corporations in their host countries) has grown more rapidly and is far larger than international trade (the global value of exports from their home countries) itself? Since international production and trade interact closely with each other in intricate ways (sometimes, mutually augmenting and at other times, substituting – but growing together over time), we should expect that *the patterns (nature and directions) of FDI, both inward and outward, also change* pari passu *with the structural transformation of the economy, since international business operations (i.e., trade and overseas direct business activities) are the driving mechanism for economic growth – and vice versa* (Ozawa, 1991, 1992).

For example, the beginning of the labor-driven stage attracts labor-seeking inward FDI. The transition from the labor-driven to the higher rungs of the development ladder (say, to heavy and chemical industrialization) begins to generate outward FDI toward lower-wage countries in labor-intensive manufacturing (and in resource extraction abroad, particularly if the home economy happens to be natural-resource-scarce) and attracts inward FDI in higher value-added industries. Similarly, a further transition toward the knowledge-driven phase beyond the assembly-driven phase brings about outward FDI in assembly-intensive goods and inward FDI in knowledge-based industries. These stages-punctuated flows of FDI in both directions are likely to occur naturally, as long as the nation pursues an unjumbled/orderly process of catch-up (i.e., 'progress of opulence' *à la* Adam Smith).

The above concomitant stages of structural transformation, trade, and FDI are illustrated in Figure 7.3. The sequential process of structural transformation can be distinguished in terms of the changing proportions of three major types of capital stock employed in a nation's overall industrial activity: natural capital (natural resources and raw labor), physical capital, and human capital. In other words, the nation grows by upgrading its structure as its factor endowments and technological level alter with the accumulation of physical and human capital (relative to natural capital): *the higher the per capita gross domestic product (GDP), the larger the per capita stock of physical and human capital relative to that of resources and the larger the per capita stock of human capital relative to that of physical capital.*

The economy continuously evolves to develop new comparative advantages by shifting from technologically less sophisticated, low-productivity products to more sophisticated, higher-productivity industrial activities (analogous to Adam Smith's sequence of 'necessities' → 'conveniences' → 'elegancies'). For example, this changing pattern of dynamic comparative advantages may be measured sequentially in terms of an index of the revealed comparative advantage in unskilled labor-intensive goods, an index of the revealed comparative advantage in physical-capital-intensive goods, and an index of the revealed comparative advantage in knowledge-intensive goods (Figure 7.3). At the same time, different stages-based patterns of FDI, both inward and outward, appear over a certain span of time, a span determined by how rapidly a given economy industrializes, as outlined above. Indeed, the stages-based evolutionary progression of FDI has been most clearly demonstrated by Japan's experience of a rapid structural transformation and its concomitant FDI in the post-WWII period.

A caveat is in order, however. Any stages model is *specific to* time and place. The global economy is in a state of constant flux, and *no* country is alike in historical experiences. Depending on a catching-up country's specific economic and geographical conditions, for example, it may skip any given stage of industrial development (as best illustrated by Hong Kong and Singapore, which did not develop heavy and chemical industries – nor, for that matter, an automobile industry – because of their geographical constraints as small city-state economies). A catching-up country's development policy may also jumble the sequence of stages. And the phenomenon of 'time compression' likewise telescopes the stages. Although there may, therefore, be a number of outlier cases, nevertheless, the underlying forces of hegemon-led growth clustering work through the evolutionary sequence of concomitant structural transformations in the economy, international trade, and international direct business operations. (In this regard, South Korea, Taiwan,

Stages: Labor-driven → scale-driven → assembly-driven → R&D-driven → IT-driven

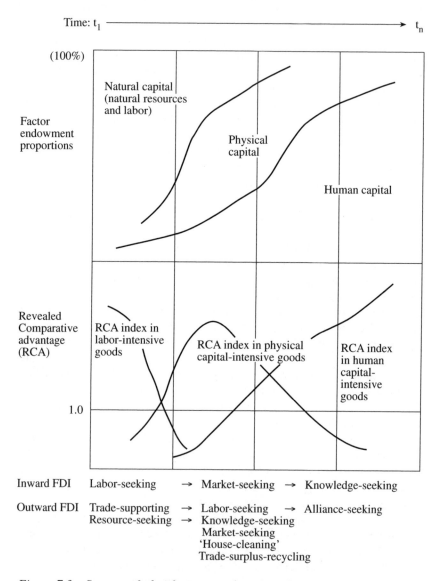

Figure 7.3   Stages of development, changing factor proportions, and dynamic comparative advantage

China, and India are also the economies that are most likely to exhibit similar patterns but with time lags.)

7.5.   KOJIMA'S PRO-TRADE (AS OPPOSED TO ANTI-TRADE) FDI – AND TRIUMVIRATE PRO-TRADE STRUCTURAL TRANSFORMATION

Focusing on the trade implications of FDI, Kiyoshi Kojima (1973, 1975) made an important distinction between pro-trade and anti-trade types of FDI from a host country's perspective and in terms of the Ricardian doctrine of comparative advantage. The first effect may be called the 'comparative advantage augmentation' principle, since the pro-trade type of FDI is a powerful augmenter of comparative-advantage-based trade. And trade is growth-inducing. Despite its significance, both theoretically and empirically, this principle of Kojima's seems so far to have been totally neglected by the conventional theories of trade and cross-border knowledge transfer.

The 'maximum' growth-inducing effect of trade is based on three interlinked key propositions (Kojima and Ozawa, 1985: 135–9):

Proposition I: Countries gain from trade and maximize their economic welfare when they export comparatively advantaged goods and import comparatively disadvantaged goods.

Proposition II: Countries gain even more from expanded trade when superior entrepreneurial assets are transferred through FDI (or any other forms of direct overseas businesses) from the home countries' comparatively disadvantaged industries or segments in such a way to improve the efficiency of comparatively advantaged (existing as well as potential) industries or segments in the host countries.

Proposition III: The process of transferring comparative-advantage-augmenting assets is facilitated when the home countries are capable of innovating new goods or industries in which they can continuously renew comparative advantages and retain full employment at home, particularly employment of those resources released from comparatively disadvantaged (hence contracting) industries.

This set of three propositions represents a country's *triple pro-trade* orientation, which can magnify both the 'comparative advantage recycling' effect of FDI and the growth-enhancing effect of trade. The first proposition is Ricardo's *pro-trade specialization* in a higher-productivity sector, specialization that is comparative (not absolute) advantage-induced; the second is *pro-trade asset transfers à la* Kojima (1990); and the third is *pro-trade structural upgrading* (analogous to Schumpeter's 'creative destruction' on the macro level and in a trade-accommodating way). All this constitutes what may be called a principle of 'triumvirate pro-trade structural transformation'.

The income growth effect envisaged in the static Ricardian theory of trade (that allows no cross-border transfer of factors and no structural change) is summarized in Figure 7.4(a). It also assumes complete free trade and no transaction costs. According to this static Ricardian theory, as gains from trade are realized through intersecteral specialization and reallocation of resources into comparatively advantaged industries at home (that is, attainment of allocative efficiency), national income rises – with no outward shift of the country's production possibility frontier, because there is neither factor growth nor technological progress. The whole purpose of the Ricardian model is to show the basis for, the direction of, and gains from, trade under static conditions – and nothing more.

By contrast, the model of triumvirate pro-trade structural transformation assumes that there are restrictions on trade and investment, particularly on the part of the developing countries. Hence, economic development accelerates once the developing countries adopt an outward-looking, export-oriented policy by way of FDI-sparked comparative advantage augmentation. So long as new competitive advantages are created on the part of the advanced countries (via pro-trade structural upgrading), trade continues to rise on the basis of dynamic comparative advantage and remains mutually beneficial. The power of trade is magnified and super-growth ensues, as illustrated in Figure 7.4(b), because (i) a strong outward orientation reduces market distortions and encourages competition at the micro level (reducing X-inefficiency), (ii) the basis for trade is expanded by comparative advantage augmenting FDI (both inward and outward), hence a greater expansion of trade, and (iii) self-propelling (self-organizing) market forces are set in motion to upgrade the country's (both home and host) industrial structure in a stages-delineated fashion, so long as a pro-business, market-friendly environment (including incentives and supportive infrastructure) is created and maintained by the government.

The mandate of pro-trade structural upgrading on the part of the advanced countries in particular is now taking on greater importance, since the adverse effect of trade and FDI on domestic employment in the advanced countries has recently risen as jobs (industrial activities) are increasingly outsourced offshore in an effort to reduce production costs, thereby coping with global competition. The resultant job losses, therefore, need to be minimized; here there is definitely room for the government to play the role of a facilitator of

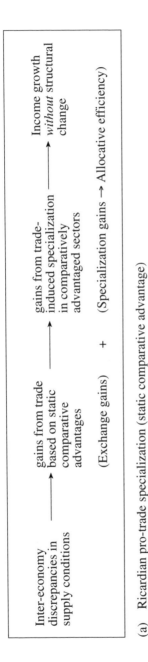

(a) Ricardian pro-trade specialization (static comparative advantage)

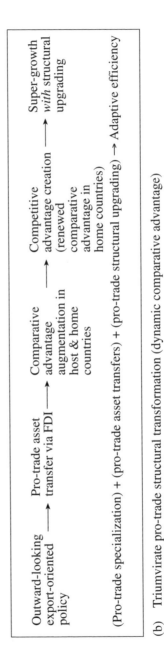

(b) Triumvirate pro-trade structural transformation (dynamic comparative advantage)

Figure 7.4 Triumvirate pro-trade structural transformation

MNC-triggered structural change by assisting investment in human resource development, promoting R&D in the private sector, and deregulating the home market so as to encourage new higher-paying jobs at home (Ozawa 1997a, 1997b). This issue is related to the 'hollowing out' of Japan's manufacturing due to 'excessive' outward FDI and the recent 'jobless recovery' of the US economy due in part to offshore outsourcing. In short, the principle of triumvirate pro-trade structural transformation is a critical frame of reference in this age of globalization.

7.5.1. FDI-Based Trade Augmentation and Ricardo's Error

In connection with the second triumvirate proposition above (i.e., Kojima's principle of trade augmentation via FDI), it is worth pointing out – and explaining – the fact that David Ricardo, the originator of the notion of comparative advantage, strangely enough, failed to understand the logic of pro-trade FDI (Ozawa, 1996a). Pro-trade FDI is actually nothing but an extended application of the comparative advantage doctrine to investment flows (in addition to trade flows). As is well known to trade theorists, David Ricardo explicitly introduced a technology (knowledge) gap into his trade theory, as reflected in the assumption of different levels of labor productivity (different unit labor requirements) between England and Portugal and the assumption of no cross-border knowledge transfer. Ricardo (1817/1888) reasoned that knowledge transfers (international factor movements) would destroy the basis for trade and cause a hollowing out in an absolutely disadvantaged country (England in his illustration):

> It would undoubtedly be advantageous to the capitalists of England, and to the consumers in both countries, that under [the circumstances of higher labor productivity in Portugal] the wine and the cloth should both be made in Portugal, and therefore that the capital and labour of England employed in making cloth should be removed to Portugal for that purpose. (p. 77, emphasis added)

According to Ricardo, then, there will be no basis for trade left once cross-border knowledge transfers are admitted: Portugal flourishes, whereas England is hollowed out and languishes. Surprisingly, therefore, it *did not dawn on Ricardo that if, instead of moving to Portugal 'the capital and labour of England employed in making cloth', the Portuguese secrets (superior knowledge) of higher productivity in cloth are transferred to England, say, through FDI or licensing, not only is England spared the hollowing out but both nations can also prosper even more, since England's comparative advantage in cloth is enhanced by such technology transfer* (Ozawa, 1996a). It is, indeed, puzzling that Ricardo failed to recognize this possibility. He did not apply to FDI flows the same logic of comparative advantage he used for trade flows.

The reason for his failure was probably because Ricardo deprived himself of a chance to study an appropriate (comparative-advantage-based) pattern of knowledge transfers by dismissing outright the issue of cross-border factor movements, since he thought that overseas investment entailed high psychological costs:

> Experience, however, shows that the fancied or real insecurity of capital, when not under the immediate control of its owner, together with the natural disinclination which every man has to quit the country of his birth and connections and entrust himself, with all his habits fixed, in *a strange government and new laws*, check the emigration of capital. (Ricardo, 1817/1888: 77, emphasis added)

In this respect, Ricardo was perhaps the very first economist who recognized what is now popularly known as the transaction costs of foreign direct investment, namely the 'costs of doing business overseas' which later came to be 'rediscovered' by Stephen Hymer (1960/1976). Be that as it may, Ricardo clearly failed to see the possibility that Portuguese entrepreneurs with superior technology and prospects for a higher profit rate would transplant their cloth manufacturing onto England, so long as the Portuguese technological advantages were sufficiently large to overcome the costs of doing business as aliens in England.

In short, so far as cross-border knowledge transfer is concerned, Ricardo's analysis was thus glaringly incomplete. Contrary to Ricardo's belief, we now know that the basis for trade will not necessarily be destroyed through knowledge transfers; on the contrary, it will be enhanced when superior knowledge is transplanted from a comparatively disadvantaged (hence contracting) industry in a lead-goose economy to a comparatively advantaged (hence expanding) industry in a follower-goose economy. In this process, both countries will gain from an expanded basis for trade, an additional gain not envisaged in the conventional trade theory. This pro-trade pattern is a natural outcome of both macro- and microeconomic market forces reinforced by government development policies as these forces are generated *endogenously* in the evolutionary course of economic development. We can claim that this process is another important 'cause of the wealth of nations' (to paraphrase Adam Smith's main tome).

7.6. THE PRINCIPLE OF 'INCREASING FACTOR INCONGRUITY'

The dynamic process of structural change involving FDI can be conceptualized as the principle of 'increasing factor incongruity' (Ozawa, 1992). The basic idea is that a growing incompatibility inevitably occurs over time between the factor and technology intensities of a good (or industry), on one hand, and the factor endowments and technological levels, on the other hand, of an economy in which a good is initially produced. This principle is useful to understand the process of structural transformation under global capitalism – and also to distinguish between the FG theory of industrial upgrading and the product cycle theory of trade.

There are two genres of the principle. The first genre occurs for an individual good, whose factor and technology intensity changes rapidly along the path of its product life cycle as it is eventually transformed from a newfangled good to a standardized one, even though the overall factor-and-technological endowments of the economy involved remain the same or are taken as a given. This inevitable factor incongruity leads to overseas production in the host countries whose factor-and-technological endowments are suitable for the standardized good. The second genre involves a situation in which an economy's overall factor endowments quickly become labor-scarcer and more capital-abundant as they do in any fast-growing economy, even though the factor intensity of the good involved remain the same. For instance, as wages rise at home in the wake of rapid growth, a good of a given input intensity, say, a relatively labor-intensive good, becomes more costly to produce – and hence is transferred to a relatively labor-abundant host country. In the meanwhile, the home country now has to produce much more capital-intensive, higher value-added goods that are commensurate with higher wages at home (Ozawa, 1995a, 1995b).

The first genre represents the product-cycle theory of trade and investment (Vernon, 1966; Hirsch, 1967), a theory briefly discussed in Chapter 1. For example, once a new good (e.g., color TVs) matures and becomes standardized in the country where it is innovated, the technical nature of the good has changed from a high to a less human-capital intensity, although the country's overall factor endowments are unchanged, resulting in a factor incongruity. The emergence of such a phenomenon is unavoidable in the dynamic Schumpeterian world of technological change where any innovation is doomed to be quickly commoditized into a standard good. Standardized goods are no longer suitable to be produced in high-wage, innovation-active advanced countries like the United States. As a result, a transplantation of production takes place from the advanced to the less advanced countries in a trickle-down fashion.

The second genre is related to the industrial upgrading model of FDI (Ozawa, 1992). The key determinant of FDI is the changing factor endowments of a rapidly industrializing country. As the country becomes more capital-abundant and labor-scarcer in the course of structural upgrading, a labor-intensive good (e.g., textiles), whose factor intensity used to be compatible with the initial state of labor abundance in the country, can no longer be produced cost-effectively at home – that is, there is factor incongruity, hence such a good should be produced in less developed countries. The product cycle theory of trade and investment is based on a quick change in the factor intensity of a new product from being human-capital-intensive to being more labor-intensive as the product matures, whereas the industrial upgrading model holds constant the factor intensity of the product involved.

In short, there are thus two essential mechanisms through which factor incongruity emerges and intensifies: one type is the *product-specific, product-cycle* phenomenon; the other is the *economy-specific, structural upgrading* phenomenon (Ozawa, 1995c). The former is microscopic in orientation with its focus on the changing technological nature of a new product, while the latter is macroscopic in perspective with its focus on the changing factor endowments of a country. The product-cycle theory is relevant to the advanced countries (lead geese) where innovations originate, whereas its industrial upgrading counterpart is appropriate to those rapidly catching-up countries (follower geese) that become less labor-abundant. This explains why some developing countries themselves begin to make overseas manufacturing investments even in the early stages of industrialization (as the Asian NIEs and the ASEAN-4 have already done, and China is now starting to do).

In either case, it is clear that an emerging/increasing factor incongruity enervates the country's trade competitiveness and compels its firms to seek a more appropriate production environment abroad by means of FDI and other cross-border direct business activities. Put differently, a country has 'a chain of comparative advantages' (Haberler, 1936), which is, however, constantly altered by dynamic economic forces in technological progress and factor growth, and whose 'weak links' inevitably appear, calling for remedial strategic measures for adjustment (inclusive of FDI) on the part of individual firms – and proactive governments.[2]

7.7.   IMPLICATIONS OF CLASSICAL GROWTH THEORIES

In addition to the phenomenon of increasing factor incongruity, there are more fundamental and more dynamic forces operating on an economy level, forcing overseas certain types of industries that are no longer appropriate for home production. These forces propel structural upgrading, impacting the *entire* economy instead of merely some individual goods and industries. Two classical growth theories provide ideal conceptual frameworks: David

Ricardo's theory of growth stagnation and Adam Smith's theory of growth élan (acceleration).

7.7.1.   The Ricardo-Hicksian Theory of Growth Bottlenecks

Ricardo's theory of growth stagnation (1817/1888) is doubtlessly the very first macroeconomic theory of secular stagnation due to profit squeezes (as opposed to a theory of long-term growth). The theory starts out with a happy state of affairs. In an early stage of development, the Ricardian economy has a small population relative to land; hence, profits, the rate of capital accumulation, and wages except rents are all relatively high. High profits lead to high capital accumulation, which expands industrial production, but simultaneously increases industry's demand for labor. As predicted by the Malthusian population principle, labor supply continues to expand, as long as the existing wages are above the subsistence level. However, since agricultural land is subject to the law of diminishing returns, as less and less fertile tracts of land are brought into cultivation in response to increases in food consumption, both rents and food prices go up, putting upward pressure on money wages. The upshot is a profit squeeze, since profits are the residual of total output after rents and wages are paid. Smaller profits mean less investment or less accumulation. For a while, however, as long as profits are positive, capital accumulation continues, and the economy grows continuously, though at an increasingly slower and slower pace. This situation finally comes to an end (a 'stationary state'), when the population reaches a point where labor earns only a subsistence wage and there are no more population increases. Now rents are so high that no profit (no residual) exists – hence there is no more capital accumulation and no more growth.

In this long-term stagnation scenario, Ricardo pessimistically saw the inevitability of a profit squeeze and a stationary state. Can the economy escape from stagnation? Ricardo pointed out that the day of reckoning could be postponed under two possible circumstances: first, if free trade is pursued, thereby allowing imports of cheap food from overseas so that rents would not rise so fast; and second, if technological progress increases productivity in both agriculture and industry. On the whole, however, Ricardo believed that the profit squeeze would not automatically lead to cheap food imports and technological progress for continuous growth, since they are considered exogenous variables.

In this regard, Ricardo apparently either failed to see or did not stress another important solution, that is, overseas investment as a means of transplanting industrial activities to new locations abroad where arable land is still plentiful and wages are still low. This solution was, however, understandably impractical for Ricardo, since he saw a prohibitively high transaction cost of doing so (as seen earlier). Because of the lack of efficient communications and transport services in his day, overseas investment meant insurmountable difficulties. However, all the three possible avenues of escape from Ricardo's bottlenecks – *trade liberalization, technological progress, and offshore production* – are now actively pursued by the advanced mature economies.

Later, Ricardo's theory of secular stagnation was strongly supported, and elaborated upon, by John Hicks (1973) in his Nobel memorial lecture. Hicks emphasized how the 'impulse of an invention' proceeds to work itself out, eventually succumbing to the law of diminishing returns in an industrialized world.[3] His model may be identified as the 'law of irremovable scarcities' and can be combined with Ricardo's theory of stagnation into what may be called the 'Ricardo-Hicksian trap of industrial development' (Ozawa, 1979a).

7.7.2. The Smithian Theory of Growth Elan

The basic elements in Ricardo's theory had been conceptualized earlier by Adam Smith (1776/1908), although not in as structured and operational a form as Ricardo's.[4] Smith, too, emphasized that economic growth depends on capital accumulation, which in turn relies on profits. He, too, was concerned with wage hikes that might cause a profit squeeze and an industrial slowdown. Smith, however, was far more optimistic than Ricardo and believed that an expansion of markets via free trade leads to the gains from increasing returns to scale, learning-by-doing (knowledge and skill accumulation), and agglomeration economies through a division of labor, which will fully offset any profit squeeze due to increases in rents and wages. His optimism is enshrined in his famous dictum: 'the division of labor is limited by the extent of the market'. In Smith's conceptualization, the dynamic *élan of growth*, i.e., the scale economies achievable through trade-led market expansion and the accompanying gains from learning-by-doing and agglomeration, are treated as *endogenous* variables within the economic system. The Smithian élan of growth is the very force that consolidates absolute advantages.

7.7.3. Relevance

What are the relevance and implications of these classical growth theories to the phenomenon of increasing factor incongruity? In our modern economy, rents represent not only the return to land and food prices, but also the prices of natural resources that are used as industrial raw materials and fuels, as well as the environmental costs of economic growth. Marshallian quasi-rents are also observable in human skills and knowledge.

The modern economy can grow continuously, provided that profits are positive, capital accumulation continues, and human wants are insatiable. This is the fundamental law of growth in the capitalist economy. Hence, any rise in real wages needs to be kept within the bounds of productivity growth. Industrial inputs (including the environment) need to be secured at the lowest possible costs (both social and private). That is to say, the potential Ricardo–Hicksian bottlenecks (rising wages and rents) that cause a profit squeeze need to be avoided. The *labor-seeking* type, the *resource-seeking* type, and the *house-cleaning* type of overseas investment are all the instruments to escape from the Ricardo–Hicksian trap of industrial development at home.

We live in a finite world where Hicks's law of irremovable scarcities eventually sets in. Modern nations are, therefore, actively engaged in the creation of the Smithian élan of growth by encouraging organizational and technological innovation and promoting trade, R&D, education, training, and skill formation, and entrepreneurial endeavors, as well as fostering industrial clusters. In fact, the more advanced the economy is, the more intensive the search for a dynamic Smithian élan of growth in order to overcome the Ricardo–Hicksian trap of industrial development that causes diminishing returns and a profit squeeze. The advanced nations need to be more strongly oriented to Smithian-élan-seeking in order to stay a step ahead of the catching-up developing nations.

This difference in motivation comes from the structural characteristics determined by stages of economic development. A country's competitiveness in the 'Heckscher–Ohlin' and 'non-differentiated Smithian' phases of industrial development is basically determined either by the domestic factor endowments (natural assets such as labor, raw materials, and fuel) or by its ability to acquire the necessary natural resources from abroad; hence, the Ricardo–Hicksian bottlenecks, including environmental damage, are the primary concern. On the other hand, the more advanced phases of growth (the 'differentiated Smithian' and 'Schumpeterian' phases of growth) are more dependent on scale and scope economies, product differentiation, and a deeper division of labor in vertically integrated production – that is, all these represented created assets. The 'McLuhan' phase is further decoupled from natural resources and is most intensive in the use of knowledge, ideas, and other intangible created resources. All these advanced phases of growth are thus directly based on the Smithian élan of growth. Put differently, *given the global development hierarchy of countries, the elimination of the Ricardo–Hicksian bottlenecks is the primary concern of any rapidly catching-up countries, while the search for Smithian growth élan should be the central strategy of business firms and governments in the advanced world.*

In this connection, it is worth noting an observation made by Lee (1984) about the earlier version of the stages model of FDI (Ozawa, 1979a, 1979b) introduced in the late 1970s:

> In Ozawa's theory an economy grows but eventually reaches the Ricardo–Hicksian trap of industrial stagnation. Direct foreign investment is only a temporary escape, because eventually the entire world will reach Ricardo–Hicksian stagnation, and there is no escape from 'spaceship Earth.' Ozawa sees an economy as an individual organism or a collective whole that goes through the cycle of birth, maturation, and then interminable senescence. With direct foreign investment an economy may slow down this progress toward stagnation, but there is no escape from this final stage … Does Ozawa's view of Japan foretell the world to come? Or is it a singular phenomenon from which we cannot generalize? Only history will be able to tell. (Lee, 1984: 720–1)

The theory Lee referred to was built on Japan's earlier phases of growth. Japan was then still in the midst of heavy and chemical industrialization ('non-differentiated Smithian') in the early 1970s, having just graduated from its labor-intensive stage in the late 1960s. Resource-indigent Japan then became the world's largest importer of resources and also began to suffer intolerable environmental problems at home. Hence, Japan was clearly caught in the Ricardo–Hicksian trap of industrial development and had to find an escape by means of overseas investments (of both the 'resources-seeking' and the 'house-cleaning' types) and industrial upgrading.

Since then, however, Japan has succeeded in transforming its industrial structure from resource-intensive industries and toward those that are more intensive in the use of created resources, particularly knowledge (a clean renewable resource). Japan's past 30-year history thus tells us how the country has managed to escape from the Ricardo–Hicksian trap of industrial development by unleashing the Smithian élan of growth.

7.8.   KNOWLEDGE ABSORPTION AND DIFFUSION

Fears of an industrial hollowing out in Japan and an offshore outsourcing of IT jobs in the United States are currently on the rise. This is an irony because the *more knowledge-based* an advanced economy becomes, the *faster* the diffusion of such knowledge (and knowledge-driven industries) overseas, since knowledge is essentially a footloose resource (an 'international public good').

A strong industrial build-up at home is thus only a fleeting event, since it creates a self-enervating condition that leads to ineluctable knowledge (industry) outflows, as conceptualized in the 'price-knowledge/industry-flow' model *à la* Hume. As already discussed in Chapter 1, Hume stressed that even if a country tries to run trade surpluses and accumulate precious metals by pursuing mercantilist policy, the precious metals thus gained in one period will necessarily be drained out of the country in the next period. This is because its domestic money supply will automatically rise, causing inflation and making its trade surplus disappear. Analogously, the more successful Japan is in acquiring technology and building up industry at home under neomercantilism, the greater the upward pressure on the yen and wages at home – hence, the eventual loss of Japan's home-based industry via outward FDI (i.e., newly acquired technologies and industries are predestined to be 'drained out' from Japan).

The inevitable outflow of knowledge and industry causes the social problems of employment adjustment. From Hume's point of view, however, such outflows signified what he called 'a happy concurrence of causes in human affairs, which checks the growth of trade and riches, and hinders them from being confined entirely to one people' (as referred to in Chapter 1). Indeed, this process is the driving/enabling mechanism of hegemon-led growth clustering that makes it possible for prosperity to spread to the follower-geese countries.

7.9. SUMMING UP

The stages approach we have used in the previous six chapters can provide a frame of reference for *dynamic* process-oriented analysis. It goes beyond a mere classification of different stages of growth. The forces at work in stage-to-stage transitions – that is, rising wages, availability of savings (hence, home-spun capital), currency appreciation, knowledge accumulation, skill formation, resource and environmental constraints, and the like – have been identified. They represent the *autocatalytic* elements that serve to self-metabolize and self-upgrade the economic structure in an evolutionary fashion, a sequential process that, however, *needs* to be simultaneously promoted and facilitated by the government in a market-compatible and reinforcing manner, since the market frequently fails, especially in catching-up (rapidly developing) countries. The market is a powerful instrument, no doubt. Yet, 'Like fire, the market is a good servant, but a bad master' (Eatwell, 1982: 33). The market is basically neither goal-determining nor goal-pursuing; it is goal-neutral at best and sometimes even goal-hindering. In essence, the market is merely a resource-allocative instrument devoid of any goals (Ozawa, 1997a).

Structural upgrading is a dynamic disequilibrium process, incessantly compelling adjustments and adaptations. In this respect, two strands of the principle of increasing factor incongruity (the product cycle theory and the structural upgrading theory of FDI) are examined and distinguished, along with the Ricardo–Hicksian trap of industrial development and the Smithian theory of growth élan. All of them can shed light on the restructuring mechanisms of a catching-up economy engaged in an expansion of international business activities, both outward and inward, as instruments of structural transformation and economic development. The 'price-knowledge/industry-flow' theory *à la* David Hume can capture the evolutionary sequence of industrial upgrading and the ineluctable cross-border dissemination of knowledge and industrial activities, which results in a time-compressed process of industry development on the part of catching-up host countries. In short, this chapter further sought to identity some more fundamental conceptual underpinnings of structural upgrading and overseas investment.

NOTES

1. On a theoretical level, what is involved above is not static *allocative* efficiency, that is, a movement along a given product possibility frontier, but dynamic *adaptive* efficiency, that is, a biased shift-out of the product possibility frontier in a trade augmentation fashion along the Rybczunski path. The industrial upgrading process itself has been state-supported but fundamentally driven, as well as tested, by the logic and rigor of market forces.
2. For more detailed and theoretical analyses (in terms of neoclassical isoquants and isocost lines) of these two phenomena, see Ozawa (1995c).
3. Hicks (1973) observes: '... For unlimited expansion of a particular kind, such as that induced by a particular invention, there is not enough space. .... Space, however, is not the only issue. Any indefinite expansion must encounter scarcities. Some [bottlenecks] ... are removable; in time they can be overcome. Others – by necessity, or in the world as it is and has been – are irremovable. It is by *irremovable scarcities* that expansion ... is brought to a stop ... When it is so interpreted (or generalised), the Ricardian theory still holds; and I maintain that it is rather fundamental' (336–48, emphasis added).
4. Letiche (1960) argues that 'Adam Smith made an important contribution to the analysis of economic growth by discussing it in terms of general economic principles, rather than in terms of a theory of economic growth' (p. 65).

PART III

Changes in institutions and industrial
organization: toward the reform-driven,
M&A-active period of growth

8. Network capitalism: industrial organization in evolution

8.1. STAGE-SPECIFIC INDUSTRIAL COORDINATION

This chapter explores how Japanese industry has organized production at different stages of growth and assesses the on-going evolution of the modalities of economic coordination and industrial organization in the Japanese economy. Japan once formulated and maintained a highly effective brand of capitalism and corporate management in the post-World War II period – up until the asset bubble bust (1987–90). Gerlach (1992) identified it as 'alliance capitalism' (along with the subtitle of 'the social organization of Japanese business'). That particular brand was created out of the tattered economic regime at the end of war to reconstruct and build up domestic industries, especially the heavy and chemical industries that Japan had already established in the prewar days but that had become dilapidated during the war. Dunning (1997a, 1997b) adopted the term alliance capitalism when he explored in more general terms the implications of this mode of capitalistic pursuit of business goals by modern corporations across national borders.

The themes of this chapter are (i) that Gerlach-type alliance capitalism – or for that matter, any other types in Japan – has proved to be merely a *transitory* regime that was suitable and instrumental only for a particular stage of Japan's structural upgrading, (ii) that networking is the underlying principle of social organization in Japan, (iii) that G.B. Richardson's trichotomy model of how economic activity is coordinated (by market, hierarchy, and network) needs to be modified to explain the evolution of Japanese-style industrial organization, (iv) that Japan is presently groping for ways to transform its business model once again into something new, something closer to the American model of 'open-systems integration', and (v) that this sequence of institutional transformation is fundamentally a function of the stages of economic growth and structural upgrading, the sequential stages examined in the preceding chapters.

8.2.   EVOLUTIONARY TRANSFORMATION

8.2.1.   Trichotomy of Economic Coordination

As illustrated in Figure 8.1, it was Adam Smith (1776/1908) who first saw inefficiency in government involvement (i.e., 'government failure') in economic affairs and advocated market-driven coordination as a way of maximizing the wealth of nations because 'the Government of Smith's day was corrupt and incompetent; it often peddled monopoly privilege' (Letiche, 1960: 68). Put in modern parlance, Smith was clearly making a distinction between 'market' and 'organization/hierarchy' (i.e., government in his day) in coordinating economic activities. And the modern economics embedded in the market mechanism thus originated with Smith's work. His notion of the 'invisible hand' epitomizes the market, a system of arm's length exchanges based on 'higgling and haggling' in primitive society but on contractual relations in modern society. In other words, a modern market economy is built on a system of jurisprudence (but with the possible downside effect of developing into a high litigation society).

One hundred sixty one years later, however, Ronald Coase (1937) theorized exactly the opposite situation; that is, why markets might be replaced by

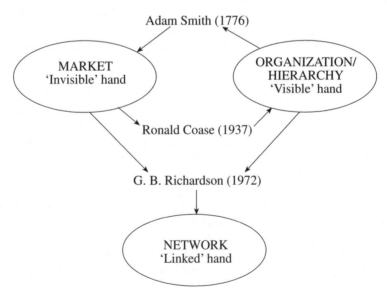

Source: Ozawa (2003d: 231)

Figure 8.1   Trichotomy of economic coordination

organization/hierarchy because of high transaction costs associated with the former (i.e., 'market failure'). Market transactions came to be perceived no longer as costless; in fact, they are often prohibitively costly when the market fails. And transaction cost economics came into existence, as elaborated most extensively by Oliver Williamson (1975, 1985).

This dichotomy between markets and hierarchies then became popular in the economics of industrial organization. But it was not long before another coordination mechanism (which had actually been known in other sciences) was brought to economists' attention for the first time by G.B. Richardson (1972):

> I was once in the habit of telling pupils that firms might be envisaged as islands of planned co-ordination in a sea of market relations. This now seems to me a highly misleading account of the way in which industry is in fact organised. (p. 883)

He then introduced the concept of networking as the third modality of economic coordination by pointing out 'the dense network of co-operation and affiliation by which firms are inter-related' (Richardson, 1972: 883). Consequently, the trichotomy of market (the 'invisible hand'), hierarchy (the 'visible hand'), and network (the 'linked hand') has come to be widely accepted.[1]

These three modalities of economic coordination are driven by different enforcers of order and stability in economic activities and relations. The market is basically driven by 'enlightened self-interest' (non-opportunistic and responsible pursuit of self-interest), the hierarchy by 'command and control', and the network by 'reciprocity, trust, and obligations' *à la* Polanyi (1944).

It should be noted in passing that while Richardson stressed the notion of *inter-firm* networking at the firm level, Karl Marx (1867) had much earlier stressed the notion of *inter-operative/agent* networking at the individual level in terms of the synergy of collective action among 'social animals' (Marx, 1867).

8.2.2.   Gerlach-Type Alliance Capitalism

Using data covering the period from the late 1960s and comparing them with these with data available for US industry, Gerlach (1992) depicted the Japanese structure specific to that period in the following way:

> Japanese business networks are shown to be strongly organized by *keiretsu* across three types of ties (dispatched directors, equity shareholding, and bank borrowing) and more weakly organized in a fourth (intermediate product trade). In all cases but product trade ... the proportion of transactions taking place with firms in the same group is over ten times higher than the average with firms in other groups, indicating an extremely strong pattern of *preferential trading* that clearly has

important implications for how we understand the nature of Japanese markets ...
Although *a variety of alliance forms* are discussed in the study, it is the diversified
groupings linking *major banks and industrial enterprise* that receive special
attention. The large corporation occupies a central position in industrialized
economies, especially in strategic sectors such as finance, basic manufacturing, and
international trade. Even in Japan, where the medium-and-small-firm sector
constitutes a substantial percentage of total employment, it is the large firm sector
that has been the primary source of Japan's financial capital, its imports and
exports, and its major technological and organization innovations. (Gerlach, 1992:
246–7, emphasis added)

The phenomenon 'preferential trading', to which he makes reference, fits in
with the analogy of *keiretsu's* growth as a 'knowledge/information creation'
effect as will be discussed below. What Gerlach describes here is basically the
keiretsu-dominated structure funded by the main banks and dominated by
large corporations, a system that existed from the late 1960s into the 1980s,
exactly the same period on which his empirical study was focused. It was,
however, a *transitory* (though relatively long) period for Japan's structural
transformation (as will be made clear below).

As to the effectiveness of the *keiretsu*-controlled structure, he raises the
issue:

Rationalized markets have long been considered efficiency-generating institutions,
yet the Japanese economy has out-performed any other major industrial
economy for much of the postwar period. If ... Japan's alliance structures
of industrial organization represent clear deviations from textbook models of
market organization, the question becomes whether the Japanese economy has
performed as well as it has despite these deviations or because of them. (Gerlach,
1992: 247)

He then characterizes the Japanese system as 'a balancing of benefits and
costs', in which the benefits far exceed the costs for the Japanese economy as
a whole, whereas the reverse is true for the rest of the world. Gerlach,
however, did not define the benefits and costs involved, nor did he explain
theoretically how the net benefit accrues to the economy. (This question will
be explored below in the 'knowledge creation' vs. 'knowledge diversion'
section.)

Although Gerlach's analysis cites and draws upon Richardson's principle of
networking, he describes Japanese-style alliance capitalism as *sui generis* –
that is, not totally explainable by such a principle alone. Those who accept
Richardson's trichotomy are likely to be perplexed by the thick
confluence/fusion of hierarchy (*keiretsu*) and network (alliance) in what is
presented by Gerlach as the unique Japanese industrial organization. But
this puzzle is to be solved by the works of Kumon (1992) and Imai (1992)
below.

8.2.3.   Network as the Underlying Principle of Social Organization

Kumon (1992) treats networking as a form of *information/knowledge management* at the corporate level and expounds a theory of networking (abstracted from the Japanese experience as distinct from – and without any reference – to Richardson's conceptualization):

> ... a network as a generic social system is one in which, no matter whether it is a complex actor or a societal system, the major type of mutual acts is *consensus/inducement-oriented* [as opposed to *threat/coercion-oriented* or *exchange/exploitation-oriented*]. Networks are organized under the premise that *information rights* are legitimately established in some form or other and at the same time *partially restricted within themselves*. The main reasons for individual actors to join in a network are to share useful information/knowledge with other members, to achieve better mutual understanding, and to develop a firm base for *mutual trust* that may eventually lead to collaboration to achieve actors' individual as well as collective goals. (Kumon, 1992: 121, emphasis added)

For Kumon, the market is thus perceived as 'exchange/exploitation-oriented', the hierarchy as 'threat/coercion-oriented', and the network (here only of the Japanese genre) as 'consensus/inducement-oriented'. To stress and explain the Japanese genre, he then presents two classifications: '(1) those that are simultaneously organizations [or hierarchies], and (2) those that are not organizations – namely, those that are societal systems', the former being called 'network organizations' (network-cum-hierarchy) and the latter 'societal networks'. In Kumon's conceptualization, then, there is *no* clear-cut Richardsonian trichotomy of markets, hierarchies, and networks. The three modalities are intricately and functionally combined as complements – *not* as substitutes or alternatives. And his principle of networking applies to *both* markets and organizations, as well as to inter-firm/organization relations and higher-order societal systems at large. Everything is rolled into one integrative whole, and networking is the basic organizational glue everywhere: 'Japanese society can be characterized as a society in which such networks are ubiquitous, not only informally but also in a formally institutionalized form' (Kumon, 1992: 121). In short, networking permeates Japan's society *at its core* as a major governing principle.

Similarly adopting the same notion of Japanese-style networking, Imai (1992) argues that Japan first organized *zaibatsu* in the pre-World War II days and then, after the war, 'business groups', and most recently 'network industrial organizations'. By business groups he specifically means *keiretsu*, which Gerlach called alliances. The combined arguments advanced by Kumon and Iami are schematically illustrated in Figure 8.2. Basically, Japanese society is extremely intensive and thick in networking, to facilitate exchanges of information and knowledge. The ubiquitous principle of networks underlies the evolution of Japan's industrial organization. *Zaibatsu* (hierarchy) first emerged as a *manifestation* of Japan's network-woven society in that particular organizational form because of market failures – that is, simply because no well-functioning market existed in an underdeveloped Japanese economy. It was not a matter of rational choice. *Zaibatsu* had to fill the lacuna of the market:

> ...the *zaibatsu* as a large-scale, family-owned conglomerate represents the institutionalization of an organizational mechanism to compensate for *the incompleteness of the market* in developing economies. In addition, the role of *zaibatsu* can be interpreted as providing organizational innovation to retain internally the profits from mutually supporting and cooperative activities in an immature market. (Imai, 1992: 203, emphasis added)

The *zaibatsu* were, in Imai's words, both 'coordinating mechanisms' and 'market-like organizers' of economic activities. And additionally, they were effective in capturing and internalizing the synergistic benefits of collective activities. The 'market-like organizers' are also called 'quasi-markets' by Imai – and 'paramarkets' by Kumon. *Zaibatsu* was simultaneously 'control networks' where their holding companies (family-owned) exercised direct control over a diversified range of industries.

Then, shortly after WWII came the 'business groups' or *keiretsu*. Imai stresses that this new organization was characterized by:

(i) the use of 'presidents' clubs' as the core place for periodic exchanges of Information,

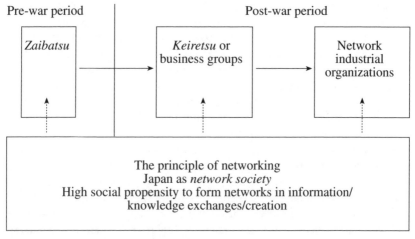

Figure 8.2   Japan as a network society and its manifestations in business organization

(ii) intercorporate holding of stock to prevent hostile takeover bids by outsiders,

(iii) the main bank system under which a large city bank served as the key lender and overseer of each group's activities, and

(iv) a general trading companies at the center of each group's trading, facilitating information gathering and dissemination about market conditions, especially overseas.

According to Imai, furthermore, a crisis was the major trigger mechanism to induce a decisive transformation from one dominant form of industrial organization to another:

> the worldwide industrial reorganization that followed the recession of the 1880s contributed to the formation of the *zaibatsu*, while the dissolution of the *zaibatsu* [after WWII], which was generally regarded as a crisis, produced the competitive postwar reorganization. Similarly, the oil crisis created a new industrial organization. (Imai, 1992: 218)

The oil crisis of 1974 was thus a blessing in disguise in compelling Japanese industry, especially in then rapidly emergent electronics and other assembly-based manufacturing, to mold a new form of business organization, which Imai calls 'network industrial organization':

> In this type of work-force specialization [in the wake of rapid technological progress and dissemination] ... units retain autonomy and yet remain closely interdependent. Unlike the hierarchical division of labor typical in automobile manufacturing, this type of specialization is characterized by self-organizing ... This specialization of the work force has been noted by M.J. Piore and C.F. Sabel, who refer to it as 'flexible specialization.' ... a more highly specialized work force necessarily creates spontaneous linkages among firms engaged in related types of specialized work. This is because when individual enterprises perform highly specialized work in the age of *system technology*, they cannot reach their full potential *unless mutual progress is made as a network*. This requires *a sharing of information among related firms that is beyond the simple information exchange in the market*. Hence, network activity, or activity with consideration for one's 'position' in the network and 'distance' from others, is the mode of action. (Imai, 1992: 218–19, emphasis added)

Given the argument that networks are the warp and weft of the fabric of Japanese society, so to speak, Imai's use of the nomenclature 'industrial network organization' (i.e., network-cum-organization/hierarchy structure) is somewhat confusing to those who are accustomed to Richardson's clear-cut trichotomy. Kumon instead calls this combined structure 'a more genuinely network-oriented form' (Kumon, 1992: 109–41). What they are really arguing is that the prewar *zaibatsu* and the postwar *keiretsu* or business groups should be regarded merely as the manifestations (derivatives) of network Japanese society.

In short, Japan's business structure has gone through metamorphoses, each of which has been triggered by a certain crisis (as posited in Imai's 'crisis-triggered metamorphosis' theory). And in Imai's view, the path of metamorphosis has so far traced out a three-stage sequence of *zaibatsu* – ➔ 'business groups' (or *keiretsu*) – ➔ 'network industrial organizations' with the principle of networking as their underlying organizational mechanism. (As will be seen later, however, this sequence will be further elaborated on and extended to the postwar five stages of 'make-shift structure'– ➔ 'keiretsu, Mark I '– ➔ 'keiretsu, Mark II' – ➔ 'systems integration, Mark I' – ➔ 'systems integration, Mark II').

8.3. WHY HAVE NETWORKS BEEN SO UBIQUITOUS IN JAPAN?

8.3.1. Legacies of Feudalism[2]

One naturally wonders why the principle of networking has been so pervasive in Japanese society. This has a lot to do with how Japan came out of 200 years' seclusion under feudalism and then plunged into modernity in the mid-nineteenth century – largely under pressure exerted from outside.

According to Veblen (1934), feudalistic traditions or experience play a positive role in economic transformation. This line of reasoning is in full agreement with a widely recognized view that feudalism contributed to the development of democracy, capitalism, and modern civilization in the Western societies, for it introduced an orderly social system based on contractually specified relationships. Some even regard feudalism as a prerequisite to civilization. Early on, indeed, feudalism in England gave rise to the practice of covenanting or contracting by specifying and formalizing a system of governance by the rule of law (Prawer and Eisenstadt, 1968). And in the end, contractual relations, the central mode of governing interpersonal commercial relations and transactions between independent operative units in modern times, have come into existence as a legacy from the evolution of feudalism. The practice of contracts (formal specifications of rights and duties among transacting parties) liberated individuals from the shackles of arbitrariness and exploitation by the powerful lords who bound their vassals in informal and often charismatic relations.

In sharp contrast, the Japanese brand of feudalism had left different evolutionary traits, traits that have survived into modern Japan:

Japan's feudalism differed from the European pattern in several important respects:

(1) the continuous importance of the imperial center in spite of its loss of political function; (2) the weakness, perhaps even total absence, of contractual elements in the relations between lords and vassals; (3) the full, personal, familistic expression of these relations; and (4) the lack of any representative institutions. (Prawer and Eisenstadt, 1968: 400)

For our analysis, the second and third features, 'the weakness, perhaps even total absence, of contractual elements in the relations between lords and vassals' and 'full, personal, familistic expression of these relations', are crucial in understanding the social system in Japan's post-feudal period and why trust-based networking has permeated Japanese society. The economies in both the West and Japan derive from their respective feudalism, but with different ways of coordinating economic transactions and interlinking relations. In the former the behaviors of micro-agents are contractually specified and explicitly rule-governed, while in Japan they are less legally particularized and bound but are more generally governed by personal ties or connections that distinctly characterize Japanese society. The Japanese operate largely on the basis of unwritten, non-contractual relations. In this respect, the Japanese modality of organizing economic transactions has some affinity with what Polanyi (1944) describes as a system of 'reciprocity' as opposed to a system of 'exchange'. In the former system, goods and services are circulated 'on the basis of familial or political obligation, reinforced by ritualistic or religious principles' – in contrast with 'the two-way transfer of equivalent values motivated by self-interested calculation that is characteristic of market exchange' (Stanfield, 1986: 20).

In the Western market economies, legal contracting and litigious proceedings are the major governing mechanisms that enforce transactional promises between economic agents. By comparison, economic transactions in Japan more strongly involve personal commitments, trust, duties, and obligations – in other words, treated more often as *social exchanges* rather than as *pure economic exchanges*. The Japanese are eager to build long-term relationships. Consequently, an atmosphere of patronage and reciprocity *à la* Polayni – rather than that of suspicion and threat – pervades the exchanges.

In this respect, as pointed out in Kay (1991), Casson's (1987) emphasis on trust and goodwill and Buckley's (1988) on forbearance and cooperation are more appropriate for Japanese-style transactions than Williamson's (1985) on opportunism, though opportunistic behavior is certainly not non-existent in Japanese society.

What is more, another important legacy of many centuries of secluded feudalism in Japan is manifested in its cultural attributes stemming from paddy rice cultivation. This type of farming, particularly in Japan's natural disaster-prone climate (with frequent typhoons and flooding), necessitated collective control over, coordinated use of, and mutual help in irrigation among the village farmers. Aoki (1988), for example, stresses this point:

> There is no doubt that through centuries of agrarian experience up to as recently as a generation ago, the Japanese developed the customs of mutual help, collective coordination, risk sharing, ad hoc and flexible adaptation to continual and incremental environmental changes, diligent work habits, and penetration of communal life into the private spheres, which are now viewed as characteristics of modern Japanese factory life. (p. 307)

In short, the unique evolution of Japan's feudalism, along with its heavy dependence on wetland farming as the major economic base, left indelible marks on how the Japanese interact with each other not only in economic affairs but also in any other types of activity. The Japanese principle of networking thus derives from their deep cultural roots.

8.4.   SYSTEMS INTEGRATION

An important question still remains unanswered: *Is Japanese-style networking based on intra-group trust and cohesiveness really equally as information/knowledge-enhancing, hence economic efficiency-increasing, as its American counterpart?*

8.4.1.   Open vs. Closed

Analyzing the resurgence of Route 128 and the recent information and communications technology (ITC) revolution in the United States, Best (2000) introduces the new concept of 'open-systems integration' as opposed to what may be called 'closed-systems integration':

> System integration is a static concept with respect to component design rules; it does not imply openness to innovation or technological change. In fact, the challenge of system integration exerts pressure to freeze technological change. *Kaizen*, or continuous improvement management, pursues experimentation and technological improvement but *holds basic technology design rules constant* … The process of integrating subsystems have dynamic feedback effects … Intel built a business model based on the concept of design modularization. Leading Japanese companies have substantial systems-integration capabilities. They, like Intel, integrate new product development with process reorganization. But *the Japanese leading electronics companies have not redesigned their business system to capture the innovation potential offered by the principle of systems integration. To do so would mean moving from a closed to an open-systems model of supplier relations and industrial organization.* (Best, 2000: 470–1, emphasis added)

For Best, the Japanese practice of incremental technical improvement, *kaizen*, is a rather static approach that cannot alter the basic technological paradigm. And the Japanese are still operating under *closed-systems* integration, unlike their American counterparts who benefit more substantially from *open-systems* integration. In other words, what Imai identified above as 'network industrial organization' is basically closed-systems integration. In order to stress the importance of transition from the closed type to the open type, we will call the former 'systems integration, Mark I', and the latter 'systems integration, Mark II'.

8.4.2. 'Knowledge/Information Creation' vs. 'Knowledge/Information Diversion'

The benefits and costs of open- vs. closed-systems integration can be theorized on a comparative basis in terms of two opposing effects: 'knowledge/information creation' and 'knowledge/information diversion'. These effects are analogous to Viner's (1960) distinction between 'trade creation' vs. 'trade diversion'. Knowledge/information creation occurs within a closely knit network, as information flows unhindered and smoothly in such a group, leading to a successful synthesis and synergy in idea generation. This benefit is, as seen earlier, stressed in both Imai (1992) and Kumon (1992). Simultaneously, however, knowledge/information diversion may result from the introversive focus of the group, neglecting and slighting ideas and practices outside the group. Kumon (1992) also touches on this undesirable aspect of the closed type of networking:

> … in networks, success tends to lead to complacency in and closedness of the system, with members becoming more introverted. Of course, they will show some interest in the outside world insofar as it continues to be the source of some useful information, or other goods and services, but they will have little genuine interest in, or sympathy for, the outside world as such. (p. 136)

So long as the knowledge/information creation (positive) effect outweighs the knowledge/information diversion (negative) effect, the group as a whole benefits. Ironically, however, the greater the knowledge/information creation effect, the more introverted and hubristic the group may become; the upshot then is a greater knowledge/information diversion effect, which eventually ossifies network relations. As will be discussed below, in the early stages of Japan's catch-up growth, the *keiretsu* groups were able to maximize the positive effect, but eventually they were overwhelmed by the negative effect as the nature of industrial technology became more sophisticated and the scope of business operations was increasingly globalized.

This conceptualization of two opposing effects is thus useful in interpreting in theoretical terms what is meant by Gerlach's 'balancing of benefits and costs' as mentioned earlier.

8.4.3.   From Comparative to Competitive Advantage

To explain the nature of Japan's network society, the theory of comparative advantage can also be used when we interpret it as the principle of *intra*-unit specialization and *inter*-unit division of labor, whether the unit happens to be a country, a network group, or an individual. The trade doctrine of comparative cost advantage originally expounded by David Ricardo (1817) looks at an individual country (entire economy) as a unit of analysis. Trade takes place because of a difference in comparative costs, inducing an expansion of comparatively advantaged (relatively higher-labor-productivity) industries and a contraction of comparatively disadvantaged (relatively lower-labor-productivity) industries. This causes a better reallocation of resources, a phenomenon called 'allocative efficiency', resulting in higher outputs and higher living (consumption) standards in trade-participating countries. According to this doctrine, even a *weak* (non-competitive) country, a country that has no absolute advantage in any single industry, can still participate in and gain from trade. In other words, it is clearly a theory of *inclusion and coexistence, not exclusion and rivalrous elimination.*

In this perspective, each *keiretsu* group can be interpreted as an organization which is built on the doctrine of comparative advantage – in the sense that each group is comprised of some several leader companies and a large number of their respective follower/affiliated companies, especially in vertical supply (input procurement and output distribution) chains. This characteristic is popularly called '*gosoh sendan* [convoy formation]' in which a group of affiliated companies/banks, large and small, advance together in mutual protection and cooperation. Strong major companies are supposed to assist and foster their closely affiliated weaker companies. In other words, each *keiretsu*'s *intra*-group transactions are based on the doctrine of comparative advantage or the principle of inclusiveness and mutual existence – and not on the doctrine of absolute advantage or the principle of exclusion and rivalrous elimination. For example, a major company in one *keiretsu* may find supplies cheater if it purchases from a company in another *keiretsu*, but the former refrains from doing so (and the latter may refuse to deal with such an out-of-group customer). Instead, the major company continues to procure whatever is needed from its own affiliated suppliers, while providing any necessary assistance (technical and financial) to make the affiliate more productive and equally competitive. In short, the idea of comparative advantage-based specialization is applicable to, and useful in, delineating the strength of intra-*keiretsu* cooperation.

8.5. STRUCTURAL UPGRADING AND BUSINESS ORGANIZATION

The postwar progression of Japan's network-based industrial organization can be juxtaposed with its sequential stages of structural upgrading, since the former has occurred *pari passu* with the evolutionary changes in Japan's industrial composition punctuated by the growth of a certain leading sector in each stage (as seen in the preceding chapters and also as shown in Figure 8.3).

The industrial progression is the sequence of 'make-shift structure' – → '*keiretsu*, Mark I' – → '*keiretsu*, Mark II' – → 'systems integration, Mark I' – → 'systems integration, Mark II', as suggested earlier. The upgrading effectiveness of each type of industrial organization is schematically illustrated in terms of how successfully Japan has performed vis-à-vis Europe and the United States (used as reference points) during the different decades since the war, starting with the 1950s.

In the early postwar period (the 1950s and 1960s), Japan was clearly far behind the West. In the 1970s, Japanese industry quickly succeeded in initiating consumer electronics as its leading growth industry (as best exemplified by the successful innovation of pocket-size transistor radios[3]). Thanks also largely to the oil crises of 1974 and 1979, Japanese-made small subcompact cars became popular because of fuel economy, providing Japan's automobile industry with a foothold in the Western markets. And by the end of the 1980s, Japan on the whole had caught up with both Europe and the United States in overall industrial and technological levels. In fact, the phrase 'the Triad' that came into vogue in the 1980s mirrored Japan's newly acquired status as an equal economic power in the global economy.

Yet, following the burst of the asset bubble of 1987–90, Japan plunged into stagnation, mainly because of its political inability to solve its banking crisis. Japan has been incapacitated for over more than a decade because it failed decisively to force the banks to cut off their 'zombie' borrowers, especially in the 'pork-barrel' industries such as construction and distribution (a topic to be explored in Chapter 9). In the meantime, the United States quickly regained its leadership and forged ahead with the information technology revolution.

These outcomes of Japan's catch-up growth at the different stages have been brought about by the efficacy of industrial organization specific to each stage. In the immediate postwar period when economic disruption and chaos initially prevailed, a 'make-shift' structure of industrial organization (whatever way they were able to organize corporate activities) was improvised. And it sufficed for the Heckscher–Ohlin stage of labor-driven economic recovery and reconstruction. *Zaibatsu* was dissolved by the order of the Occupation authorities, and *keiretsu* formation was still inchoate. In order to earn precious foreign exchange, Japan exported whatever manufactures it

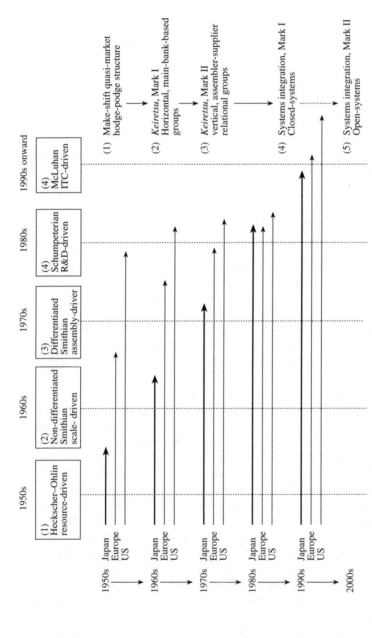

Note: Arrows indicate the relative positions of each economy in stages of growth during different postwar decades

Source: Ozawa (2003d: 243)

Figure 8.3 Japan's catch-up in structural upgrading under different forms of business organization

180

was capable of producing with an abundance of relatively well-trained, disciplined, and low-cost labor in the aftermath of wartime destruction and defeat. Japan's famous 'lifetime employment' was still inchoate, and so was the 'main bank' system of corporate finance and governance.

The 1960s began to witness the birth and rapid growth of the six main-bank-based groups (Mitsui, Mitsubishi, Sumitomo, Fuyo, Sanwa, and DKB), a form of industrial organization that may be identified as '*keiretsu*, Mark I'. They were *horizontally* conglomerated and diversified in industrial activity under the so-called 'one-set' principle which compelled each *keiretsu* group to vie vigorously with each other in establishing an almost identical set of key industries, such as steel, heavy machinery, shipbuilding, petrochemicals, and trading (in the form of *sogo shosha* (general trading companies)) – all in an oligopolistic fashion. *Keiretsu,* Mark I proved effective for the non-differentiated Smithian stage of scale-driven heavy and chemical industrialization.

These groups were also financially governed by their respective main banks, which were in turn controlled by the Bank of Japan – that is, by the Ministry of Finance because of the lack of independence of Japan's central bank. But *keiretsu*, Mark I soon began to evolve into *keiretsu*, Mark II, as assembly-based industries such as consumer electronics and automobiles emerged as the leading growth sector in the 1970s (as seen in Chapter 4). They grew more *vertically* conglomerated through the supply chains of parts, components, and accessories. *Keiretsu,* Mark II was thus specific to the differentiated Smithian stage of assembly-based manufacturing.

As electronics became increasingly more sophisticated with rapid product/process innovations, however, systems integration emerged as a new form of industrial organization. Computers began to be applied to on-line order placement and procurement and 'just-in-time' delivery. But this new form of industrial organization, 'systems integration, Mark I', was carried out within the closed system of the *keiretsu* tradition – and was, therefore, accompanied by the negative effect of knowledge/information diversion (as discussed above).

In the past few years, however, the landscape of Japanese industry has begun to change dramatically. The *keiretsu* started to break down in its original formation. First of all, the six main banks, which used to lead and jealously guarded their respective *keiretsu* groups, have merged with each other into mixed-up entities. For instance, Sumitomo Bank (the flagship bank of the Sumitomo group) merged with Sakura Bank (the Mitsui group) to create Sumitomo Mitsui Banking Corp., and Fuji Bank (the Fuyo group) joined forces with Dai-Ichi Kangyo Bank (the DKB group), along with the Industrial Bank of Japan and Yasuda Trust, to form Mizuho Holdings, the world's largest bank in terms of assets.

Left in the lurch, group companies themselves began to engage in inter-*keiretsu* tie-ups. For example, Sumitomo Chemical merged with Mitsui Chemical. Strategic alliances were forged between Kawasaki Steel (the DKB group) and NKK (the Fuyo group), and between two of Japan's largest *sogo-shosha*, Marubeni Corporation (the Fuyo group) and Itochu (the DKB group), in steel trading. Although the *keiretsu* firms are still not yet as uninhibited and as flexible as American firms, they are becoming more profit-conscious than loyalty-bound. Their networking is now pragmatically extending *beyond and across* their group affiliations.

Some may regard this new business restructuring merely as a regrouping of *keiretsu*, but it is more appropriate to view it as a move toward the new and more flexible form of 'systems integration' pioneered by the electronics industry where rapid technological progress is crucial for business survival and where the forces of globalization and competition are relentlessly compelling the producers to restructure through strategic alliances and M&As. They can no longer operate under the principle of comparative advantage (inclusiveness and coexistence) but must perform on the basis of competitive advantages. Yet, they have not yet quite graduated from closed-systems integration, 'systems integration, Mark I'. With deregulation and trade liberalization, Japanese industry is clearly in search of a new business model, 'systems integration, Mark II', which is closer to, if not identical with, American-style, market-driven, open systems integration. The 'McLuhan' information-driven stage of growth requires a flexible and open business model in order to survive in ever-intensifying global competition in this age of the IT revolution.

8.6. SUMMING UP

Japan's network capitalism has evolved, and is evolving, taking different transitory shapes in industrial organization. Gerlach's description of *keiretsu* as alliance capitalism fits only one form of evolutionary manifestation of the Japanese principle of networking, a form that prevailed mostly during the Smithian (both non-differentiated and differentiated) stages of scale-and assembly-driven industrialization (mid-1950s through 1970s), involving the 'metal-bashing'-type production of steel, basic chemicals, heavy machinery, and early-generation automobiles.

The Schumpeterian R&D-driven stage was initially accommodated by systems integration, Mark I, especially in electronics and other high-tech industries where technological progress is pronounced and the product cycle is increasingly shortened. Yet the advent of the IT revolution and its accompanying 'McLuhan' stage calls for a more open and flexible organizational structure, systems integration, Mark II. Japan is clearly in the throes of transition to this new phase of industrial organization. The principle of networking is, nevertheless, the governing doctrine of Japanese society in all walks of life, and the different business models have been reflective of the structural requirements of their respective corresponding stages of industrial transformation.

The notions of 'knowledge/information creation vs. knowledge/information diversion' and 'inclusiveness vs. exclusiveness' were introduced as the analytical frameworks within which to evaluate the benefits and costs of Japanese-style networking based on intra-group trust and cohesiveness.

NOTES

1. The phrase, 'visible hand', is adopted from Chandler (1977).
2. This section draws in part on Ozawa and Phillips (1994).
3. OECD (1970) recognized that small transistor radios were Japan's first significant innovation after WWII.

9. Out of an institutional quagmire? International business to the rescue

9.1. MATRICES OF INSTITUTIONS, OUTER VS. INNER

When we talk about institutions and international business, it is important to keep in mind that there are two layers of institutional setting: one is an 'outer' (supra-national) set of global institutions and the other is an 'inner' (nation-specific) set of domestic institutions in each individual country. Both sets evolve as their surrounding politico-economic conditions alter over time. The outer set is currently arranged under the Pax Americana, which sends forth the forces of globalization. In this age of hegemon-led globalization, therefore, the outer set is dominant over the inner set, forcing accommodation and compliance of the latter with the norms of the former. Yet, some inner institutions retain their own logic of survival, resisting changes. Most of the time, international business activities react and adapt to – and even arbitrage between – these different institutional surroundings, but they themselves serve as *agents of institutional homogenization* throughout the world.

As stressed by Douglass North (1990, 1999), the overall economic performance of a given economic unit is largely determined (enhanced or retarded) by its institutional regime. Such a regime can also be called 'an *institutional matrix* that defines the *incentive* structure of society' against the backdrop of 'the belief system' that connects 'reality' to the institutions (North, 1999: 9, emphasis added). In addition, the belief system is a product of local mores and traditions in the individual countries. North was thus talking about the role of an institutional matrix in a *given* individual country – that is, an inner set alone. However, his concept of institutional matrix can be extended to the global economy in which outer and inner institutions interact with each other, staking out a dominant position on a global stage.

In particular, ever since the collapse of the Soviet Union, the Pax Americana has been ruling the world with the ideology of global capitalism embedded in the Anglo-American belief system of market liberalism and free enterprise. Since the inner institutions are still molded by the individual countries' belief systems, conflicts and tensions are naturally expected to arise. As stressed by Gerschenkron (1962), developing countries in particular, as latecomers to industrialization, tend to become reliant on institutional arrangements rather than on the market – for the very simple reason that the market mechanism has yet to be developed. And early postwar Japan was no exception; it started out its reconstruction and recovery by adopting a renovated set of inner institutions which strongly reflected Japan's own belief system – and which was suitable for its own purposes – despite the fact that Japan assimilated many new democratic and market-based institutions of the Pax Americana. It is in terms of this broad analytical framework of political economy and institutional economics that this chapter interprets and explores the postwar – and current – experiences of Japan with its institutional setups.

Japan's postwar economy was once well known for a number of unique institutions such as state-controlled bank-based finance, the main bank system, *keiretsu*, company unions, lifetime employment, consensus decision-making, and the seniority system of promotion and wages (although these peculiar institutions once considered 'culturally' embedded and unalterable have lately begun to change). Japanese society has been disposed to collective welfare maximization with equitable income distribution rather than individualistic (self-interest-centered) welfare maximization. All these constitute an inner matrix of interwoven institutions. And each of them has already been exhaustively examined by many scholars from a variety of perspectives and in great detail. But so far they have only been studied separately and not as a coherent system of *interdependent and mutually reinforcing* institutions that is subject to the forces of path dependence (Ozawa, 2001a). Less well-known and left unexplored, moreover, is another important organizational setup, the so-called dual industrial structure. This chapter focuses on this particular feature, though references to other related institutions are also made whenever appropriate.

The leitmotif of this chapter is as follows: (i) that the origin of Japan's dual structure had a lot to do with the outer set of global institutional arrangements that once prevailed in the early postwar period (especially the Allies' occupation policy, which drastically changed in the wake of communist threat), (ii) that Japan's pre-crisis phenomenal growth was built on its unique *dirigiste* set of inner institutions, (iii) that the new forces of globalization (i.e., stepped-up international business activities) that emanate from the outer set are currently compelling Japan to renovate its inner institutions – that is to say, the only way out of its present imbroglio is to adapt more closely, if not totally, to the norms of the newly altered outer matrix of institutions and the drastically transformed global environment, and (iv) that Japan's slow pace of reform is largely explainable in terms of the politico-economic difficulties associated with the dismantling of its early postwar – now obsolete and burdensome – internal institutions.

9.2. THE OUTER MATRIX OF GLOBAL INSTITUTIONS IN EVOLUTION

Early postwar Japan serendipitously benefited from a favorable external economic environment. As discussed in Chapter 2, at the war's end, the Allied Forces planned to strip industrial machinery and equipment from Japanese factories and ship them out as war reparations to other Asian nations which had suffered Japanese occupation. Japan was supposed to revert to an agrarian subsistence economy devoid of industrial capability to wage another war. With the start of the Cold War, however, this radical punishment plan was quickly scrapped, and the US began to assist Japan in reconstructing itself as a bastion against communism. The communists' takeover of China in 1949 and the resultant Sino-Soviet Alliance was taken as a big threat to the Free World. The US immediately began to wage 'economic cold war' ('negative economic diplomacy' or 'economic embargo') (Zhang, 2001) against the communist bloc – and at the same time, 'positive economic diplomacy' towards US allies. This diplomacy was designed to ensure Asia's 'continuous orientation toward Washington' (Cumings, 1984). The Korean War of 1950–53 was a godsend to the Japanese economy, which was assigned the task of supplying the UN forces. It jump-started the reconstruction and modernization of Japan's heavy and chemical industries.

On the political front, as detailed below, a conservative government was soon created. Agriculture in particular was restructured in such a way as to serve as a powerful support base for a pro-business (pro-America) political party, the Liberal Democratic Party (LDP), that would preside over Japan in the subsequent four decades of rapid growth. Furthermore, the United States tolerated Japan's protectionist catch-up strategy and even willingly provided technology and market access – all in the name of fighting against communism even at the cost of America's economic interests.

A stable monetary system was established in the form of the Bretton Woods regime of pegged exchange rates. It also gave Japan temporary immunity from the prohibition against free capital flows and foreign exchange convertibility. At the time of entry to the IMF in 1949, the Japanese yen was on the whole set at a somewhat undervalued rate relative to the US dollar, favoring Japanese exports, and the yen became even more undervalued as Japanese industry gained competitiveness in the world market. By the time when the Bretton Woods regime was officially replaced by a managed float in 1973, the Japanese economy had already been well industrialized so that it was strong enough to withstand the volatility of the yen's value against the US dollar.

In short, the Cold War and the original IMF system no doubt provided an externally favorable period for Japan to succeed in catching up with – and even surpassing in some industrial sectors – the West. The United States allowed – and even encouraged – Japan to pursue a *dirigiste* development policy so that the latter would quickly reconstruct and strengthen its economy. In other words, Japan's interventionist way of conducting economic affairs was tolerated, and some of its distinctive institutional arrangements, such as the *keiretsu* formation, the main bank system, and company unions, were even promoted by the United States as instruments of quick economic recovery and political stability. No wonder, then, when the Berlin wall tumbled down, that Chalmers Johnson aptly observed: 'The Cold War is over; Japan has won'.

But towards the end of the Cold War (ever since President Nixon's visit to China in 1972 and the subsequent start of China's open-door policy), US trade policy started to switch from unilateral free trade policy to reciprocity (the 'level playing field' principle). For example, the United States initiated a series of bilateral trade negotiations with Japan, starting with the Market-Oriented Sector-Selective (MOSS) talks (1985–6 during the Reagan administration) and proceeding to the Structural Impediments Initiative (SII) talks (1989–90 during the Bush administration) and the Framework (or Bilateral Comprehensive Economic) talks (from 1993 onward under the Clinton administration) (Schoppa, 1997). The MOSS round signaled a shift in US focus from restraining Japanese imports into the US to opening up *specific* Japanese markets for American exports (Mikanagi, 1996). In contrast, the SII talks involved *economy-wide* issues, such as macroeconomic policy (centered on savings and investment relationships which influence the trade balance), the distribution system, land policy, and *keiretsu*. Then, the Framework talks reverted to, and refocused on, the sector-specific approach by aiming at tangible results as 'indicators' of market opening (Ozawa, 2001b).

The disappearance of the communist threat with the demise of the Soviet empire in 1989 ushered the world decisively into a new era of US economic and political dominance. The United States began ever more strongly to demand reciprocity in openness for trade and investment. True, the September 11 attacks moderated America's unilateralism, but the success the US has so far achieved in the war against terrorism in Afghanistan and elsewhere has fortified its resolve for 'enduring freedom'. In his 2002 state-of-the-union message, President Bush called on the rest of the world to adopt the three tenets of market democracy: 'open market', 'open trade', and 'open society'. These ideologies epitomize the nature of the current outer matrix of global institutions under the Pax Americana, which is the driving force of globalization.

Meanwhile, the international monetary system had already become more market-dependent with the adoption of a managed float (i.e., flexible exchange rates with behind-the-scene interventions) in 1973 after the abandonment of the Bretton Woods regime (i.e., pegged exchange rates) which required – and justified – state interventions to maintain fixed rates.

9.3.   THE INNER MATRIX OF DOMESTIC INSTITUTIONS IN EVOLUTION

Japan as a defeated nation began its reconstruction and modernization under the aegis of the United States. Japan's political system in particular was overhauled so as to introduce democracy and to eliminate any feudalistic remnants of the prewar years. Most important of all, once the communist threat emerged, a conservative government was quickly handpicked by the United States. Nobusuke Kishi (who became a prime minister in 1957), minister of munitions in Tojo's wartime cabinet, was freed from war crime charges and released from prison, along with others. Many war-time economic planners, who once were engaged in the Greater East Asian Co-prosperity Sphere program, came back to Japan's *dirigiste* bureaucracy and started to introduce a series of industrial policies. The Japanese government, once granted independence under the San Francisco Peace Treaty of 1951, began a so-called *sengo kaikaku* (postwar reforms) to renovate Japan's early postwar matrix of inner institutions, even revising some of the occupation-imposed measures, such as the Anti-Trust Law.

9.3.1.   New Structural Dualism: An Outgrowth of Japan's Matrix for FG Catch-Up

Blessed on the whole by favorable external market conditions and under its unique matrix of institutions, the postwar Japanese economy was successful in nurturing dynamic comparative advantages and climbing up the ladder of industrial upgrading. This was accomplished by way of dynamic infant-industry protection (import-substitution-cum-export promotion), initially involving heavy protection of domestic industries. It was only when Japanese enterprises became competitive that trade and investment barriers were gradually removed. In fact, the 1950s can be characterized largely as a period of strict import restrictions, the 1960s as a period of gradual liberalization, and the 1970s onwards as a period of more 'committed' trade liberalization (Ozawa, 1986). Although there was constant pressure from the United States on Japan to open up its market, Japan was on the whole allowed to schedule trade liberalization on its own terms. As pointed out earlier, as the Cold War intensified, the US opted for a foreign policy in favor of security rather than in its own economic interests.

As explored in earlier chapters, in terms of an FG-style structural upgrading, Japan started out with labor-intensive industries such as textiles, toys, and sundries in the early postwar years (the 'Heckscher–Ohlin' stage of growth). From there, Japan quickly developed competitiveness in a ladder-climbing fashion – first in steel, ships, and other heavy and chemical industries during the 1960s (the 'non-differentiated Smithian' stage); in small compact automobiles and early-generation electronics (e.g., color TVs and calculators) during the 1970s (the 'differentiated Smithian' stage); and in robotics, new materials, microchips, and luxury higher-end automobiles – and then on to latest-generation electronics (e.g., lap-top and palm-size computers, specialty chips, and play-stations) during the 1980s and through the mid-1990s (the 'Schumpeterian' stage). Japan is now eagerly catching up in new Internet-driven industries (the 'McLuhan' stage). And all these stage-delineated competitive industries have developed in, and come to constitute, what may be called the *outer-focused* (OF) sector.

During the course of structural transformation, Japan has transplanted overseas, notably to its neighboring Asian countries, via FDI those industrial activities in which Japan had lost competitiveness, as envisaged in the FG paradigm of comparative advantage recycling. This 'industrial shedding' activity was instrumental in reallocating resources from comparatively disadvantaged to comparatively (also competitively) advantaged industries, raising overall industrial efficiency and productivity.

In the meantime, however, Japan has ended up creating a slew of once heavily regulated and protected inefficient industries – protected from competition, both domestic and foreign. Foreign competition in imports and inward FDI was fended off if not by outright legal restrictions, by the built-in bias of regulations and red tape. These industries, which are hereafter called the *inner-dependent* (ID) sector, are agriculture, forestry, fisheries, food and beverage, telecommunications, transportation, wholesaling and retailing, construction, health, banking, finance, insurance, real estate and other domestic-market-focused services.

These bifurcated sectors are under the jurisdiction of different government ministries. The OF sector has been mainly under the purview of the Ministry of International Trade and Industry – whose name was changed to the Ministry of Economy, Trade and Industry in 2001. Because of its task of managing external diplomatic relations, the Ministry of Foreign Affairs ought to be added as an indirect supporter – and beneficiary – of the OF sector. The ID sector, on the other hand, was under the supervision of a variety of inner-focused ministries: the Ministry of Agriculture, Forestry, and Fisheries, the Ministry of Construction, the Ministry of Health and Welfare, the Ministry of Post and Telecommunications, the Ministry of Finance, the Ministry of Labor, and the Ministry of Home Affairs.

It should be noted that these two structurally demarcated sectors which have come into existence are not totally separate entities but interconnected in a variety of ways. For example, the automobile industry is in the OF sector, but its distribution, auto finance, and some of its suppliers of inputs are in the ID sector. Japan's carmakers established their own networks of exclusive dealerships as well as their own multi-layered systems of parts suppliers. And there is little doubt that their tight controls on distribution have been one important hindrance to car imports. A similar situation exists in the consumer electrical/electronics goods sector. In other words, the *keiretsu* groups inevitably straddled both the OF and the ID sectors.

Government ministries have been the home of the interventionists promoting the development of domestic industries under their jurisdiction, thus continuing the bureaucratic tradition established by the Meiji government, Japan's first modern administration, after the Meiji Restoration of 1868. As a latecomer nation, government ministries and agencies were created, as Johnson (1982) so aptly put it, not so much as 'civil servants' per se, as in the US, but rather as 'task-oriented mobilization and development agencies' whose main functions were originally 'to guide Japan's rapid forced development in order to forestall incipient colonization by Western imperialists'. That is to say, their current predispositions toward controls are path-dependent – and justified from a nationalistic point of view.

As dynamic comparative advantages were acquired in the OF sector, Japan's rising trade surplus began to cause a sharp appreciation of the yen and ever-rising competitive pressure on the ID sector. The OF sector thus came to represent a competitive tradables sector, while the ID continued to be an ever protected and inefficient non-tradables sector, as illustrated in Figure 9.1.

Up until 1971, the yen was nominally fixed at 360 yen to the dollar. This meant a continuous *real* depreciation (namely undervaluation) of the yen as Japanese industry gained export competitiveness. However, once exchange rates were subject to market forces, the yen quickly began to appreciate. To cope with the ever-rising yen, the OF sector had to keep raising productivity to remain export-competitive. As the sector succeeded in this endeavor, however, it again faced another round of yen appreciation because the ID sector did not absorb imports sufficiently to relieve the upward pressure on the currency. In other words, the OF sector came to be trapped in a treadmill: a vicious cycle running from a struggle for productivity improvement and a greater trade surplus, to an ever-appreciating yen, and to an even greater need for cost cutting. The upshot was that over the 1973–83 period, for example, labor productivity growth in Japan's tradables sector outstripped that in the non-tradables sector by as much as 73.2 per cent (compared to the US tradables sector which exhibited 13.2 per cent higher productivity growth than in its non-tradables sector) (Marston, 1987).

9.3.2. The ID Sector as the LDP 'Pork-Barrel', the Japanese Disease, and Hollowing Out

This intersectoral effect via the foreign exchange market is the Japanese

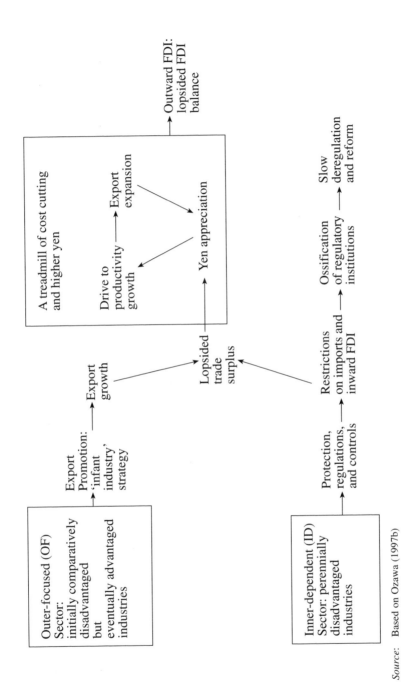

Source: Based on Ozawa (1997b)

Figure 9.1 Distorted structural dualism

version of the 'Dutch disease' (Ozawa, 1997a). Imports should have become available to Japanese consumers at cheaper and cheaper prices in yen terms, but they were either hindered by trade and inward FDI barriers or not delivered (passed through) at cheaper retail prices (i.e., the foreign exchange gains were simply pocketed by the highly regulated and protected distribution sector). In other words, a stronger yen was a hidden subsidy for the ID sector. The OF sector began to escape from the *disadvantages* of producing at home by shifting production abroad via FDI. The high yen also subsidized this investment outflow. The upshot was a one-sided imbalance in Japan's FDI account: a huge investment outflow but a miniscule investment inflow.

There is strong evidence that during the abnormally overvalued yen period of 1985–95, Japanese firms transplanted production abroad 'excessively' – excessively because outward FDI was induced not so much because they lost real comparative advantages, but rather because the abnormally high yen made it distortedly more costly to produce at home than abroad. The 'price distortion' effect of the foreign exchange rate was thus the primary cause of the sharp growth in Japan's outward FDI in the 1985–95 period. Put differently, Japan became a high-cost country, and many Japanese firms moved offshore, not so much because they were genuinely attracted to overseas host countries that offered promising local markets or truly favorable industrial milieus but because they had to escape from the ever-increasing cost burden of home-based production. This anomaly was caused by the over-regulated structure of the ID sector. One official study reveals a close correlation of outward FDI with 'internal and external price differentials', as demonstrated in Figure 9.2.

What made things worse was that instead of letting competitive forces rationalize the ID sector, the government held onto – and even reinforced through administrative guidance – its regulatory involvement to further shelter the ID sector. The reason was that this sector as a whole (but especially agriculture, construction, distribution, and finance) was the key political power base and financial source of the LDP, Japan's long-reigning political regime ever since 1955. In this respect, the ID sector can be most appropriately identified as a 'pork-barrel sector,' a political economy institution developed basically as a legacy of the occupation authorities that succeeded in installing the conservative administration.

This characteristic is most pronounced particularly in agriculture, construction, and *chusho-kigyo* (small and mid-sized businesses). Early on (for example, in 1955), agriculture was the major political base of the LDP when that sector provided employment for as much as 39 per cent of Japan's workforce and yielded 21 per cent of GDP (Argy and Stein, 1997). In fact, this pork-barrel was created as a result of drastic land reform introduced by the occupation authorities (the United States) to emancipate peasants. Under this

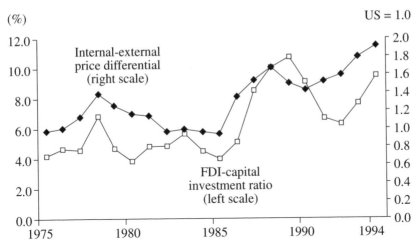

Source: Small and Medium Enterprise Agency (1996: 268), as cited in Ozawa (1997b)

Figure 9.2 '*Internal and external differentials' and outward FDI*

reform, up to 1950, about 1.5 million landlords lost their farmland (except about five hectares for their own use), while about 4 million peasant households acquired new land (Nakamura, 1994; Takahashi, 1968). Consequently, the tenant farmers all but disappeared. The occupation authorities under General MacArthur also converted the prewar and wartime hierarchy of agricultural associations into a democratic agricultural cooperative system. These well-organized agricultural cooperatives became a powerful political lobbying bloc on par with other lobbying groups such as labor unions and the Japanese Medical Association.

Thus, agricultural regions themselves, along with their surrounding semi-urban farm-linked areas (where farm-related activities such as dairy, food processing, farm supplies, and services are centered), became a major political power base for the LDP. In fact, these farm districts came to be overrepresented electorally. 'Although eligible voters in the agricultural sector made up only 20 per cent of the national electorate in 1976, the rural and semi-urban districts in Japan decided about 30 per cent of the seats in the Lower House of parliament' (Okimoto, 1989: 183).

In addition, throughout Japan, but especially in the urban districts, construction firms and their workers (estimated to be over 6 million workers, approximately 10 per cent of Japan's labor force) have been staunch supporters of the LDP.

Beside contributing to leading politicians who throw business their way the [construction] companies hire senior officials from the central government and from larger subnational jurisdictions and public corporations that are responsible for serious amounts of construction orders [i.e., *amakudari* or 'descent from heaven'] … Japan is a construction state, in contrast to being a military-industrial state or a welfare state. The circular flow is from taxpayers to construction companies for massive development projects, bridges and tunnels, highways, and airports. The money goes to favored construction companies, who provide kickbacks from these regional development projects, to the LDP politicians who keep the money flowing. (Tabb, 1995: 172–3)

In addition, small businesses in both manufacturing and distribution (wholesale and retail) constitute an important political base for the LDP, as Japan's primary sector contracted while the secondary and tertiary sectors expanded – *pari passu* with rapid economic growth. Wholesale and retail businesses (including restaurants) have been squarely in the highly protected and regulated ID sector. In short, it is thus important to realize how the ID sector was built up as the pork-barrel of LDP politicians, many of whom are popularly identified as a 'farm tribe', a 'construction tribe', a 'road tribe', and so on as they represent their particular constituencies.

9.4. LIBERALIZATION, THE BUBBLE, AND ITS AFTERMATH

As repeatedly – but so far to little avail – called for by Junichiro Koizumi (a supposedly maverick prime minister, who took office in April, 2001), Japan is in dire need of reform. The reforms required can be classified broadly into two types: public-domain and private-sector. The former includes budgetary reform, privatization of the postal services system, the elimination or privatization of 'special public corporations' whose existence is only for the purpose of providing post-retirement plums for high-ranking bureaucrats, and a host of deregulations designed to increase competition, especially in the hitherto sheltered ID sector.

As an example of public-domain reform, in April, 2004, at the third anniversary of its administration as one of the longest-lasting cabinets in Japan, Koizumi succeeded in letting the Council on Economic and Fiscal Policy draw up an interim blueprint for gradual privatization over the following five to ten years of Japan Post, a state-run agent of bloated postal services. The editorial of the *Asahi Shimbun*, Japan's largest newspaper, zeroed in on the nature of the problems facing Japan's postal services:

The productivity of mail delivery operations is seriously undermined by a slew of inefficient 'family companies,' or firms that thrive on favorable business contracts provided by the operator of postal services, usually in exchange for cushy jobs for retiring post officials. The same problem became an issue in the debate over the privatization of the four public corporations operating toll roads.

Since its establishment a year ago, Japan Post, a public entity now operating the postal services, has been trying to reduce costs and streamline its operations by adopting a competitive bidding process for its contracts and introducing efficient methods developed by Toyota Motor Corp. for mail delivery services [through the dispatch of a crack team of efficiency experts from Toyota]. While it deserves some credit for these efforts, Japan Post will not be able to protect its workers' jobs if it carries out restructuring without knowing exactly what kind of organization it will become after privatization.[1]

On the other hand, private-sector reform involves, for example, quick disposal of non-performing bank loans, swift restructuring of corporations (via discarding unprofitable business units), and a switch from a seniority-based to a merit-based system of wages and promotion inside companies. Needless to say, the public-domain reforms are prerequisites of or simultaneously needed to induce the private-sector reforms.

All these recognized needs for reform stem from the fact that the postwar system which once did wonders for Japan's catch-up growth is *no longer in sync with the drastically altered economic conditions/environs, both inside and outside Japan* – altered conditions such a system itself contributed to. In other words, the syndrome of *institutional incongruity* set in – because institutions, once set up, become too 'sticky' (socio-politically rigidified) to be easily removed or altered, particularly when they are tied to special political interests (Olson, 1982).

9.4.1. Bank-Loan Capitalism

The OF-ID dual structure was also responsible for the ballooning and burst of the asset bubble (1987–90). As is well known, Japan's high growth (1950–74) was financed mostly by bank loans under the so-called 'main bank' scheme (Aoki, 1994; Aoki and Patrick, 1994; Teranishi, 1994). Although the stock market was initially a relatively important source of funds for corporate investment, bank loans were soon deliberately promoted for corporate finance – as the essential financial strategy of overall FG development notably during the catch-up phase of heavy and chemical industrialization – and equity finance quickly became secondary to bank loans. In order to control credit expansion, moreover, the government prohibited corporations from issuing bonds (up until the mid-1980s). A bond-issuing privilege was granted only to those financial institutions (mainly, three long-term credit banks) and utilities that were specifically designed to finance public purpose long-term projects (Patrick, 1994a). Consequently, there was early on no choice on the part of corporations but to borrow from banks. Under central bank-based finance, the Bank of Japan pumped reserves into the six major city banks (Mitsui,

Mitsubishi, Sumitomo, Fuji, Sanwa, and DKB), which in turn extended industrial loans to their own groups of closely affiliated corporations, the six groups known as the bank-led *kinyu keiretsu* (financial conglomerate).

Dependence on bank loans thus became the critical mechanism through which a policy of financial repression was implemented by keeping interest rates low, controlling market competition (via entry regulations in key industries), and channeling capital to policy-targeted sectors and projects. In those days, the strength of the main bank system was 'its strong information collecting, related monitoring capabilities, and management consulting' (Patrick, 1994b: 359) – reducing uncertainty and increasing commercial information, although it was also accompanied by weaknesses such as preferential access to information among participants, secretive and opaque relationship banking, and limited public disclosure.

Furthermore, bank-created money (both the central bank's credit and the banking industry's multiple-expansion of deposits and loans) did not lead to any serious inflation, because (i) the funds were carefully invested in supply-increasing industrial projects, (ii) the monetary spigot was turned off as soon as Japan encountered a balance-of-payments deficit, a deficit caused by such an expansionary monetary policy (Wallich and Wallich, 1976), (iii) during Japan's high-growth period (early 1950s to early 1970s), domestic savings increased dramatically, and were channeled into business investment (instead of consumer credit, whose facilities were still repressed), and (iv) the government maintained a balanced budget; hence, the absence of open-market operations (to monetize national debts) (Patrick, 1994b). That central-bank augmented credit creation for growth (mainly via the discount window) was a *classic* case of development finance in the early stage of industrial capitalism as envisaged and theorized by Schumpeter (1934), who even called the banks 'the headquarters of the capitalist system'. (Schumpeter recognized the role of equities and bonds in finance but considered them basically byproducts or derivatives of the very process of economic development made possible by bank loans in the first place.)

The state-augmented banking system naturally produced a 'moral hazard' effect, because high-risk investments were encouraged and the central bank always stood ready to bail out any *keiretsu* bank at the first sign of financial difficulty; they were *strategically too significant to fail*. The upshot was that bank operations became extremely asset-expansive as they eagerly extended loans – especially in the context of inter-*keiretsu* oligopolistic rivalry where the *keiretsu* competed vigorously with each other in setting up a similar set of industries, a phenomenon that was called the 'one-set' principle (as discussed in Chapter 3).

Banks – and their *keiretsu* customers – were thus all the more willing to take risks because they could count on government help. Moral hazard was actually needed to serve as an inducement to promote large-scale risky investments in capital-intensive, scale-driven industries, since these industries imposed high financial risks on the private sector. Without government support and the *keiretsu* formation, individual enterprises alone might have been reluctant to plunge into new large-scale ventures during Japan's heavy and chemical industrialization (from the mid-1950s to the early 1970s). A rise in national output capacity (aggregate supply) had to be induced to match the liquidity (aggregate demand) pumped into the economy by the central bank's credit creation in order to prevent inflation (as emphasized by Schumpeter). This type of moral hazard, then, can be identified as the *socially justifiable* type (Ozawa, 1999b), because it induced socially desirable investments in the modern sector, thereby facilitating a swift industrial transformation. Indeed, this was the financial side story of Japan's FG strategy, which resulted in unusually rapid growth during the 'non-differentiated Smithian' stage of heavy and chemical industrial modernization.

Ironically, however, the main bank system has proved to be self-destructive; the more effective it was in facilitating Japan's catch-up industrialization, especially in capital-intensive heavy and chemical industries during the high-growth period by way of subsidized capital infusion, the faster its loss of effectiveness. The process of globalization (i.e., the inevitable deregulations Japan had to implement in its financial sector) accelerated this paradoxical outcome.

9.4.2. Unfolding of the Bubble

With the above unique features of Japan's institutional matrix for FG catch-up as the backdrop, a number of developments quickly unfolded (Ozawa, 2001a):

(i)   Thanks to the low-cost capital made available under the main bank system, large-sized firms, particularly those in the *keiretsu* groups in the OF sector, began to grow and accumulated internal reserves very rapidly. This accumulation of retained earnings made the banks' clients less dependent on loans. At the same time, as Japan left behind the stage of heavy and chemical industrialization and moved up to the next stage of assembly-based, more consumer-oriented industries (notably cars and electronics), there soon emerged new world-class manufacturers (such as Toyota, Honda, Sony, and Matsushita just to name a few). They were Japan's new maverick companies which began actively to issue new stocks at market prices, breaking the *keiretsu*-pleasing custom of issuing new equities at par value on a pre-emptive basis. These successful Japanese corporations were also soon able to tap into international capital markets for their financing needs at lower cost as restrictions on borrowings from abroad were lifted with the amendment of the Foreign Exchange Control Law in 1980.

In fact, several of these firms did not originate as *keiretsu* firms that were supposedly best coached by their main banks. They started out as outsiders (non-*keiretsu* upstarts) and have largely remained as such, though they themselves formed their own supply-chain-based (as opposed to finance-based) *keiretsu* later on. Toyota Motor Corporation is a prime example that has had no affiliation with either any *zaibatsu* or financial *keiretsu* since its establishment in 1937. It has persistently avoided external debts. Toyota's internal reserves became enormous, so much so that Toyota itself came to be known as the 'Toyota Bank'. Also, Honda was an independent upstart (though now 'affiliated' to the Tokyo-Mitsubishi Bank). So was Sony. Matsushita Electric Industries likewise accumulated huge internal funds.

(ii)   Consequently, the banks began to lose major customers for lending. The popular phrase *ginko banare* (departure from banks) came to describe this phenomenon. Having been used as the key policy instrument of bank loan capitalism, however, the banks still felt protected by the government and guaranteed for bailout if anything went wrong. In fact, the Ministry of Finance itself publicly announced that no bank would be allowed to fail. (Until the failure of Hanwa Bank in November 1996, a mid-sized regional bank, no Japanese bank had ever gone out of business since WWII. Even faltering banks were protected under the so-called *goso sendan* (convoy) policy, which compelled stronger banks to help out weaker ones.)

(iii)   It was against this backdrop that banks' imprudent lending resulted in a short-lived bubble from 1987 to 1990. The Plaza accord of 1985 soon drove up the yen phenomenally. Fearing a 'high-yen' recession, the Bank of Japan pumped money into the economy. This made the banks awash in liquidity. Having lost many large borrowers, they had to look for new, smaller, riskier borrowers. The banks found small- and mid-sized enterprises, real estate firms, construction companies, and finance firms in the ID sector as their new customers. In particular, they channeled loans through non-bank banks (that is, housing loan companies and consumer credit firms), since the latter were less strictly regulated than the banks themselves. These non-bank loans accounted for as much as 37.8 per cent of the total loans the real estate industry secured (Noguchi, 1992).

Low interest rates and the abundance of liquidity fuelled the rising prices of stocks and real estate. Many Japanese firms issued new shares at home and bonds abroad (including so-called 'warrants'), but actively put the proceeds back into the stock market, driving share prices even higher. This speculative mania was even lauded as *zai-tekku* (financial engineering). The banks became all the more anxious to lend to anyone, especially those who had land, since the value of land as collateral soared due to speculation. The rising stock prices in banks' portfolios increased their capacity to make even more loans. Thus, a speculative spiral began. The bubble was nothing but the outcome of the main bank system gone astray.

(iv) The bursting of the bubble began in early 1990, following the rise in the discount rate. The stock market reached its peak on the last trading day in 1989, and the urban land price started to fall shortly thereafter. The debacle was a disaster for borrowers in real estate, construction, distribution, and finance, as well as for banks as lenders – all in the ID's pork-barrel sector. The banks thus came to be saddled with ever-rising amounts of bad loans – at one time (April 2001) estimated to be between $338 billion ('non-performing' loans only) and $1.23 trillion (inclusive of 'problem' loans).[2]

In sum, the bubble was created largely in the ID sector into which the banks poured liquidity since they were no longer the critical source of corporate funds in the OF sector. True, the ID sector has done its job in supporting and keeping Japan's pro-business party in power, thereby enabling Japan to achieve its dream of catching up with the West and joining the ranks of the most advanced. But the very institutional setup of dualism eventually culminated in a devastating economic downturn.

9.5. WHY HAS THE JAPANESE GOVERNMENT BEEN SO DILATORY IN CLEANING UP THE BANKING MESS?

Everybody knows that the core of Japan's drawn-out economic doldrums has been its troubled banking industry which has until recently been the victim of a vicious circle of 'triple deflation' (simultaneous declines in the prices of goods, property, and equity shares – though at the time of writing, the trend may finally be reversed). As a legacy of the main bank system, the banks still hold a large amount of shares of their customers. Although these cross-shareholdings have declined somewhat recently, the 'dishoarding' process still has a long way to go, since nearly a half of Japan's total outstanding stocks are still held by financial institutions. Hence, the declined stock prices before the 2003–4 market recovery considerably reduced their lending capability, especially under the Basel Accord that imposed an 8 per cent capital requirement for risk-weighted assets.

As already discussed above, forcing the banks to reduce problem loans abruptly means the bankruptcies of an enormously large number of heavily indebted companies, in construction, distribution, and small businesses – all in the LDP's pork-barrel sector. It is political suicide. The failure of the Koizumi administration to impose limits on savings deposit insurance stems from the fear that the limited deposit guarantee will induce depositors to shift money to stronger banks, thereby making weaker banks collapse. They cannot bear a cold-turkey treatment of the type the US successfully used to solve its savings-and-loan crisis of the 1980s. Hence, the government keeps propping up the banks, which in turn prop up their customers.

Furthermore, a recent avalanche of corporate scandals in the US has considerably dampened the enthusiasm some Japanese once had towards the US shareholder model of corporate governance. And this episode has been used by reform opponents as a justification for not rushing to emulate American-style capitalism.

9.6. INTERNATIONAL BUSINESS AND THE IT REVOLUTION TO THE RESCUE

While the government muddles on, some promising developments have occurred. Ironically, the very external market forces Japan used to suppress and control are now coming to the rescue of Japan in carrying out major reforms – without much fanfare. Although the process is admittedly a gradual one, dramatic changes are cumulatively in motion, creating promising roles and opportunities for foreign investors as well as the potential for Japan to realize a new economic vitality (Ozawa, 2001c).

Beginning in the latter half of the 1990s, signs of fundamental change began to appear – with the collapse of the ID sector. Yamaichi Securities, Japan's oldest securities firm (bankrupted in 1997), was sold to Merrill Lynch. In 1999, the Long-Term Credit Bank of Japan, one of Japan's three major quasi-public institutions designed to provide long-term capital to infrastructure projects throughout Japan's high growth period (1950–73), was bought by Ripplewood Holdings (United States) and was renamed the Shinsei Bank. Japanese companies were in dire financial straits, and only foreign companies had expressed interest in acquiring the Long-Term Credit Bank. Politically, the American side treated these deals as examples of Japan's sincerity about opening its financial markets to foreign participation under the program of financial deregulation referred to as the 'Big Bang'.[3] Second-tier Kofuku Bank and Tokyo Sowa Bank were also quickly purchased by a Texas-based equity fund, Lone Star. Two of Japan's mid-sized consumer finance companies fell into the hands of AFCC (a subsidiary of US Citigroup). Foreign investors from

France, Switzerland, and the US also had a field day, as they bought up six of Japan's troubled insurance companies.

In 1999, Renault of France took a 36.8 per cent stake in and assumed the management of Nissan Motor, Japan's number-two automaker. The company began an impressive turnaround under the French executive Carlos Ghosn, who is popularly known in Japan as 'le cost cutter'. Only a few years before, who would have imagined that this world-class Japanese carmaker – whose vehicles were rated higher in quality, reliability, emissions control, and fuel efficiency than any Western-made car – would have to be rescued by French management?

But the once-touted Japanese-style management quickly lost its luster. Those Japanese company with excess capacity were simply unable to restructure. Japanese management was not prepared to retrench through ruthless, Western-style cost-cutting measures that would have thrown tens of thousands of workers out of their jobs. French management, however, swiftly moved to reduce Nissan's global workforce, to close excess assembly plants, and drop its inefficient suppliers, thereby restoring profitability in 2001.[4] Moreover, in 2004, Nissan achieved a rate of operating profit, 11 per cent, which proved to be even higher than Toyota's (9 per cent) and Honda's (7 per cent).

Similar restructuring efforts have been under way at Mazda, Fuji Heavy Industries (Subaru), and Mitsubishi Motors, all of which had fallen into the hands of foreign multinationals. It is indeed a sea change, now that Prime Minister Koizumi has specifically endorsed Renault's takeover and the impressive turnaround of Nissan as an exemplary way of restructuring Japanese businesses in this age of globalization. In other words, the OF sector itself, once admired as Japan's export juggernaut, now suffers from its overcapacity, overstaffing, and ever-rising overhead costs, although some management-savvy corporations such as Toyota and Canon have been able to stay trim and competitive.

Japan's distribution sector (wholesaling and retailing) – once off-limits under the Large-Scale Retail Law that protected small, mom-and-pop stores in the ID pork-barrel sector – is now attracting a number of large-scale distributors and retail stores. While competition comes from both domestic and foreign sources, it is particularly keen from foreign multinational discount chains, such as Toys'R'Us, Office Depot, the Gap, Boots, Sephora, Starbucks, Carrefour, and Costco Wholesale. Most recently, Wal-Mart acquired a minority stake of 37.7 per cent in Seiyu, Japan's fifth largest supermarket group, whose affiliated companies have been burdened with huge debts – and is stirring up Japan's retail industry with its super-efficient Wal-Mart way.

During the bubble of 1987–90, such a large number of golf courses were built recklessly with borrowed money that many of them became insolvent after the bubble burst. Reportedly, 265 courses went bankrupt in 2000–3.[5] They are now being actively rescued by Western 'vulture' investors who buy their assets at depressed prices. Goldman Sachs, for example, has more than 100 Japanese golf courses under its control, while Lone Star has so far invested in over 60 golf courses, more than any of Japan's largest golf course operators, such as the Tokyu Corp. group, the Seibu Group, and the Nitto Kogyo group.[6] Ripplewood also acquired the Phoenix Seagaia Resort (with four hotels, a convention center, golf courses, and the world's largest indoor water park) that was built in a semitropical city, Miyazaki, on Kyushu Island during the bubble but went bankrupt with more than $3 billion in debt.

Furthermore, Japan's telecommunications industry, only recently deregulated, has quickly attracted Vodafone Group and British Telecommunications (both of the UK) as new shareholders in J-Phone Group, one of Japan's three major wireless phone companies. The pharmaceutical industry which has long been protected (above all to give opportunities to Japanese doctors to sell drugs directly to their patients) is now being deregulated, and foreign drug makers are entering the market. The foreign multinationals operating in Japan as a group have been continually outperforming the Japanese companies (all of them taken together) in profit margins of at least two to one (i.e., they are twice as profitable).[7]

The suddenly rising FDI in Japan is boosting the presence of foreign business interests. They now form an increasingly effective *lobbying group* that is pressuring the Japanese government to create a more business-friendly environment through deregulation and by rewriting Japan's archaic commercial codes. It is no coincidence that Howard Baker, the US ambassador to Japan, called for US opportunities to invest in Japan that would be comparable to Japan's freedom to invest in the United States.

Business restructuring requires the disposal of non-profitable businesses through M&As. The recent corporate tax reform is a welcome development, since it enables companies to reorganize around their holding companies by way of either 'spinning-off' or 'spinning-in', as illustrated in Figure 9.3. Holding companies are thus now increasingly used to spin off and separate unprofitable business units (e.g., divisions, departments, and subsidiaries) from profitable ones so that not only are there tax advantages to be gained but also the non-competitive units can be disposed of in the M&As market. At the same time, they allow specialized companies to diversify their business activities by acquiring new businesses.[8] The holding company model also matches the needs of those entrepreneurs who are in-house bred (i.e., 'intrapreneurs') and spun off from their 'mother' companies to operate more autonomously. Alternatively, independent entrepreneurs can be spun in to be become a part of a larger business entity and to be financially supported for their growth. In this respect, the holding companies are a corporate

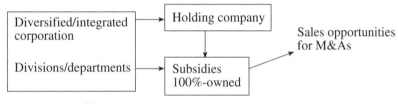

A. 'Spinning-off' approach

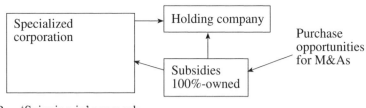

B. 'Spinning-in' approach

Source: Based on Ozawa (2003b)

Figure 9.3   Corporate tax reform and business restructuring

organizational form most suitable for the high-tech, high-information New Economy industries where business entries and exits are quickening through M&As. Foreign multinationals themselves are consolidating their recent acquisitions of Japanese businesses by setting up holding companies in Japan.

Japan's sudden opening to inward FDI is reflected in the value of such investments. (Inward FDI in 1998 ($10.47 billion) was nearly double that in 1997 ($5.53 billion). It dipped to $6.24 billion in 2001, but rose back to $9.25 billion in 2001 (JETRO, 2001, 2002, 2003).) True, the ratio of inward FDI stock to GDP is still minuscule compared with other advanced countries; in 2001, it was merely 1.2 per cent for Japan as opposed to 25.1 per cent for the United States, 38.8 per cent for Britain, 24.2 per cent for Germany, and 42.8 per cent for France (JETRO, 2003). Japan's willingness to host foreign multinationals, nevertheless, has risen vastly in the space of a few years, especially in the ID sector: 'The industries that have been realigned the most by the influx of foreign capital are the telecommunications, retail, electricity-power generation and insurance and consumer finance sectors' (JETRO, 2002: 23). Indeed, the non-manufacturing sector accounted for 62.4 per cent of inward FDI in 2003.

Inward M&As have likewise jumped in recent years, especially since 2002.

The total number of cases, for example, stood at 1728 in 2003, more than triple the number in 1994. And at the time of writing, the first half of 2004 alone has already seen a record number of M&As, as many as 1017 cases.[9] And for the first time in 2003, the 'in-out' type of M&As (Japanese firms acquiring foreign firms) was taken over in value by the 'out-in' type. Now that the prospect for Japan's economic rebound has become bright, foreign investors are acquiring Japanese companies in order to benefit from their future growth – instead of merely buying out struggling companies.

Concerned about its lopsided FDI deficit (outward FDI overwhelming its inward counterpart), the Japanese government has recently launched a campaign to double Japan's cumulative stock of inward FDI in five years. JETRO (Japan External Trade Organization), in charge of this initiative has run a series of full-page advertisements in the *Wall Street Journal* in an effort to attract more foreign investments in Japan. For example, it posted the following advertisement:

> Unlocking the Awareness Barriers: Reading any newspaper over the past three decades, from a distance it would be easy to conclude foreign firms in Japan had gone from frying pan to fire.
>
> In the now-distant days when Japan seemed poised to be the world's number one economy, the keyword was 'barriers'. Beyond thickets of legal and regulatory obstacles, foreign firms often found themselves shut out by Japan's business world and consumers alike. Throughout the mid-1980s, a complex, multi-player distribution system sent imported canned soup (and most other products) through a dozen or more wholesalers en route to retailers. The final wholesale transaction? Typically, six cans to a corner grocer – on consignment.
>
> Worse, holding a job with the foreign importer of that same soup was often seen as a sign of failure. And, by the same measure, foreign products were often seen as inferior.
>
> Twenty years on, you might find that corner grocer buying Campbell's soup by the case at one of four nationwide outlets run by the Japan unit of Issaquah, Washington-based Costco Wholesale Corp. And, says Ken Theriault, vice president Japan Operations, 'when we advertised about 200 job openings at our newest warehouse in Tokyo's western suburbs, we got thousands of applicants – many with university degrees'. (JETRO, 2004: A21)

It is thoroughly interesting that JETRO has turned the table on foreign multinationals, saying that it is the latter who have 'the awareness barriers', now that Japan as a host has dramatically changed as a result of the removal of its FDI barriers. Distribution used to be one of the most strictly regulated and sheltered industries that exemplified the ID sector. It has seen a dramatic sea change from heavy protection to a spirited promotion of competition via inward FDI, a phenomenal reversal of the market conditions that can be summarized as the paradox of 'FDI aversion as FDI promotion'.

What is more, as discussed in Chapter 6, the advent of the IT revolution has thrust Japan abruptly into a new stage of growth that intensively employs IT and intellectual capital. Along with FDI in Japan, the IT revolution is providing an autonomous, market-driven impetus for Japan to deregulate its business milieu so as to promote entrepreneurial Internet-based ventures. In other words, the marked increase in arrivals of foreign multinationals in the Japanese markets and the institutional (deregulation) mandate of the IT revolution are thus the two key elements that are compelling both the government and industry to remake Japan's inner set of institutions more aligned and compatible with the norms of the outer set established under the Pax Americana. In this regard it is worth noting that the formerly state-run institutions of higher learning, including the University of Tokyo, are being 'privatized', and that in order to survive financially these ivory towers are turning to industry for funding – and participate in – their research projects. For example, the University of Tokyo Graduate School of Information Science and Technology is reportedly establishing its 'branch campus' at the heart of Tokyo's famous Akihabara electronics district for the purpose of training IT experts and promoting industry–academia tie-ups in research, product development, and test-marketing.[10]

The new roles of inward FDI and IT both as a corporate restructuring agent and as an institutional reform facilitator (Ozawa, 2001a) are much more pronounced in Japan than anywhere else.

9.7. SUMMING UP

The Japanese experience provides a fascinating case study on the interactions between the outer matrix of evolving global institutions and the inner matrix of domestic setups. Early postwar Japan was skillful in setting up a unique matrix of domestic institutions designed to facilitate its catch-up growth under the leadership – and protection – of a pro-business political party, the LDP. The party's power was built on a large segment of voters and campaign fund contributors in ID industries such as agriculture, construction, distribution, and small businesses, which were long sheltered from competition, especially competition from foreign multinationals' FDI. All this *dirigiste* inner set of institutions was largely tolerated by the United States, the hegemon of the Pax Americana, because of Japan's unique geography as the forefront bastion against communism in the Cold War – that is, until the détente and final collapse of the Soviet Union in 1989.

In the meantime, the successful growth of the OF sector and the continued protection of the ID sector led to a dual industrial structure, which was in large measure responsible for the bubble of 1987–90 and its aftermath, the present banking crisis. And herein lies the inability of the currently ruling LDP to adopt a cold-turkey treatment to cure the bad loan problem; it would be political suicide to do so.

Yet the Japanese government and industry have begun to welcome and host foreign multinationals' active participation in local businesses *earnestly for the first time* since the end of World War II. Indeed, this new open-door policy is often referred to as the 'third opening of Japan' (Kojima, 2000/2001). It follows two other major transformations, the Meiji opening of 1868 and the postwar opening of 1945. It should be noted, however, that the earlier two openings were *not* autonomous (not of Japan's own volition), and that they were driven by external pressures. The current third opening is no exception. Nevertheless, the difference this time around is that this new movement toward economic liberalization has been fundamentally compelled by *market forces* rather than led by the government. It is largely the result of Japan's *own* necessity to break the impasse of the rigidities and newly arisen incompatibilities of inner institutions with *both* its own status as an advanced country and the drastically altered milieu of the world economy. True, the end of the Cold War did change America's foreign policy toward Japan, exerting greater pressure on Japan to open up. More importantly, however, even without the breakup of the Soviet Union, Japan's catch-up success itself made its existing matrix of inner institutions obsolete and it would have had to carry out the necessary reforms in any event.

Two key market imperatives have been forcing Japan to bring itself more in line with the outer matrix of institutions. The first is corporate Japan's pressing need to dispose of non-performing loans, excess capacity, and distressed businesses while acquiring new managerial skills and expertise in business restructuring. The second is the advent of the IT revolution, which calls for deregulation and a more market-oriented milieu, where entrepreneurship, with its free-spirited ideas, can flourish. Thus, these market imperatives are engendered by international business activities and competitions. In the past, Japan has excelled in innovating new technologies and business practices. These alone are not now enough to cope with the recent decline of industrial vitality. Japan is now groping for new and better institutions, which can replace or renovate the now obsolescent inner matrix that was established many decades (a half century) ago and has been ossified to the detriment of the present Japanese economy.

Indeed, foreign multinationals, which are now eagerly welcomed by Japan to revitalize its corporate business sector, are serving as renovators that can remodel Japan's inner set of institutions more closely in accordance with the norms of the outer set. In other words, Japan can no longer afford not to capitalize on the forces of institutional homogenization via inward FDI and the IT revolution in the economic sphere toward a more unified structure of the global economy. Yet, Japan's political interests, deeply rooted in its inner set of institutions, are a big hindrance to this new effort – and Japan continues to muddle through.

NOTES

1. *Asahi Shimbun*, April 27, 2004, as translated into English and published in the International Herald Tribune, 'Postal Services reform: Any plan designed to please everybody will fail', April 28; p. 26.
2. At 122.52yen = $1.00, as reported in 'Debate persists on size of loan problem in Japan, clouding Tokyo's ability to act', *Wall Street Journal*, April 24, 2001. More recently (as of March 31, 2004), however, non-performing loans at all banks fell to 26.6 trillion yen ($240 billion). *Wall Street Journal*, August 11, 2004.
3. A detailed story of Ripplewood's takeover is told in Tett (2003).
4. 'Japanese corporate restructuring: Uncut', *The Economist*, July 20, 2002.
5. As reported in James Brooke, 'American Investors put Japan's resorts in play', *New York Times* (on the Web), January 6, 2004.
6. 'Foreign firms' drive revitalizes golf clubs', *International Herald Tribune (the Asahi Shimbun)*, May 5, 2004; 'Foreign investors see green in struggling golf courses', *Nikkei Weekly*, February 24, 2003.
7. 'Japanese corporate restructuring: Uncut', *The Economist*, July 20, 2002.
8. Yet, there is dubious way in which this new holding company structure has begun to be used, a way in which some parent companies are merely fudging their announced layoff plans for corporate restructuring by creating new, unlisted subsidiaries and hiving workers off the parent's books.
9. 'Japan sets record in terms of M&A, but lags globally', *Wall Street Journal*, July 6, 2004.
10. 'Akihabra reinventing itself', *Nikkei Weekly*, July 26, 2004.

Bibliography

Abegglen, James C. and George Stalk, Jr. (1985), *Kaisha: The Japanese Corporation*, New York: Basic Books.

Abo, Tetsuo (1994), *Hybrid Factory: The Japanese Production System in the United States*, New York: Oxford University Press.

Abromowitz, Morton, and Stephen Bosworth (2003), 'Adjusting to the New Asia', *Foreign Affairs*, **82** (4), 119–131.

Akamatsu, Kaname (1935), 'Wagakuni Yomo Kogyohin no Boeki Suisei [The Trend of Japan's Foreign Trade in Woolen Manufactures]', *Shogyo Keizai Ronso* [Journal of Nagoya Higher Commercial School], Vol. unknown, 129 *ff*.

Akamatsu, Kaname (1961), 'A Theory of Unbalanced Growth in the World Economy', *Weltwirtschaftliches Archiv*, **86**, 196–215.

Akamatsu, Kaname (1962), 'A Historical Pattern of Economic Growth in Developing Countries', *Developing Economies*, preliminary issue No. 1 (March–August), 1–23.

Aoki, Masahiko (1988), *Information, Incentives, and Bargaining in the Japanese Economy*, Cambridge and New York: Cambridge University Press.

Aoki, Masahiko, K. Murdock and M. Okuno-Fujiwara (1997), 'Beyond the East Asian Miracle: Introducing the Market-Enhancing View', in M. Aoki, H.-K., Kim, and M. Okuno-Fujiwara (eds), *The Role of Government in East Asian Economic Development*, Oxford: Clarendon Press, 1–40.

Aoki, Masahiko, and Hugh Patrick (1994), *The Japanese Main Bank System: Its Relevance for Developing and Transforming Economies*, Oxford: Oxford University Press.

Aoki, Masahiko, and Hiroshi Yoshikawa (1999), 'Demand Creation and Economic Growth', Center for International Research on the Japanese Economy, Faculty of Economics, University of Tokyo, Discussion Paper No. F-43, March.

Argy, Victor, and Leslie Stein (1997), *The Japanese Economy*, New York: New York University Press.

Arisawa, H. (ed.) (1967), *Nihon Sangyo Hyakunenshi* [A 100-year History of Japanese Industry], vols. 1 and 2, Tokyo: Nihon Keizai.

Arrighi, Giovanni (1994), *The Long Twentieth Century*, London: Verso.

Arrow, Kenneth (1962), 'The Economic Implications of Learning by Doing',

Review of Economic Studies **29**, 155–176.

Balassa, Bela (1965), 'Trade Liberalisation and Revealed Comparative Advantage', *Manchester School of Economic and Social Studies*, **33**, 99–123.

Balassa, Bela (1989), *Comparative Advantage, Trade Policy and Economic Development*, New York: New York University Press.

Baumol, William J. (2002), *The Free-Market Innovation Machine: Analyzing the Growth Miracle of Capitalism*, Princeton: Princeton University Press.

Bell, John F. (1953), *A History of Economic Thought*, New York: Ronald Press.

Berri, David, and Terutomo Ozawa (1997), 'Pax Americana and Asian Exports: Revealed Trends of Comparative Advantage Recycling', *International Trade Journal*, **11** (1), Spring, 39–67.

Best, Michael H. (2000), 'Silicon Valley and the Resurgence of Rout 128: Systems Integration and Regional Innovation', in John Dunning (ed.), *Regions, Globalization, and the Knowledge-based Economy*, Oxford: Oxford University Press.

Bhagwati, Jagdish N., and T.N. Srinivasan (1983), *Lectures on International Trade*, Cambridge: MIT Press.

Bieda, Ken (1970), *The Structure and Operation of the Japanese Economy*, New York: Wiley.

Boltho, Andrea, and Gerald Holtham (1992), 'The Assessment: New Approaches to Economic Growth', *Oxford Review of Economic Policy*, **8** (4), Winter, 1–14.

Bonacich, Edna, and David V. Waller (1994), 'Mapping a Global Industry: Apparel Production in the Pacific Rim Triangle', in E. Bonacich, L. Cheng, N. Chinchilla, N. Hamilton, and P. Ong (eds), *Global Production: The Apparel Industry in the Pacific Rim*, Philadelphia: Temple University Press, 21–41.

Buckley, Peter (1988), 'Organisational Forms and Multinational Companies', in S. Thompson, and M. Wright (eds), *International Organisation, Efficiency and Profit*, Oxford: Philip Allen.

Buckley, Peter (1994), 'Review Article: World Investment Report 1994: Transnational Corporations, Employment and the Workplace', *Transnational Corporations*, **3** (3), 91–100.

Casson, Mark (1987), *The Firm and the Market*, Oxford: Blackwell.

Caves, Richard E. (1974), 'Industrial Organization', in John Dunning (ed.), *Economic Analysis and the Multinational Enterprise*, London: George Allen & Unwin.

Chandler, Alfred D., Jr. (1977), *The Visible Hand: The Managerial Revolution in American Business*, Cambridge, MA: Harvard University Press.

Chandler, Alfred D. Jr., (2001), *Inventing the Electronic Century: The Epic*

Story of The Consumer Electronics and Computer Industries, New York: Free Press.

Chen, Edward K.Y. (1993), 'Economic Restructuring and Industrial Development in the Asia-Pacific: Competition or Complementarity', *Business & the Contemporary World*, **5** (2), 67–88.

Chenery, Hollis B. (1960), 'Patterns of Industrial Growth', *American Economic Review*, **50** (4), 624–654.

Chenery, Hollis B. (1979), *Structural Change and Development Policy*, Oxford: Oxford University Press.

Chenery, Hollis B. and Moshe Syrquin (1975), *Patterns of Development, 1950–1970*, Oxford: Oxford University Press.

Chenery, Hollis B., and Lance J. Taylor (1968), 'Development Patterns among Countries and over Time', *Review of Economics and Statistics*, **50** (November), 391–416.

Clark, Colin (1935), *The Conditions of Economic Progress*, London: Macmillan.

Coase, Ronald (1937), 'The Nature of the Firms', *Economica*, **4**: 386–405.

Cumings, Bruce (1984), 'The Origins and Development of the Northeast Asian Political Economy', *International Organization*, **38**: 149–153.

Curtis, Philip J. (1994), *The Fall of the U.S. Consumer Electronics Industry: An American Trade Tragedy*, Westport, Conn.: Quorum Books.

Cusumano, Michael A. (1989), *The Japanese Automobile Industry: Technology and Management at Nissan and Toyota*, Cambridge, Mass.: Harvard University Press.

Donohue, Peter (1992), 'Free Trade, Unions and the State: Trade Liberalization's Endorsement by the AFL-CIO, 1943–1962', *Research in Political Economy*, **13**, 1–73.

Dunning, John H. (1981), 'Explaining the International Direct Investment Position of Countries: Toward a Dynamic or Developmental Approach', *Weltwirtschaftliches Archiv*, **119**, 30–64.

Dunning, John H. (1991), 'The Eclectic Paradigm of International Production: A Personal Perspective', in Christos Pitelis, and Roger Sugden (eds), *The Nature of the Transnational Firm*, London and New York: Routledge, 117–133.

Dunning, John H. (1992), 'The Global Economy, Domestic Governance, Strategies and Transnational Corporations: Interactions and Policy Implications', *Transnational Corporations*, **1** (3), 7–45.

Dunning, John H. (1997a), 'Advent of Alliance Capitalism', in John Dunning, and Khali Hamdani (eds), *The New Globalism and Developing Countries*, New York: United Nations University Press.

Dunning, John H. (1997b), *Alliance Capitalism and Global Business*, London: Routledge.

Dunning, John H. (2003), 'Relational Assets, Networks and International Business Activity', in John Dunning, and Gavin Boyd (eds), *Alliance Capitalism and Corporate Management: Entrepreneurial Cooperation in Knowledge Based Economics*, Cheltenham, UK: Elgar, 1–23.

Dunning, John H., and Rajneesh Narula (1996), 'The Investment Development Path Revisited', in J. Dunning and R. Narula (eds), *Foreign Direct Investment and Governments*, London and New York: Routledge, 1–41.

Dutta, Manoranjan (2000), 'The Euro Revolution and the European Union: Monetary and Economic Cooperation in the Asia-Pacific Region, *Journal of Asian Economics*, **1** (1), 1–12.

Eatwell, John (1982), *Whatever Happened to Britain?* London: BBC.

Economic Planning Agency (1971), *Economic Survey of Japan, 1970–1971*, Tokyo: Finance Ministry Printing Office.

Elmslie, Bruce T. (1995), 'Retrospectives: The Convergence Debate between David Hume and Josiah Tucker', *Journal of Economic Perspectives*, **9** (4), 207–16.

Friedman, Thomas L. (1999), *The Lexus and the Olive Tree*, New York: Anchor Books, 2000.

Fujimoto, Takahiro (1995), 'A Note on the Origin of the "Black Box Parts" Practice in the Japanese Motor Vehicle Industry', in Haruhito Shiomi and Kazuo Wada (eds), *Fordism Transformed: The Development of Production Methods in the Automobile Industry*, New York and Oxford: Oxford University Press, 184–218.

Galbraith, John K. (1973), *Economics and the Public Purposes*, Boston: Houghton Mifflin.

Gerlach, Michael L. (1992), *Alliance Capitalism: The Social Organization of Japanese Business*, Berkeley, Cal.: University of California Press.

Gerschenkron, Alexander (1962), *Economic Backwardness in Historical Perspective*, Cambridge, Mass.: Harvard University Press.

Glyn, Andrew, Alan Hughes, Alain Lipietz, and Ajit Singh (1990), 'The Rise and Fall of the Golden Age', in Stephen Marglin and Juliet Schor (eds), *The Golden Age of Capitalism: Reinterpreting the Post-War Experience*, Oxford: Clarendon Press, 39–125.

Gray, H. Peter (1999), *Global Economic Involvement: A Synthesis of Modern International Economics*, Copenhagen: Copenhagen Business School Press.

Gregory, R.G. (1986), 'Overview', in H. Mutoh et al. (eds), *Industrial Policies for Pacific Economic Growth,* Sydney: Allen & Unwin, 1–22.

Haberler, Gottfried von (1936), *The Theory of International Trade with its Applications to Commercial Policy*, London: William Hodge.

Hagel, John III (2002), *Out of the Box: Strategies for Achieving Profits Today and Growth Tomorrow through Web Services*, Boston, Mass.: Harvard Business School Press.

Hara, Akira (1991), 'Sage of an Economic Diplomat (1): Saburo Okita: "America was Generous and Open"', *Tokyo Business Today*, July 1991, 48.

Hatch, Walter, and Kozo Yamamura (1996), *Asia in Japan's Embrace*, Cambridge: Cambridge University Press.

Hersh, Jacques (1993), *The USA and the Rise of East Asia since 1945: Dilemmas of the Postwar International Political Economy*, New York: St Martin's Press.

Hicks, John R. (1973), 'The Mainspring of Economic Growth', *Swedish Journal of Economics*, **54**: 258–266.

Hirsch, Seev (1967), *Location of Industry and International Competitiveness*, Oxford: Oxford University Press.

Hume, David (1754/1985), *Essays: Moral, Political and Literary*, edited by Eugene Miller, Indianapolis, Indiana: Liberty Fund.

Hymer, Stephen (1960/1976), *The International Operations of National Firms*, PhD Dissertation completed in 1960 at MIT; published under the same title in 1976, Cambridge, Mass.: MIT Press.

Ichimura, Shin'ichi (ed.) (1988), *Azia ni Nezuku Nihonteki Keiei* [Japanese-Style Management Takes Root in Asia], Tokyo: Toyo Keizai Shimpo.

Ikari, Yoshiro (1981), *Nohon no Jidosha Kogyo* [Japan's Automobile Industry], Tokyo: Nihon Noritsu Kyokai.

Imai, Ken-ichi (1992), 'Japan's Corporate Networks', in Shumpei Kumon, and Henry Rosovsky (eds.), *The Political Economy of Japan Vol. 3: Cultural and Social Dynamics*, Stanford, Cal.: Stanford University Press, 198–230.

Itagaki, Hiroshi, and Tetsuo Abo (1993), 'Kankoku-Taiwan ni okeru Nihongata Seisan shisutemu [The Japanese Production System in Korea and Taiwan]', *Shakai Kagaku Kenkyu*, **45** (3), 73–148.

Itami, Hiroyuki (1991), *Nihon no Kagaku Sangyo: Naze Sekaini Tachiokretanoka* [Japan's Petrochemical Industry: Why has it Fallen behind Others in the World], Tokyo: NTT.

Itami, Hiroyuki (1994), *Nihon no Jidosha Sangyo: Naze Kyubureiki ga Kakkata noka?* [Japan's Automobile Industry: Why a Sudden Brake?], Tokyo: NTT.

Ito, Takatoshi (2001), 'Growth, Crisis, and the Future of Economic Recovery in East Asia', in Joseph Stiglitz, and Shahid Yusuf (eds), *Rethinking the East Asia Miracle*, New York: Oxford University Press, 55–94.

JETRO (2001), *JETRO Toshi Hakusho* [JETRO White Paper on Foreign Direct Investment], Tokyo: JETRO.

JETRO (2002), *JETRO White Paper on Foreign Direct Investment 2002: Growth in Global Foreign Direct Investment Slows (Summary)*, JETRO web site: www.jetro.go.jp.

JETRO (2003), *JETRO White Paper on International Trade and Foreign*

Direct Investment (Summary), JETRO web site: www.jetro.go.jp.

JETRO (2004), 'Investing in Japan: A More Open-Minded Society Offers New Incentives for Foreign Investors', special advertising section, *Wall Street Journal*, March 23, A21.

Johnson, Chalmers (1982), *MITI and the Japanese Miracle: The Growth of Industrial Policy, 1925–1975*, Stanford, Cal.: Stanford University Press.

Johnstone, Bob (1999), *We Were Burning: Japanese Entrepreneurs and the Forging of The Electronic Age*, New York: Basic Books.

Jorgenson, Dale W. (1995), *Productivity, Vol. 2: International Comparison of Economic Growth*, Cambridge., Mass.: MIT Press.

Jorgenson, Dale W., and Kazuyuki Motohashi (2004), 'Potential Growth of the Japanese and U.S. Economies in the Information Age', Discussion Paper Series No. 88, Economic and Social Research Institute, Cabinet Office, Tokyo.

Kanasaki, Takashi (1982), *Kaden Industry* [The Household Electric Appliance Industry], Tokyo: Kenkusha.

Kay, Neil M. (1991), 'Multinational Enterprise as Strategic Choice: Some Transaction Cost Perspectives', in Christos Pitelis, and Roger Sugden (eds), *The Nature of the Transnational Firm*, London: Routledge.

Kenen, Peter B. (1960), *Giant among Nations: Problems in United States Foreign Economic Policy*, New York: Rand McNally.

Kenney, Martin, and Richard Florida (1993), *Beyond Mass Production: The Japanese System and Its Transfer to the US*, New York and Oxford: Oxford University Press.

Kibi, Masato (1980), *Kiseki o Umitsuzukeru Takokuseki Kigyo: Sony* [Miracle-spawning Multinational Enterprise: Sony], Tokyo: Asahi Sonorama.

Kindleberger, Charles P. (1967), *Europe's Postwar Growth: The Role of Labor Supply*, Cambridge, Mass.: Harvard University Press.

Kindleberger, Charles P. (1969), *American Business Abroad*, New Haven: Yale University Press.

Koike, Kazuo (1996), 'Skill Formation Systems and Technology Transfer', *Developing Engineering*, **2**, 43–53.

Koike, Kazuo, and Takenori Inoki (1990), *Skill Formation in Japan and Southeast Asia*, Tokyo: University of Tokyo Press.

Koizumi, Hideo (1990), *Kaden Gyokai* [The Household Electric Industry], Tokyo: Kyoikusha.

Koizumi, T., and K.J. Kopecky (1977), 'Economic Growth, Capital Movements, and the International Transfer of Technical Knowledge', *Journal of International Economics*, **7**, 45–65.

Kojima, Kiyoshi (1958), 'Nihon Keizai no Aankokeitaiteki Hatten to Boeki no Yakuwari [Flying-Geese Style Growth of the Japanese Economy and the

Role of Trade]', in K. Kojima (ed.), *Nihon Boeki no Kozo to Hatten* [The Structure and Growth of Japan's Trade], Tokyo: Shiseido.

Kojima, Kiyoshi (1973), 'A Macroeconomic Approach to Foreign Direct Investment', *Hitotsubashi Journal of Economics*, **12**, 1–21.

Kojima, Kiyoshi (1975), 'International Trade and Foreign Investment: Substitutes or Complements', *Hitotsubashi Journal of Economics*, **16**, 1–12.

Kojima, Kiyoshi (1990), *Japanese Direct Investment Abroad*, Tokyo: International Christian University.

Kojima, Kiyoshi (1996), *Trade, Investment and Pacific Economic Integration: Selected Essays of Kiyoshi Kojima*, Tokyo: Bunshindo.

Kojima, Kiyoshi (2000/2001), 'The "Flying-Geese" Model of Asian Economic Development: Origin, Theoretical Extensions, and Regional Policy Implications', *Journal of Asian Economics,* **11**, 375–401.

Kojima, Kiyoshi (2003), *Gankogata Keizai Hattenron: Vol. 1, Nihon Keizai, Azia Keizai, and Sekai Keizai* [The Flying-Geese Theory of Economic Development, Vol. 1, The Japanese Economy, the Asian Economy, and the World Economy], Tokyo: Bunshindo.

Kojima, Kiyoshi (2004), *Gankogata Keizai Hatten Ron: Vol. 2, Azia to Sekai no Shin Chitsujo* [The Flying-Geese Theory of Economic Development: Vol. 2, Asia and the New World Order], Tokyo: Bunshindo.

Kojima, Kiyoshi, and Terutomo Ozawa (1984a), 'Micro- and Macro-economic Models of Direct Foreign Investment: Toward a Synthesis', *Hitotsubashi Journal of Economics,* **25** (1), 1–20.

Kojima, Kiyoshi, and Terutomo Ozawa (1984b), *Japan's General Trading Companies: Merchants of Economic Development*, Paris: OECD.

Kojima, Kiyoshi, and Terutomo Ozawa (1985), 'Toward a Theory of Industrial Restructuring and Dynamic Comparative Advantage', *Hitotsubashi Journal of Economics*, **26** (2), 135–45.

Komiya, Ryutaro (1990), *The Japanese Economy, Trade, Industry, and Government*, Tokyo: University of Tokyo Press.

Komiya, Ryutaro, Masahiro Okuno, and Kotaro Suzumura (1988), *Industrial Policy of Japan*, Tokyo: Academic Press.

Kondo, Masayuki (1996), 'Industrial Technology Strategy of Malaysia to Enhance Industrial Competitiveness', *Developing Engineering*, **2**, 77–95.

Korhonen, Pekka (1994), *Japan and the Pacific Free Trade Area*, London and New York: Routledge.

Korhonen, Pekka (1998), *Japan and the Asia Pacific Integration,* London: Routledge.

Krasner, S.D. (1987), *Asymmetries in Japanese-American Trade: The case for specific reciprocity*, Berkeley, Cal.: Institute of International Studies, University of California.

Krugman, Paul R. (1984), 'Import Protection as Export Promotion:

International Competition in the Presence of Oligopoly and Economies of Scale', in Henryk Kierzkowski (ed.), *Monopolistic Competition and International Trade*, Oxford: Clarendon Press, 180–193.

Krugman, Paul R. (1984), 'Import Protection as Export Promotion: International Competition in the Presence of Oligopoly and Economies of Scale', in Henryk Kierzkowski (ed.), *Monopolistic Competition and International Trade*, Oxford: Clarendon Press, 180–193.

Krugman, Paul R. (1991), *Geography and Trade*, Cambridge, Mass.: MIT Press.

Krugman, Paul R. (1994), 'The Myth of Asia's Miracle', *Foreign Affairs*, **73** (6), 62–93.

Kudo, Akira (1995), 'Western Multinationals in Japan: Missed Opportunities and Lessons from Inter-war Business History', *Asia Pacific Business Review*, **2** (1), 20–36.

Kumon, Shumpei (1992), 'Japan as a Network Society', in Shumpei Kumon, and Henry Rosovsky (eds), *The Political Economy of Japan, Vol. 3 Cultural and Social Dynamics,* Stanford: Stanford University Press, 109–41.

Landes, David S. (1969), *The Unbound Prometheus*, Cambridge and New York: Cambridge University Press.

Lee, Chung H. (1984), 'On Japanese Macroeconomic Theories of Direct Foreign Investment', *Economic Development and Cultural Change*, **32** (4), 713–723.

Letiche, J.M. (1960), 'Adam Smith and David Ricardo on Economic Growth', in Bert Hoselitz (ed.), *Theories of Economic Growth*, New York: Free Press.

Lewis, W. Arther (1954), 'Economic Development with Unlimited Supplies of Labour', *Manchester School of Economics and Social Studies*, **12**, May, 139–191.

List, Friedrich (1841), *The National System of Political Economy*, translated by S. Lloyd, New York: Longmans, Green & Co., 1904.

Lynn, Leonard H. (1982), *How Japan Innovates: A Comparison with the U.S. in the Case of Oxygen Steelmaking*, Boulder, Col.: Westview Press.

Lyons, Nick (1976), *The Sony Vision*, New York: Crown.

Marshall, Alfred (1920), *Principles of Economics*, London: Macmillan.

Marston, Richard C. (1987), 'Real Exchange Rates and Productivity Growth in the United States and Japan', in Sven Arndt, and David Richardson, *Real-Financial Linkages among Open Economies*, Cambridge, Mass.: MIT Press: 71–96.

Marx, Karl (1867), *Capital, vol. 1. A Critical Analysis of Capitalist Production*, London: Swan Sonnenschein, Lowry & Co (reproduced by International Publishers, 1967).

McLuhan, Marshall, and Quentin Fiore (1967), *The Media is the Message*, New York: Random House.

McLuhan, Marshall, and Bruce R. Powers (1989), *The Global Village: Transformations in The World Life and Media in the 21st Century*, New York: Oxford University Press.

McNulty, Paul J. (1972), 'Predecessors of the Multinational Corporation', *Columbia Journal of World Business*, **7**, June, 73–80.

Meier, Gerald M. (1980), *International Economics. The Theory of Policy*, New York: Oxford University Press.

METI (2001), *White Paper on International Trade*, on the web, Tokyo.

METI (2002), *White Paper on International Trade*, on the web, Tokyo.

Mikanagi, Yumiko (1996), *Japan's Trade Policy: Action or Reaction?* London and New York: Routledge.

Mill, John Stuart (1848/1909), *Principles of Political Economy*, London: Longmans, Green.

Ministry of Education, Culture, Sports, Science and Technology (2002), *Annual Report On the Promotion of Science and Technology*, on the web.

MITI (1986), *Kokusai Kyocho Jidai no Sangyo Kozo Bijyon* [A Vision for Industrial Structure in the Age of International Cooperation], Tokyo: Finance Ministry Printing Office.

MITI (1996), *Daihenkaku suru Nihon no Kenkyu Kaihatsu* [A Big Structural Change in Japan's R&D], Tokyo: MITI.

Miyazaki, Yoshikazu (1980), 'Excessive Competition and the Formation of Keiretsu', in Kazuo Sato (ed.), *Industry and Business in Japan*, White Plain, New York: Sharpe, 53–73.

Morita, Akio (1986), *Made in Japan: Akio Morita and Sony*, New York: Dutton.

Mutoh, Hiromichi (1988), 'The Automotive Industry', in R. Komiya, M. Okuno and K. Suzumura (eds), *Industrial Policy of Japan*, Tokyo: Academic Press, 307–331.

Myint, Hla (1958), 'The "Classical Theory" of International Trade and the Underdeveloped Countries', *Economic Journal*, **68**, No. 270, June, 317–337.

Myint, Hla (2001), 'International Trade and the Domestic Institutional Framework', in Gerald Meier, and Joseph Stiglitz (eds), *Frontiers of Development Economics. The Future in Perspective*, New York: Oxford University Press, 2001, 520–528.

Nakamura, Takafusa (1994), *Lectures on Modern Japanese Economic History 1926–1994*, Tokyo: LTCB International Library Foundation.

Narula, Rajneesh (1996), *Multinational Investment and Economic Structure: Globalisation and Competitiveness*, London: Routledge.

Nelson, Richard R., and Sydney G. Winter (1982), *An Evolutionary Theory of*

Economic Change, Cambridge, Mass.: Harvard University Press.

Noguchi, Yukio (1992), *Baburu no Keizaigaku: Nihon Keizai ni Naniga Okkotanoka* [Economics of the Bubble: What has Happened to the Japanese Economy?], Tokyo: Nihon Keizaisha.

North, Douglass C. (1990), *Institutions, Institutional Change and Economic Performance*, Cambridge, UK: Cambridge University Press.

North, Douglass C. (1999), *Understanding the Process of Economic Change*, London: Institute of Economic Affairs.

OECD (1970), *Gaps in Technology: Analytical Report*, Paris: OECD.

OECD (1972), *The Industrial Policy of Japan*, Paris: OECD.

Ohno, Tai'ichi (1978), *Toyota Seisan Hoshiki: Datsu-kibo no Keiei o Mezashite* [Toyota Production Formula: Toward Non-scale-based Management], Tokyo: Daiyamondo.

Okazaki, Saburo (1954), *Nippon Shihonshugi no Hatten Dankai* [Stages of Development of Japanese Capitalism], Tokyo: Kawade Shobo.

Okimoto, Daniel I. (1989), *Between MITI and the Market: Japanese Industrial Policy for High Technology*, Stanford: Stanford University Press.

Olson, Mancur, Jr. (1982), *The Rise and Decline of Nations: Economic Growth, Stagnation and Social Rigidities*, New Haven: Yale University Press.

O'Rourke, Kevin H., and Jeffrey G. Williamson (1999), *Globalization and History: The Evolution of a Nineteenth-Century Atlantic Economy*, Cambridge, Mass.: MIT Press.

Ozawa, Terutomo (1974), *Japan's Technological Challenge to the West, 1950–1974: Motivation and Accomplishment*, Cambridge, Mass.: MIT Press.

Ozawa, Terutomo (1979a), 'International Investment and Industrial Structure: New Theoretical Implications from the Japanese Experience', *Oxford Economic Papers*, **31** (1), March, 72–92.

Ozawa, Terutomo (1979b), *Multinationalism, Japanese Style: The Political Economy of Outward Dependency*, Princeton: Princeton University Press.

Ozawa, Terutomo (1980), 'Government Control over Technology Acquisition and Firms' Entry into New Sectors', *Cambridge Journal of Economics*, **4** (June), 133–146.

Ozawa, Terutomo (1985), 'Macroeconomic Factors Affecting Japan's Technology Inflows and Outflows', in Nathan Rosenberg, and Claudia Frischtak (eds), *International Technology Transfers*, New York: Praeger.

Ozawa, Terutomo (1986), 'Japanese Policy toward Foreign Multinationals: Implications for Trade and Competitiveness', in Thomas Pugel (ed.), *Fragile Interdependence: Economic Issues in U.S.-Japanese Trade and Investment*, Lexington, Mass.: Lexington Books, 141–168.

Ozawa, Terutomo (1987), 'Can the Market Alone Manage Structural

Upgrading? A Challenge Posed by Economic Independence', in John Dunning, and M. Usui (eds), *Structural Change, Economic Interdependence and World Development*, London: Macmillan.

Ozawa, Terutomo (1991), 'Japanese Multinationals and 1992', in B. Burgenmeier, and J.L. Mucchielli (eds), *Multinationals and Europe 1992: Strategies for the Future*, London: Routledge.

Ozawa, Terutomo (1992), 'Foreign Direct Investment and Economic Development', *Transnational Corporations*, **1** (1) (February), 27–54.

Ozawa, Terutomo (1993), 'Foreign Direct Investment and Structural Transformation: Japan as a Recycler of Market and Industry', *Business & the Contemporary World*, **5** (2) (Spring), 129–150.

Ozawa, Terutomo (1995a), 'The Flying-geese Paradigm of Tandem Growth: TNC's Involvement and Agglomeration Economies in Asia's Industrial Dynamism', paper presented at the 1995 AIB annual meeting in Seoul, Korea, 15–18 November.

Ozawa, Terutomo (1995b), 'Structural Upgrading and Concatenated Integration: The Vicissitudes of the Pax Americana in Tandem Industrialization of the Pacific Rim', in Denis Simon (ed.), *Corporate Strategies in the Pacific Rim*, London: Routledge, 1995, 215–248.

Ozawa, Terutomo (1996a), 'Professor Kojima's "Trade Augmentation" Principle and the "Flying-Geese" Paradigm of Tandem Growth', *Surugadai Economic Studies*, **5** (2), March, 269–296.

Ozawa, Terutomo (1996b), 'The Russian Far East: The Role of Japan', in P. Artisien-Makismenko, and Y. Adjubei (eds), *Foreign Investment in Russia and Other Soviet Successor States*, London: Macmillan, 157–176.

Ozawa, Terutomo (1996c), 'Japan: The Macro-IDP, Meso-IDPs, and the Technology Development Path (TDP)', in John Dunning, and Rajneesh Narula (eds), *Foreign Direct Investment and Governments*, London: Routledge, 142–173.

Ozawa, Terutomo (1997a), 'Japan', in John Dunning (ed.), *Governments, Globalization, and International Business*, Oxford: Oxford University Press, 377–406.

Ozawa, Terutomo (1997b), '"Excessive" FDI and Dilemmas of Technology Transfer', *Development Engineering*, **3**, 27–42.

Ozawa, Terutomo (1997c), 'Images, Economies of Concatenation, and Animal Spirits: Dependency vs. Emulation Paradigm', in Brian Toyne, and Douglas Nigh (eds), *International Business: An Emerging Vision*, Columbia, SC: University of South Carolina Press, 204–220.

Ozawa, Terutomo (1997d), '"Managed" Growth, Relocation and Restructuring: The Evolution of Japan's Motor Industry into a Dominant Multinational Player', in Peter Buckley, and Jean-Louis Mucchielli (eds), *Multinational Firms and International Relocation*, Cheltenham, UK:

Edward Elgar, 161–188.

Ozawa, Terutomo (1997e), 'Strategic Organization and Structural Dynamism: Spatial Underpinning of Japan's Phased-Based Industrial Competitiveness', *CEMS Business Review*, **2** (suppl.), 519–535.

Ozawa, Terutomo (1998), *Recycling Japan's Surpluses for Developing Countries*, Paris: OECD.

Ozawa, Terutomo (1999a), 'Pacific Economic Integration and the "Flying Geese" Paradigm', in Alan Rugman, and Gavin Boyd (eds), *Deepening Integration in the Pacific Economies: Corporate Alliances, Contestable Markets, and Free Trade*, Cheltenham, UK: Edward Elgar, 55–91.

Ozawa, Terutomo (1999b), 'Bank Loan Capitalism and Financial Crises: Japanese and Korean Experiences', in Alan Rugman, and Gavin Boyd (eds), *Deepening Integration in the Pacific Economies: Corporate Alliances, Contestable Markets, and Free Trade*, Cheltenham, UK: Edward Elgar, 214–248.

Ozawa, Terutomo (2000), 'Small- and Medium-Sized MNCs, Industrial Clusters and Globalization: The Japanese Experience', in Neil Hood, and Stephen Young (eds), *The Globalization of Multinational Enterprise Activity and Economic Development,* London: Macmillan.

Ozawa, Terutomo (2001a), 'The "Hidden" Side of the "Flying-Geese" Catch-up Model: Japan's *Dirigiste* Institutional Setup and a Deepening Financial Morass', *Journal of Asian Economics*, **12** (4), Winter, 471–491.

Ozawa, Terutomo (2001b), 'Japan in the WTO', in Alan Rugman, and Gavin Boyd (eds), *The World Trade Organization in the New Global Economy*, Cheltenham, UK: Edward Elgar, 191–215.

Ozawa, Terutomo (2001c), 'Putting the Pieces in Place for Japan's Economic Recovery', *Asia Pacific Issues*, No. 57, December (a publication of the East-West Center, Honolulu, Hawaii), 1–8.

Ozawa, Terutomo (2003a), 'Pax Americana-led Macro-clustering and Flying-geese-style Catch-up in East Asia: Mechanisms of Regionalized Endogenous Growth', *Journal of Asian Economics*, **13** (6): 699–713.

Ozawa, Terutomo (2003b), 'Japan in an Institutional Quagmire: International Business to the Rescue?' *Journal of International Management*, **9** (3), 219–236.

Ozawa, Terutomo (2003c), 'Towards a Theory of Hegemon-Led Macro-Clustering', in Peter Gray (ed.), *Extending the Eclectic Paradigm in International Business: Essays in Honor of John Dunning*, Cheltenham UK, Elgar, 143–158.

Ozawa, Terutomo (2003d), 'Japan's Network Capitalism in Evolution', in John Dunning and Gavin Boyd (eds), *Alliance Capitalism and Corporate Management: Entrepreneurial Cooperation in Knowledge Based Economies*, Cheltenham, UK: Elgar, 230–248.

Ozawa, Terutomo (2003e), 'The Hegellian Dialectic and Evolutionary Economic Change: Special Reference to the Flying-Geese Paradigm of Industrial Upgrading', Presidential address delivered at the 13th International Conference of the International Trade and Finance Association, Vaasa Polytechnic, Vaasa, Finland, May 28–30.

Ozawa, Terutomo (forthcoming), *Regionalized Endogenous Growth in Asia: The Flying-Geese Paradigm of Tandem Catch-Up*, Working Paper in progress, Department of Economics, Colorado State University.

Ozawa, Terutomo, and David Berri (1997), 'Pax Americana and Asian Exports: Revealed Trends of Comparative Advantage Recycling', *International Trade Journal*, **11** (1), Spring, 39–67.

Ozawa, Terutomo, and Christine Ferror (1997), 'Strategic Organization and Structural Dynamism: Spatial Underpinnings of Japan's Phase-Based Industrial Competitiveness', *CEMS Business Review*, **2** (Suppl.), S19–S35.

Ozawa, Terutomo, and Ronnie J. Phillips (1994), 'Persistence of the Veblenian "Old Japan": Organizational Efficiency as a Wellspring of Competitiveness', *Rivista Internazionale di Scienze Economiche e Commerciali*, **16** (9), September, 721–740.

Palma, G. (1978), *Underdevelopment and Marxism: From Marx to the Theories of Imperialism and Dependency*, Thames Papers in Political Economy, London: Thames Polytechnic.

Patrick, Hugh (1986), 'Japanese High Technology Industrial Policy in Comparative Context', in Hugh Patrick (ed.), *Japan's High Technology Industries: Lessons and Limitations of Industrial Policy*, Seattle: University of Washington Press, 3–33.

Patrick, Hugh (1994a), 'Comparisons, Contrasts and Implications', in Hugh Patrick, and Y.C. Park (eds), *The Financial Development of Japan, Korea, and Taiwan*, New York: Oxford University Press, 216–244.

Patrick, Hugh (1994b), 'The Relevance of Japanese Finance and its Main Bank System', in Masahiko Aoki, and Hugh Patrick (eds), *The Japanese Main Bank System: Its Relevance for Developing and Transition Economies*, Oxford: Oxford University Press, 353–408.

Patrick, Hugh, and Henry Rosovsky (eds) (1976), *Asia's New Giant: How the Japanese Economy Works*, Washington, DC: The Brookings Institution.

Peck, Merton J. (1976), 'Technology', in Hugh Patrick and Henry Rosovsky (eds), *Asia's New Giant: How the Japanese Economy Works*, Washington, DC: Brookings Institution.

Phelps, N.A., and T. Ozawa (2003), 'Contrasts in Agglomeration: Proto-industrial, Industrial and Post-industrial Forms Compared', *Progress in Human Geography*, **27** (5), 583–604.

Polayni, Karl (1944), *The Great Transformation: The Political and Economic Origins of Our Time*, Boston, Mass.: Beacon Press, 1957.

Porter, Michael E. (1990), *The Competitive Advantage of Nations*, New York: Free Press.

Prawer, Joshua, and Samuel N. Eisenstadt (1968), 'Feudalism', in *International Encyclopedia of the Social Sciences*, vol. 5, New York: Crowell Collier and Macmillan.

Prime Minister's Office (Naikakufu) (2004), *Kagaku Gijutsu to Shakai ni kansuru Yoron Chosa* [A Survey on Public Opinions about Science and Technology], Tokyo.

Radelet, Steven, and Jeffrey Sachs (1997), 'Asia's Reemergence', *Foreign Affairs*, **76** (6), 44–59.

Rapp, William V. (1967), 'A Theory of Changing Trade Patterns under Economic Growth: Tested for Japan', *Yale Economic Essays*, Fall, 69–135.

Rapp, William V. (1975), 'The Many Possible Extensions of Product Cycle Analysis', *Hitotsubashi Journal of Economics*, **16** (1), 22–29.

Ricardo, David (1817/1888), 'Principles of Political Economy and Taxation', in J.R. McCulloch (ed.), *The Works of David Ricardo*, London: John Murray, 1–584.

Richardson, G.B. (1972), 'The Organization of Industry', *Economic Journal*, **82** (327) (September), 883–896.

Rodrik, Dani (2000), 'How Far Will International Economic Integration Go?', *Journal of Economic Perspectives*, **14** (1), 177–187.

Rostow, W.W. (1960), *The Stages of Economic Growth: A Non-Communist Manifesto*, Cambridge, UK: Cambridge University Press.

Rostow, W.W. (1990), *Theorists of Economic Growth from David Hume to the Present*, New York: Oxford University Press.

Samuels, Richard J. (1994), *'Rich Nation, Strong Army': National Security and the Technological Transformation of Japan*, Ithaca, NY: Cornell University Press.

Sano, Shinya, and Atushi Degawa (1993), *Konputa* [Computer], Tokyo: Nihon Keizai Shimbunsha.

Saxonhouse, Gary R. (1986), 'Industrial Policy and Factor Markets: Biotechnology in Japan and the United States', in Hugh Patrick (ed.), *Japan's High Technology Industries: Lessons and Limitations of Industrial Policy*, Seattle: University of Washington Press, 36–97.

Schoppa, Leonard J. (1997), *Bargaining with Japan*, New York: Columbia University Press.

Schumpeter, Joseph A. (1934), *The Theory of Economic Development*, originally published in German; English translation, New York: Oxford University Press, 1961.

Schumpeter, Joseph A. (1942), *Capitalism, Socialism and Democracy*, New York: Harper & Row.

Science and Technology Agency (1997), *Kagaku Gijutsu Hakusho* [White

Paper on Science and Technology], Tokyo: Finance Ministry Printing Office.

Science and Technology Agency (1998), *Kagaku Gijutsu Hakusho* [White Paper on Science and Technology], Tokyo: Finance Ministry Printing Office.

Sekiguchi, Sueo (1997), 'Chokusetsu Toshi to Gijutsu Iten: Sangyo no Kokusai kan Iten to Toshikoku, Hitoshikoku [FDI and Technology Transfer: Industrial Migration and the Home and Host Countries]', *Kaigai-Toshi-Kenkyusho-Ho* [Journal of Research Institute for International Investment and Development], **23** (3), March, 4–23.

Sen, Amartya K. (1999), *Development as Freedom*, New York: Knopf.

Shimada, Haruo (1988), *Humanware no Keizaigaku: Amerika no Nakano Nihon Kigyo* [Economics of Humanware: Japanese Ventures in America], Tokyo: Iwanami Shoten.

Shimokawa, Koichi (1985), *Jidosha* [Automobiles], Tokyo: Nihon Keizai Shmbunsha.

Shinjo, Koji (1988), 'The Computer Industry', in R. Komiya, M. Okuno, and K. Suzumura (eds), *Industrial Policy of Japan*, Tokyo: Academic Press, 333–354.

Shinohara, Myohei (1972), *Growth and Cycles in the Japanese Economy*, Tokyo: Institute of Economic Research, Hitotsubashi University.

Shinohara, Myohei (1982), *Industrial Growth, Trade, and Dynamic Patterns in the Japanese Economy*, Tokyo: University of Tokyo Press.

Small and Medium Enterprise Agency (1996), *White Paper on Small and Medium Enterprises*, Tokyo: Finance Ministry Printing Office.

Smith, Adam (1776/1908), *An Inquiry into the Nature and Causes of the Wealth of Nations*, London: Routledge, reproduced: New York: E.P. Dutton, 1908.

Smitka, Michael (1991), *Competitive Ties: Subcontracting in the Japanese Automobile Industry*, New York: Columbia University Press.

Sony Corporation (2003), *History: Milestones in Product Development*, www. Sony.net.

Soriano, Emanuel V. (1996), 'A Case Study Analysis for the Evaluation of Technological Innovation', *Development Engineering*, **2**, 15–30.

Stalk, George, Jr., and Thomas Hout (1990), *Competing against Time: How Time-based Competition is Reshaping Global Markets*, New York: Free Press.

Stanfield, Ron J. (1986), *The Economic Thought of Karl Polanyi*, London: Macmillan.

Stolper, W.F., and P.A. Samuelson (1941), 'Protection and Real Wages', *Review of Economic Studies*, **9** (November), 58–73.

Suzuki, Yoshio (ed.) (1987), *The Japanese Financial System*, Oxford:

Clarendon Press.

Tabb, William K. (1995), *The Postwar Japanese System: Cultural Economy and Economic Transformation*, New York and Oxford: Oxford University Press.

Takahashi, Masao (1968), *Modern Japanese Economy since 1868*, Tokyo: Kokusai Bunka Shinkokai.

Tatsuno, Sheridan M. (1990), *Created in Japan: From Imitators to World-Class Innovators*, New York: Ballinger.

Teranishi, Juro (1994), 'Japan: Development and Structural Change of the Financial System', in Hugh Patrick, and Yung Chul Park (eds), *The Financial Development of Japan, Korea, and Taiwan*, New York: Oxford University Press, 27–80.

Tett, Gillian (2003), *Saving the Sun*, New York: Harper Collins.

Tsuru, Shigeto (1993), *Japan's Capitalism: Creative Defeat and Beyond*, Cambridge, UK: Cambridge University Press.

Uchino, Tatsuro (1983), *Japan's Postwar Economy: An Insider's View of Its History and its Future*, Tokyo and New York: Kodansha.

UNCTAD (1995), *World Investment Report*, New York and Geneva: United Nations.

United Nations (1970), *Demographic Yearbook*, New York: United Nations.

Veblen, Thorstein (1927), *The Theory of Business Enterprise*, New York: Charles Scribner's Sons.

Veblen, Thorstein (1934), *Essays in Our Changing Order*, New York: Viking Press.

Vernon, Raymond (1966), 'International Investment and International Trade in the Product Cycle', *Quarterly Journal of Economics*, **80** (2), May, 190–207.

Vernon, Raymond (1970), 'Future Multinational Enterprise', in Charles Kindleberger (ed.), *The International Corporation: A Symposium*, Cambridge, Mass.: MIT Press, 373–400.

Vernon, Raymond (1979), 'The Product Cycle Hypothesis in the New International Environment', *Oxford Bulletin of Economics and Statistics*, **41** (4), 255–268.

Vernon, Raymond (1983), *Two Hungry Giants: The United States and Japan in the Quest For Oil and Ores*, Cambridge, Mass.: Harvard University Press.

Viner, Jacob (1960), *The Customs Union Issues*, New York: Carnegie Endowment for International Peace.

Wallich, Henry C., and Mabel I. Wallich (1976), 'Banking and Finance', in Hugh Patrick and Henry Rosovsky (eds), *Asia's New Giant: How the Japanese Economy Works*, Washington, DC: Brookings Institution, 249–315.

Williamson, Oliver E. (1975), *Markets and Hierarchies: Analysis and Antitrust Implications*, New York: Free Press.

Williamson, Oliver E. (1985), *The Economic Institutions of Capitalism: Firms, Markets, Relational Contracting*, New York: Free Press.

Womack, James P., Daniel T. Jones, and Daniel Roos (1990), *The Machine that Changed the World*, New York: Macmillan.

Yamawaki, Hideki (1988), 'The Steel Industry', in Ryutaro Komiya, Masahiro Okuno, and Kotaro Suzumura (eds), *Industrial Policy of Japan*, Tokyo: Academic Press, 281–305.

Yamawaki, Hideki (1992), 'International Competition and Japan's Domestic Adjustment', in Kym Anderson (ed.), *New Silk Roads: East Asia and World Textile Markets*, Cambridge and New York: Cambridge University Press, 89–118.

Yamazaki, Mitsuru (1980), *Japan's Community-based Industries: A Case Study of Small Industry*, Tokyo: Asian Productivity Organization.

Yamazawa, Ippei (1988), 'The Textile Industry', in R. Komiya, M. Okuno, and K. Suzumura (eds), *Industrial Policy of Japan*, Tokyo: Academic Press, 395–419.

Yamazawa, Ippei (1990), *Economic Development and International Trade: The Japanese Model*, Honolulu, Hawaii: East-West Center.

Yoshikawa, Hiroshi (2000), 'Technical Progress and the Growth of the Japanese Economy—Past and Future', *Oxford Review of Economic Policy*, **16** (2), 34–45.

Yoshino, Michael Y., and Srinivasa Rangan (1995), *Strategic Alliances: An Entrepreneurial Approach to Globalization*, Boston, Mass.: Harvard Business School Press.

Zhan, James, and Terutomo Ozawa (2001), *Business Restructuring in East Asia: Cross-Border M&As in the Crisis Period*, Copenhagen: Copenhagen Business School Press.

Zhang, Shu Guang (2001), *Economic Cold War: America's Embargo against China and the Sino-Soviet Alliance, 1949–1963*, Washington, DC: Woodrow Wilson Center Press.

Index